Indigenous Peoples and Colonialism

Indigenous Peoples and Colonialism

Global Perspectives

Colin Samson and Carlos Gigoux

polity

First published in 2017 by Polity Press

Polity Press
65 Bridge Street
Cambridge CB2 1UR, UK

Polity Press
350 Main Street
Malden, MA 02148, USA

ISBN-13: 978-0-7456-7251-9
ISBN-13: 978-0-7456-7252-6(pb)

A catalogue record for this book is available from the British Library.

Library of Congress Cataloging-in-Publication Data

Names: Samson, Colin, author. | Gigoux, Carlos, author.
Title: Indigenous peoples and colonialism : global perspectives / Colin Samson, Carlos Gigoux.
Description: Malden, MA : Polity Press, 2016. | Includes bibliographical references and index.
Identifiers: LCCN 2016013425 (print) | LCCN 2016025561 (ebook) | ISBN 9780745672519 (hardcover : alk. paper) | ISBN 0745672515 (hardcover : alk. paper) | ISBN 9780745672526 (pbk. : alk. paper) | ISBN 0745672523 (pbk. : alk. paper) | ISBN 9781509514564 (mobi) | ISBN 9781509514571 (epub)
Subjects: LCSH: Indigenous peoples--Colonization. | Indigenous peoples--Government relations. | Indigenous peoples--Ethnic identity. | Self-determination, National.
Classification: LCC JV305 .S36 2016 (print) | LCC JV305 (ebook) | DDC 323.11--dc23
LC record available at https://lccn.loc.gov/2016013425

Typeset in 10.5 on 12 pt Plantin by Servis Filmsetting Ltd, Stockport, Cheshire
Printed and bound in the UK by CPI Group (UK) Ltd, Croydon

For further information on Polity, visit our website: politybooks.com

Contents

Acknowledgements

The idea for this book is inspired by indigenous peoples' continued resistance to colonialism, their enlivening worldviews and their respect for the natural world we inhabit. We are indebted to many of them for sharing with us their knowledge, hospitality and friendship. Our work is also a consequence of our collaborative research and teaching in the Department of Sociology and the Centre for Interdisciplinary Studies at the University of Essex. We are truly grateful to our students for their questions and critical comments when discussing indigenous issues.

Colin Samson I thank George Rich of Natuashish, Canada, and Napess Ashini, Marcel Ashini and Anthony Jenkinson of Sheshatshiu, Canada, for constant friendship and solidarity; Caskey Russell, Tory Fodder and the American Indian Students Alliance (University of Wyoming) for their hospitality and introductions to the indigenous worlds in Wyoming; Jennifer Hays (University of Tromsø) for help in Namibia; Hideo Ichihashi (Saitama University) for help in Hokkaidō; also Pierrot Ross Tremblay (Laurentian University), Maria Sapignoli (McGill University), Damien Short (University of London), James Wilson, Fiona Watson and Jony Mazower (Survival International), Stephen Small (University of California, Berkeley), Charles Watters (University of Sussex), Rob Schehr (Northern Arizona University) and Sarah Sandring (Nirgun Films); and Nicola Gray for support and patience.

Carlos Gigoux I would like to thank my parents Carlos and María Elena for their love, constant support and motivation. I am grateful to Mihoko Fukushima (University of Miyazaki) for welcoming me to

Japan and for organizing the seminars that we teach on indigenous peoples and sustainable development. I would like to express my gratitude to Richard Siddle (University of Hokkaido), Jeffry Joseph Gayman (University of Hokkaido) and Jolan Hsieh (National Dong Hwa University) for their friendly welcome and for our many hours of conversations.

Warm thanks to Jonathan Skerrett for his guidance in publishing the book and to Sarah Dancy and India Darsley for their thorough editing of the manuscript.

Preface

In 2007 the United Nations adopted the Declaration on the Rights of Indigenous Peoples (UNDRIP). Its success was largely the result of the dedicated and persistent activism of indigenous social movements in the face of resolute opposition from states with indigenous populations. Although it is not legally binding, the Declaration means that the relationships between national governments and indigenous peoples can no longer be consigned to matters of 'domestic' policy only. The demands by members of indigenous communities for designated international rights for indigenous peoples emerged from longstanding colonial occupation, dispossession and induced transformations of distinct peoples, often justified as an inevitable consequence of modernity.

Our book underlines the connections between modernity and colonialism. In particular, it focuses on colonialism as a modern and contemporary experience. We aim to contribute to an understanding of these dynamics by examining how indigenous peoples have been dealt with under European and other types of geopolitical expansion and how they continue to be treated today as their lands are targeted for settlement, agriculture, industrialization and fossil fuel extraction. The main ideology that legitimates these modern processes is Western liberalism, a body of ideas that has most often been represented as universal and emancipatory. We attempt to show how liberal ideas are applied differentially and selectively and how they often masquerade for decidedly illiberal policies and actions. Social scientific and literary writers as diverse as W. E. B. Du Bois, Frantz Fanon, Aimé Césaire, Hannah Arendt, bell hooks, Vine Deloria, Edward Said, Paul Gilroy and Enrique Dussel have extended the critique of modernity into this domain. Furthermore, numerous contemporary indigenous scholars such as Linda Tuhiwai Smith, Aileen Moreton-Robinson, Pamela Palmater, Devon Mihesuah, Taiaiake Alfred, Glen Sean Coulthard, Audra Simpson, Leanne Simpson, Robert Warrior, James Fenelon, Dale Turner, Duane Champagne, Gerald Vizenor, N. Scott Momaday, Leslie Marmon Silko and scores of younger indigenous writers, academics, activists, and commentators are daily adding to the varied corpus of knowledge of the ongoing colonial aspects of modernity.

Our discipline, sociology, has not made the study of colonialism a priority. Instead, it has primarily looked at 'society' parochially from the vantage point of nineteenth- and twentieth-century theories that argued that developments such as democracy, rationalism, the state and industrialism made the West uniquely progressive. Although sociologists have examined empires, they have largely excluded indigenous societies from modernity, and indigenous scholars, writers and orators have rarely been used as sources of authority. The omission of indigenous peoples in sociology can be explained by the fact that, although many rejected elements of the social evolutionist ideology of early social science (Kurasawa 2004), they constructed 'stages' of human society which positioned indigenous peoples further back in history. Consequently, 'founding fathers' such as Weber, Durkheim and Marx made the rise of Europe their main focus (Samson and Short 2006). The study of indigenous peoples was left to anthropology and various types of natural science, including the subfield of scientific racism. These academic divisions have yet to be completely transcended. Sociologists who in the past analysed colonialism and empires have been retroactively assigned to anthropology (Steinmetz 2013: 1), and sociologists such as us are often assumed to be anthropologists simply because of our interests in indigenous societies.

The Eurocentric nature of the social sciences is of course well noted by numerous scholars around the world. It has provided an impetus for new theorizations from the 'global South' (Connell 2007) and attempts to reconceptualize the discipline of sociology as less parochial (Bhambra 2007; Bhambra 2014). However, while colonialism and global historical connections are forefronted, the concern in Bhambra's important works, for example, is principally with academic disciplinary politics. The main point of contrast to European conceptualizations of modernity is the global South, a meaningless category for indigenous peoples. By contrast, scholars from indigenous communities are developing a body of literature that incorporates transcultural methodologies and indigenous knowledge. Many are creating genuinely transdisciplinary knowledge and,

although located in university departments, are rejecting identification with established academic disciplines. At the same time,
indigenous writers frequently affirm that academic products are not
solely for the benefit of universities, the state or corporations, but are
important means of promoting self-determination and control over
indigenous territories and resources. Indigenous researchers have
been centrally concerned with the antagonistic relationship between
the Western project of modernity, its embodiment in academia, and
indigenous peoples. As the Maori scholar Linda Tuhiwai Smith
(2012: 62) argues: 'The development of scientific thought, the exploration and "discovery" by Europeans of other worlds, the expansion
of trade, the establishment of colonies, and the systematic colonization of indigenous peoples in the eighteenth century are all facets of
the modernist project.'

   A further dimension of our book is that it is global and comparative. Although living in different locations around the world and
developing highly varied ways of life, indigenous peoples nonetheless
are affected by similar patterns of dispossession and violence. Hence,
we will highlight the features of domination, the ideologies behind
them, and the effects, responses and resistance of indigenous peoples
to them. While we will cover indigenous peoples in many areas of
the world, it is important to caution that generalizations will always
have their limitations and readers should look to specialist accounts
for more detail on specific issues. Similarly, while we discuss many
different indigenous groups and trace some of their histories and contemporary circumstances, we cover only a fraction of the diversity.

   One of our aims is to locate indigenous peoples in a global process
in order to offer an alternative to the largely national orientation
of commentaries in the various literatures. A global and comparative approach will always subvert the tendency to view policies and
practices as unique to particular nation-states. Looking at indigenous peoples *only* in national contexts reinforces the often-made
assumption that they are simply administrative units within states.
Frederick Hoxie's (2008: 1154) statement that 'historians have dif-
ficulty viewing American Indian topics apart from the history of
the American state' applies more widely. The problems and issues
raised in this book are seen differently when we view patterns in
different contexts. Both state policies and indigenous resistance to
them in North America, South America, Europe, Africa, Asia and
Australasia show striking similarities, and these are associated with
the ubiquity of colonial processes. We will look at some of these
dynamics by putting First and Third World countries on the same

page, and rejecting the conceit of Western liberalism to be the basis of a uniquely fair, democratic and benign form of society.

Finally, the book uses colonialism to explore the relationship between modernity, the nation-state and indigenous peoples. Rather than understanding colonialism as a purely historical process, we argue that it remains crucial to the structuring of indigenous peoples' lives today. Colonialism is a political, social, economic and cultural structure nourished by powerful drives for land and authority. It operates most transparently through nation-state institutional structures. These rely on governmental claims to dominion over distinct peoples using land dispossession, exclusion, violence and racist knowledge to consolidate and legitimate itself. There has been no meaningful decolonization applied to indigenous peoples. The decolonization movements that swept the globe in the mid-twentieth century led only to the formation of new nation-states and with them possibilities for renewed colonialism. Those who came to be called indigenous people in decolonized states were often groups depicted by political elites as practising ways of life that were outside the modernizing agenda inherited from their former colonizers. The experience of colonialism is therefore common to indigenous peoples, and dispossession of land, autonomy, and self-representation 'continues to inform the dominant modes of Indigenous resistance and critique that this relationship has provoked' (Coulthard 2014: 13).

This book is divided into six chapters. The first, 'Identity', sets the context for the understanding of indigenous peoples in the contemporary world. It introduces readers to general facts like geographical distribution, social indicators, population numbers and distinctions between the ways of life of today's indigenous peoples by drawing on the UN report, *State of the World's Indigenous Peoples* (UN DESA 2009). At the same time, we will consider indigenous identity through scholarly debates on the subject as well as how identity is configured in the seminal definition elaborated by Martínez Cobo (UN ECOSOC 1986) and more recently in UNDRIP. We will then proceed to examine how the establishment of nation-states has become a profound determinant of indigenous identity. Geographical and cultural differences in conceptions of indigenous identity and the recognition of this identity will also be discussed. This will include looking at the meaning of being indigenous in settler states, where migrant populations established governments and created societies based on racial taxonomies, as well as in post-independence states, such as those in Africa and Asia that often claim that 'everyone is indigenous', and states like Mexico where a kind of hybrid (*mestizaje*) identity was embraced.

The second chapter, 'Colonization', examines past and present colonial ideologies and structures that affect indigenous peoples. We will summarize some of the early contact encounters and argue that, in addition to extreme violence, these were accompanied by religious, legal and philosophical representations that were carried over into subsequent relationships between colonizing and colonized peoples. While much space will be devoted to the North American experience, we aim to show in the latter part of the chapter that the experiences of many indigenous peoples in Africa, Latin America, Northern Europe and Russia, Asia and Australia are similar to those in North America and that the common factor is colonialism.

In the third chapter, 'Land', we turn to the actual social and cultural processes central to colonialism; the removal of indigenous peoples from their lands. This begins with an account of the enclosure policies by which indigenous peoples in North America were reduced to living on small reserves, reservations or in villages. This involves the displacement and relocation of many groups, as well as the sedentarization of mobile peoples. Crucial to these ongoing processes was the introduction of assimilation policies, prominently including wage labour and state education. We then proceed to look at the similar and contrasting dynamics involved in various colonial configurations in Latin America, Southern Africa, Scandinavia and Siberia, and Japan. We end the chapter by examining the dramatic social effects of land dispossession in other spheres of indigenous life such as gender roles, family life and the profound and painful experience of state schooling.

Chapter 4, 'Environment', will move the focus to the position of indigenous peoples relative to pressing concerns over the destruction of our natural world. We will begin by outlining the architecture of European and colonial thought towards nature. Fundamental to this was the belief in the necessity of transforming and controlling nature. These ideas have been channelled through the 'development' agenda which often pits indigenous beliefs about living in tandem with nature against the neoliberal industrial mandate to dominate it. This has resulted in a number of contemporary practices that are taking place across the globe. Because 'the race for what's left' (Klare 2012) is currently being run on indigenous lands ever more remote from the main corridors of colonial expansion, land grabbing and environmental racism are making serious inroads into indigenous territories. The chapter concludes by showing how the transformation of indigenous lands also led to urbanization of many indigenous families, a policy that unites measures such as the US Relocation

Acts of the 1950s and Canadian termination policies with contemporary Israeli and Chinese mandates to urbanize Bedouin and Tibetan herders respectively.

The fifth chapter, 'Rights', examines the relationship between indigenous peoples and rights. We will discuss the development of strategic actions of resistance centred on social mobilization, networking and alliances both at national and international levels. These led to the advancement of indigenous rights at the United Nations, which in turn has created a legal framework that indigenous peoples have used to seek justice. We will balance these advances against some serious limitations. In the current international system, rights can ultimately only be enforced by the same states that are the adversaries to indigenous peoples in the recognition of these very rights. There are tensions also between the collective rights for indigenous peoples articulated in international legal instruments and individual rights favoured by states. Some key court cases will also be discussed, involving the recognition of Free Prior and Informed Consent as a required condition for fossil fuel and other resource extraction projects in indigenous territories.

The sixth and final chapter, 'Culture', addresses how creative and visual arts have become a powerful platform for the articulation of indigenous identities and means to resist colonialism. This chapter looks at culture as a site of struggle in which indigenous peoples have engaged with educational institutions, museums, galleries and the film industry to articulate themselves after centuries of silencing. They have also developed their own grassroots artistic and creative stages for asserting cultural sovereignty. We conclude that their alternative visions of the world are on the side of social justice, cultural pluralism and human survival.

Lastly, it is important to situate ourselves as authors. Together, we have more than four decades of combined experience working with, visiting and writing about the impacts of colonialism on indigenous peoples as diverse as the Innu, Arapaho and Shoshone in North America, Ainu in Japan, San in Namibia, Hadzabe and Maasai in Tanzania and the Selk'nam in Tierra del Fuego. In our journeys, we have learned from the experiences of communities, indigenous and non-indigenous researchers and NGOs working in Africa, South America and Asia. We are both non-indigenous and, having been raised in Chile (Carlos Gigoux) and England and the US (Colin Samson), our academic perspectives are obviously products of the societies where we grew up.

The perspectives we bring to this book have not emerged from being born, raised and socialized within an indigenous society. We therefore make no attempt to speak for anyone other than ourselves, but write as two people who have found inspiration in indigenous peoples' refreshing views of the world, knowledge, creativity, active resistance to colonialism, and their more considerate and invigorating connections to the natural environment. Although constantly under threat, many indigenous societies have developed ways of being and seeing that are not bound by the competitive individualism, sterile materialism and plunder under which our own society labours. Therefore, we write as friends and scholars trying to understand and resist.

Abbreviations

AANDC	Aboriginal Affairs and Northern Development Canada
ACHPR	African Commission on Human and Peoples' Rights
AFN	Assembly of First Nations (Canada)
AIDESEP	Asociación Interétnica de Desarrollo de la Selva Peruana
AIM	American Indian Movement (USA)
AIWN	Asian Indigenous Women's Network
ANCSA	Alaska Native Claims Settlement Act
BIA	Bureau of Indian Affairs (USA)
CAAMA	Central Australian Aboriginal Media Association
CDI	Comisión Nacional para el Desarrollo de los Pueblos Indígenas (Mexico)
CERD	Committee on the Elimination of Racial Discrimination (UN)
CFR	Code of Federal Regulations
CHT	Chittagong Hill Tracts
CIMI	Conselho Indigenista Missionário
CJS	criminal justice system
CKGR	Central Kalahari Game Reserve
CLACPI	Coordinadora Latinoamericana de Cine y Comunicación de los Pueblos Indígenas
CONADI	Corporación Nacional Indígena (Chile)
CONAIE	Confederation of Indigenous Nationalities of Ecuador
CIMI	Conselho Indigenista Missionário (Brazil)
CIPCA	Centro de Investigación y Promoción del Campesinado
CPA	Cordillera Peoples Alliance (Philippines)
CWIS	Centre for World Indigenous Studies
ECLAC	Economic Commission for Latin America and the Caribbean

ENIAR	European Network for Indigenous Australian Rights
FIMI	Foro Internacional de Mujeres Indígenas (International Indigenous Women's Forum)
FPCN	Friends of Peoples Close to Nature
FPIC	free, prior and informed consent
FUNAI	Fundação Nacional do Índio (Brazil)
HCA	High Court of Australia
HREOC	Human Rights and Equal Opportunity Commission
HRW	Human Rights Watch
IACHR	Inter-American Commission on Human Rights
ICTs	information and communication technologies
IITC	International Indian Treaty Council
ILO	International Labour Organization
IMF	International Monetary Fund
IPACC	Indigenous Peoples of Africa Coordinating Committee
IWGIA	International Work Group for Indigenous Affairs
IPRA	Indigenous Peoples' Rights Act (Philippines)
IWGIA	International Work Group for Indigenous Affairs
KPF	Kalahari Peoples Fund
MRG	Minority Rights Group
NAFTA	North American Free Trade Agreement
NCAI	National Congress of American Indians
NCIP	National Commission on Indigenous Peoples (Philippines)
NGO	nongovernmental organization
NPS	National Park Service (USA)
NWAC	Native Women of Canada Association
OFA	Office of Federal Acknowledgement
OIPC	Office of Indigenous Policy Coordination (Australia)
ONIC	Organización Nacional Indígena de Colombia
RCAP	Royal Commission on Aboriginal Peoples
SPI	Serviço de Proteção ao Indio (Brazil)
UDHR	Universal Declaration of Human Rights
UNDP	United Nations Development Programme
UNDRIP	United Nations Declaration on the Rights of Indigenous Peoples
UNHRC	United Nations Human Rights Council
UNI	União das Nações Indígenas
UNPFII	United Nations Permanent Forum on Indigenous Issues
VCP	Vanishing Cultures Project (USA)

WGIP   Working Group on Indigenous Populations (UN)
WIMSA   Working Group of Indigenous Minorities in Southern
            Africa

1

Identity

> For Aboriginal and Torres Strait Islander peoples it is our beliefs, our
> culture, and our family histories that contribute to our sense of who we
> are and what we mean to others. They are our source of belonging –
> and they anchor us and steer our course through our lives.
>
> Mick Gooda (2011)

Writing for *The Sydney Morning Herald*, Mick Gooda, the Aboriginal
and Torres Strait Islander Social Justice Commissioner, referred to
his Aboriginal identity as a dynamic and interactive process of self-
recognition firmly rooted in tradition, culture and community values.
For him, indigenous identity is a collective identity that provides a
sense of self, purpose and direction. Castells (2004: 6) argues that
'identity refers to the process of construction of meaning on the
basis of a cultural attribute, or a related set of cultural attributes,
that is given priority over other sources of meaning'. However, for
indigenous peoples the process of self-identification goes beyond the
attachment to the cultural attributes of a community and extends to
the special relationship with the lands where those cultural attributes
are formed, exercised and given meaning. Indigenous individuals
often recognize themselves as being part of distinct and independent,
although often changing and overlapping, communities, which in
turn are linked to territories. As a result, the choice to self-identify
is a fundamental principle in the struggle for indigenous rights.
However, this principle is often denied. Past and present colonial
governments have not only deprived indigenous peoples of their
lands and resources but also prevented self-identification through
imposed administrative definitions as to who indigenous peoples are.
This chapter sets the scene for the understanding of indigenous

peoples in the contemporary world by discussing a number of
general considerations around identity, including self-identification
and imposed identities.

Numbers of indigenous peoples

According to the UN report *State of the World's Indigenous Peoples* (UN
DESA 2009: 21), there are approximately 370 million indigenous
peoples around the world and, although they represent 5 per cent of
the world population, they constitute 15 per cent of the world's poor.
This poverty is exacerbated by the geographical fragmentation of
whole peoples across regions and national borders. For example, the
Aymara peoples live in Peru, Bolivia, Chile and Argentina; the San
peoples in Botswana, South Africa, Namibia, Angola, Zambia and
Zimbabwe; the Mohawk or Haudenosaunee peoples are spread across
the US–Canada border; Inuit live in the United States, Canada,
Greenland and Russia; the Mapuche peoples in Chile and Argentina;
and the Saami in Norway, Finland, Sweden and Russia. As a consequence of assimilation policies and adverse social conditions, large
numbers of indigenous peoples live in non-indigenous settings such
as cities, settlements, reservations, stations, government-built villages
and urban enclaves, but significant numbers inhabit their traditional
territories in rainforests, highlands, deserts, plains and tundra, much
of which constitute the world's last remaining areas of high biodiversity. In these regions, indigenous peoples' ways of life vary from pastoralists and hunter-gatherers to small-scale farmers.

Table 1.1 provides a general overview of the population distribution of indigenous peoples in selected countries around the world
according to national censuses. Indigenous peoples live in both rich
and poor countries, and in some cases they represent large propor-
tions of the overall state population. However, statistics from official
sources must be treated with scepticism because of varying and
often unreliable data collection methods and political manipulation
in many places. This notwithstanding, current official numbers of
indigenous peoples represent dramatic population declines as a result
of the violence and disease that accompanied colonization almost
everywhere.

In most countries, there are many distinct indigenous groups. For
example, in the United States there are 566 federally recognized
tribes, while Canada recognizes 630 First Nations governments.
In Mexico, there are around 60 different indigenous groups, while

Table 1.1   Number and percentage of indigenous peoples in selected countries

Country	Number of indigenous peoples	% of total population
Bolivia	6,216,026	62.2
Guatemala	5,881,009	41.0
Mexico	16,933,283	15.1
New Zealand	598,605	14.9
Philippines	12–20,000,000	10–20
Chile	1,805,243	11.0
India	84,300,000	8.2
Ecuador	1,018,176	7
Namibia	122,000–129,000	5.7–6.1
Canada	1,400,685	4.3
Australia	669,900	3
Botswana	50–60,000	3
Taiwan	533,600	2.28
United States	5,226,034	1.7
Republic of Congo	50,000	1.2
Norway	55,700	1
Malaysia	178,197	0.6
South Africa	316,500	0.6
Brazil	817,963	0.44
Russia	260,000	0.2
Japan	16,996	0.0179

Sources: ECLAC 2014; USCB 2010; SSB 2014; SNZ 2013; IWGIA 2015; Canada's NHS 2011; IBGE 2010; COAC 2015; EYROC 2014; ABS 2011

in Bolivia there are 36 such groups recognized by the state. In Australia, there are several hundred Aboriginal groups, while in Japan there is only one. However, states often configure indigenous peoples into conveniently segmented or conglomerate colletivities and manipulate the criteria for indigenous identity in order to exclude and/or underrepresent for political and economic purposes (Axelsson and Sköld 2011: 1). State control over indigenous peoples is often organized through state bureaucracies that deal specifically with them. Examples of these include the Bureau of Indian Affairs (BIA) in the United States, Aboriginal Affairs and Northern Development Canada (AANDC), the Corporación Nacional Indígena (CONADI) in Chile, the Comisión Nacional para el Desarrollo de los Pueblos Indígenas (CDI) in Mexico, the National Commission on Indigenous Peoples (NCIP) in the Philippines, the Fundação Nacional do Índio (FUNAI) in Brazil, the Office of Indigenous Policy Coordination

(OIPC) in Australia and, in Malaysia, the Orang Asli Affairs
Department. These state bureaucracies play a central role in defining
indigenous identity as well as formulating social policies, allocating
resources and even approving research.

Indigenous peoples' ways of life are hugely diverse. Thousands
of languages containing distinct ways of conceptualizing the world
are spoken. Indigenous peoples inherit a huge range of cultural pat-
rimonies and have adopted many different kinds of social organizations. Despite their uniqueness, imposed changes have dramatically
affected their wellbeing and cultural integrity. *State of the World's
Indigenous Peoples* (UN DESA 2009: 1) describes the social, economic and cultural consequences of these changes:

> The situation of indigenous peoples in many parts of the world con-
> tinues to be critical: indigenous peoples face systemic discrimination
> and exclusion from political and economic power; they continue to be
> over-represented among the poorest, the illiterate, the destitute; they
> are displaced by wars and environmental disasters; the weapon of rape
> and sexual humiliation is also turned against indigenous women for the
> ethnic cleansing and demoralization of indigenous communities; indig-
> enous peoples are dispossessed of their ancestral lands and deprived of
> their resources for survival, both physical and cultural; they are even
> robbed of their very right to life. In more modern versions of market
> exploitation, indigenous peoples see their traditional knowledge and
> cultural expressions marketed and patented without their consent or
> participation. Of the some 7,000 languages today, it is estimated that
> more than 4,000 are spoken by indigenous peoples. Language special-
> ists predict that up to 90 per cent of the world's languages are likely to
> become extinct or threatened with extinction by the end of the century.
> This statistic illustrates the grave danger faced by indigenous peoples.

As well as all the other losses, the startling decline and disappearance of indigenous languages is emblematic both of the problem of
indigenous cultural survival and the larger loss of valuable human
knowledge that disappears with languages.

Constructions of indigenous identity in Western thought

While self-recognition is an important principle of indigenous peoples'
identity, indigenous communities almost always prioritize collective
over individual identity. However, in the Western liberal democratic
world in which nation-states constitute the predominant authorities,
collective identity is problematic in two ways. First, modern Western

constructions of the self emphasize the individual as the primary agent in relation to government, law and the economy. The prioritization of the individual extends back to the European Enlightenment and continued in influential twentieth-century US sociological conceptions of individual identity in the works of Cooley (1902), Mead (1934), Goffman (1959) and Riesman (1961), the latter articulating how twentieth-century middle-class Americans had made individualism a matter of group conformity. The individual is also privileged by psychoanalysis. Deriving from Freud (1927) and Jung (1916) and later thinkers such as Lacan (2006), the individual self is constructed either as something created by the conditions of society or as having particular psychic qualities inherent in human nature. If this is who we are, indigenous peoples' special relationship with their lands as the foundation for a collective sense of identity has little place.

Second, and somewhat contradictorily, colonial policies imposed collective identities on indigenous peoples through the racial classifications that were (and are) used for administrative and conceptual purposes. Writing on the experience of the Anishinaabeg (also known as Chippewa or Ojibwe), Vizenor (1984: 19) explains how indigenous group identity was created: 'The cultural and political histories of the Anishinaabeg were written in colonial language by those who invented the Indian, renamed the tribes, allotted the land, divided ancestries by geometric degrees of blood, and categorized identities on federal reservations.' Furthermore, the notion of what Vizenor terms the *indian* represents an epistemological imposition of colonial power: 'the *indian* is the absence, natives the presence, and an absence because the name is a discoverable, and a historical simulation of distinct native cultures' (Vizenor and Lee 1999: 84). The colonial concept of the 'Indian' was a political act of defining people in order to dominate them and their lands.

This construction of indigenous identity as a kind of 'absence' is a legacy of contested legal, political and cultural debates embodied in philosophical, social scientific and other Western texts. Both individualization and racialization of indigenous identities are built upon ideological frameworks that accompanied colonial processes. As Miller (1998: 101) points out, prominent non-indigenous historians have told native histories 'by disregarding . . . living generations', and in doing so reproduce familiar patterns of colonial extraction.

A vital part of the justification for the colonization of indigenous peoples and their lands was (and to some extent remains) the claim that indigenous peoples are individually, psychologically and collectively deficient in the various qualities that comprise what Europeans and other colonists saw as civilization. Comparisons made by European observers revealed faults in indigenous societies and economies and in their psyches. These became both an important rationale for colonization and a means to situate indigenous peoples. It is therefore no accident that these comparisons coincided with the Great Land Rush (Weaver 2003), which included the westward expansion in North America, colonial settlement across Australia and New Zealand, and throughout Africa. Hence, it is important to underline that the principle of self-identification adopted at the international level is the preferred means of establishing identity, and that in many respects this is a reaction to a history in which identities were attributed to indigenous peoples in order to demean them and justify exercising authority over them (Cobo 1986: para. 381; UNDRIP 2007: Art. 33. 1).

Undoubtedly, the seeds of these imputed identities were present earlier in the writings of many of the important Enlightenment figures (Eze 1997) as well as in the pre-Enlightenment imagination of non-European peoples. Various images of monstrous creatures, wild men, giant Amazonian women and amalgams of humans and animals had circulated in the Greco-Roman world, medieval texts and encyclopaedias (Jahoda 1999). These frightening depictions are seen in engravings by artists such as Albrecht Dürer and Andrea Mantegna, and world maps such as the Mappa Mundi of 1300 in Hereford Cathedral, England. Early European explorers who encountered indigenous peoples from Columbus onwards were imbued with this medieval imagery and knowledge. Hence, the first explorers saw the New World in 'preconceived terms' (Moseley 1983: 32), but these terms varied. *The Travels of Sir John Mandeville* provides a wondrous vista of the world seen from Europe, as he records voyages to the Middle East, North Africa, India and China. It is a literary and imaginative work drawing on recorded facts and fantasies, and can be seen to 'provide a moral and political perspective for Europe. Europeans' assumptions about their superiority in politics, law, virtue and religion are either directly or ironically challenged' (Moseley 1983: 16). Similarly, the Early Modern essayist Michel de Montaigne (1993/1580) refused to judge the newly 'discovered' inhabitants of the New World as cannibals or savages, but praised their egalitarianism, intelligence, wise approach to nature and personal character.

In the course of European exploration and expansion, however, it was the fearful interpretations of indigenous customs that held sway, fuelling the use of the term 'savage' for indigenous peoples throughout the Americas. The term, derived from the Latin word for a person

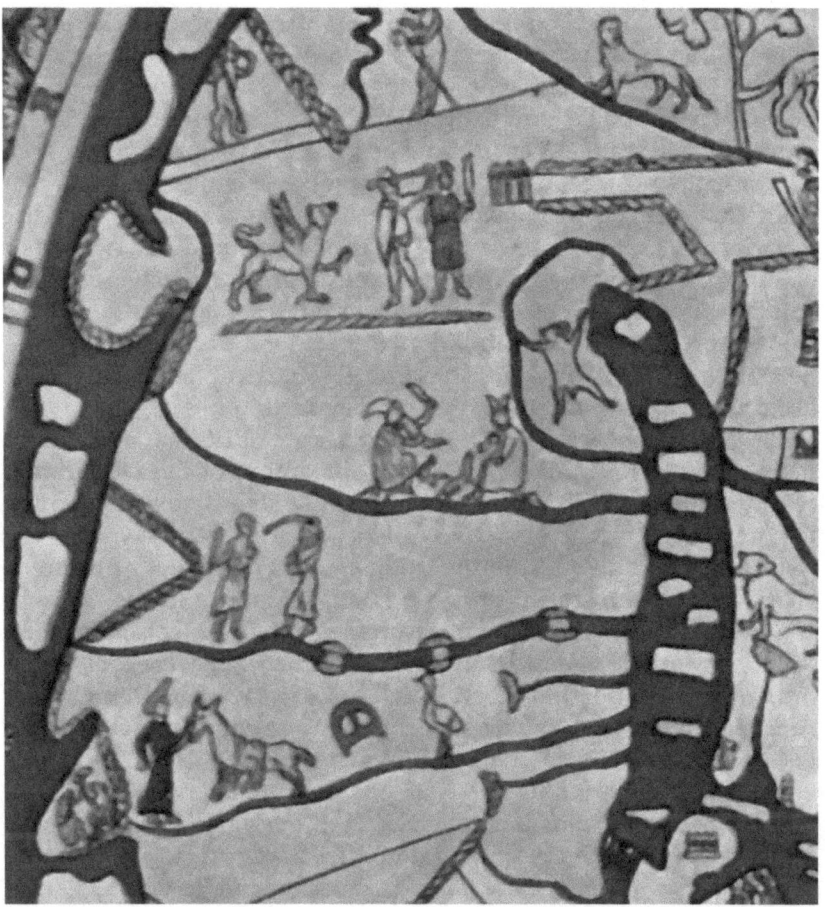

1.1 Essedones, in centre, shown enjoying a cannibalistic meal in a detail from the Mappa Mundi of Hereford Cathedral. Medieval maps and other images depicted non-Europeans as monstrous and semi-human.

Source: Universal History Archive/UIG via Getty Images

of the woods, was used well into the twentieth century. Although having slightly different connotations in various European languages, it was mostly used as a point of semantic contrast with 'civilization', a quality associated with Christianity, agriculture, machine technology and social institutions, which Europeans believed that they possessed in greater abundance or complexity. The savage departed significantly from civilization in ways of life, practices and customs. To many North American colonists in the early phases of occupation, the savages were lacking decent clothes, manners and settled communities. They were not literate and did not have great institutions such as schools, churches, government and law. They were often portrayed as childlike and malleable at one extreme and violent and unpredictable at the other (Berkhofer 1978; Pearce 1988).

Although most reports on the physique of indigenous peoples described them as attractive, muscular and agile, the notion that American Indians, for example, were stunted and inferior types of humans was also a common supposition of several prominent Scottish and French late Enlightenment figures, the most famous of whom were Lord Kames and the naturalist and evolutionist Comte de Buffon (Bieder 1986: 7). Buffon believed that Native Americans lived in environments so harsh that they could only degenerate. In his view, the temperate climate and landscape of Europe produced a more robust civilization. In response, the author of the Declaration of Independence and third US President, Thomas Jefferson, seemed to come to the rescue of Native Americans. In his *Notes on the State of Virginia*, we find an extensive and laboured refutation of Buffon's views replete with statistical comparisons of species in the Old and New World with weights and measurements. Jefferson also defended American Indians against Buffon's charge that they were dull, citing the example of Indian oratory, which he compares favourably to the Ancient Greeks, and challenging Europe to produce more eloquent orators than the Indian chiefs of Virginia (Jefferson 1975/1787: 99). However, throughout his life Jefferson, as a prominent enslaver, was never above embracing ideas of white supremacy. He supported laws sequestering indigenous lands and policies advancing rapid assimilation. Much of his defence of Native Americans can be seen as part of his nationalist defence of the American settler colonial society.

While Buffon's views can easily be seen today as crude and self-aggrandizing prejudices, a wider set of naturalistic ideas regarding indigenous peoples, having roots in the writings of late Enlightenment philosophers, scientists, explorers, colonists and politicians, became entrenched. Ideas about national and racial superiority were pervasive across European empires in the nineteenth century. They were dignified by science through cultural evolutionism and social Darwinism. Such theories extrapolated from biological evolutionism and held that lesser adapted cultures and races would inevitably be subordinated or made extinct by the better adapted European race. The main human distinctions were depicted as based on geographical origins and physiological characteristics. Race helped explain what were deemed inequalities of faculties and abilities between

Europeans and non-Europeans. The turn to this crude and hardened determinism (Russett 1976: 3) in the social sciences and politics displaced the free-thinking, more romantic, transcendentalist thinking that had briefly flourished in Europe and North America in the nineteenth century.

The influence of anthropological constructions of indigenous identity

The nineteenth-century social science of anthropology inherited Western assumptions about non-Europeans and adopted cultural evolutionism as its main founding theory. Having established itself as an authoritative voice on the identities of indigenous peoples, it emerged from a broader line of racial and evolutionary commentary and was based on ethnographic observation of cultures. In the process of analysing other cultures, many European anthropologists fed useful information to colonial administrators to help maintain imperial control (Dieckmann 2007: 61–3; Samson 2008). This was particularly important in South Africa, where the measurements of indigenous peoples' bodies and brains through physical anthropology gave credence to apartheid policies (Maylam 2001). Anthropological observation and measurement was also an important source of assimilation measures, such as the schooling of indigenous peoples in New Zealand and other British colonies (Simon 1998).

Reports, treatises and foundational anthropological texts boldly claimed to have verified that non-Europeans existed in a prior state of human civilization. Prominent among the functionaries straddling anthropology and colonial administration was the jurist and social scientist Sir Henry Maine, an architect of indirect rule whose influence on both anthropology and colonialism was immense (Mantena 2010; Mamdani 2012: 7). In the twentieth century anthropologist Malinowski (1945: 138–50) gave advice on indirect rule, reinforcing the idea that colonialism was an enterprise involving the meeting of peoples of vastly unequal capacities. Across the channel in France, the move away from biological determinism in anthropology by the likes of Paul Rivet and Marcel Mauss was based on appealing to the value of knowledge about indigenous peoples to the French Empire, and ethnology was promoted as essential to colonial rule (Conklin 2013: 191, 220). Similar connections between the anthropological images of indigenous knowledge and colonial rule can be drawn from the works and actions of US anthropologists studying American

Indians during the frontier period (Biolsi and Zimmerman 1997: 12–14). More profoundly, Taussig (1987: 220) points out that many societies bind together through secrets. These may be of a sacred nature, and help form the identities of peoples. In this respect, one of anthropology's most 'enduring contributions' is the unveiling of secrets, and these serve the interests of imposing order. By revealing a secret, the way is clear to control the peoples from whom the secret emerges.

Many nineteenth-century anthropologists, such as the 'founding fathers' Edward Tylor and Lewis Henry Morgan, as well as their counterparts in sociology, advanced the idea that differences in the qualities of cultures around the world could be understood as representing increments on a scale of human civilization. For many European and Euro-American anthropologists and sociologists, the act of looking at the non-European was akin to looking into Europe's own past. Hence, in concluding his 1878 work *The Early History of Mankind*, Tylor (1964: 233) asserts that 'there is reason to suppose that our ancestors in remote times made fire with a machine much like that of the modern Esquimaux [Inuit], and at a far later date they used the bow and arrow, as so many savage tribes still do'. The message that Europeans and indigenous peoples were not contemporaries was very clear.

Actual physical indexes of these temporal differences were considered to be bases of discrete races, and evidence that the level of civilization could be read from measurements of the human body. Here, social and natural science were in alliance. As Gould (1981: 35–6) pointed out in his influential book *The Mismeasure of Man*, the three greatest naturalists of the nineteenth century, Georges Cuvier, Charles Lyell and Charles Darwin, were all convinced of the inferiority of indigenous peoples, especially Australian Aborigines, Kalahari Bushmen and the natives of Tierra del Fuego. The real proof of inferiority was held to emerge from anthropometric measurements and photographs, showing that there existed racial differences in cranial capacity and other physical qualities, such as facial appearance and skull shape, and that these corresponded with various indices of group traits such as a propensity towards crime or intelligence. Anthropologists around the world also collected skulls and bones to make judgments on the characteristics of indigenous peoples in comparison to each other and to other racial types. In the first third of the twentieth century, the South African Museum was active in making casts of skulls of deceased Khoisan-speaking peoples taken from various sites (Dieckmann 2007: 102).

Being members of a culturally less developed race implied that improvements to indigenous communities would be brought about by the tutelage of colonial rulers and settlers. Early American anthropology, in particular, contributed greatly to enlarging the use of the concept of race, and this influenced politicians' views and institutional policies that in turn prejudiced the position of people of non-European descent in US society (Baker 1998: 52–3). The inescapable conclusion from social and natural science in a multi-racial society like that of the United States was that non-Caucasians were likely to fail or do worse than whites in the areas of education, employment and citizenship. The best that could be hoped for them was through remedial programmes. Race-based policies would then legitimate American and European colonial control around the world, since they could easily be interpreted as benign enterprises to uplift backward peoples.

Some anthropologists, while still adhering to cultural evolution-ism, which depicted their indigenous informants below them in the hierarchies of civilization – notably Frank Cushing and Lewis Henry Morgan – had close associations with Native Americans and were advocates for them in their conflicts with the US government (Strong 2004: 347). This concern was often of a paternal nature. Morgan, for example, begins his classic work on the Haudenosaunee with a plea for readers to be empathic to the American Indians in order to assist with 'his capabilities for future elevation' (1962/1851: ix). Less pater-nalistic and more concerned with adding to the corpus of Western professional knowledge was A. R. Radcliffe-Brown, who conducted his research on Australian Aborigines under the aegis of brutal cus-todial authority in 'lock hospitals' (Lindqvist 2007: 112–16). At around the same time, German anthropologists were undertaking research on Bushmen prisoners rather than in 'the field' (Dieckmann 2007: 55). And at the turn of the twentieth century, A. L. Kroeber, generally thought of as a liberal anthropologist, put the Northern California Yahi genocide survivor Ishi on live display at the Phoebe Hearst Museum of Anthropology in San Francisco; after Ishi's death, Kroeber delivered his brain to the Smithsonian Institution for further research (Scheper-Hughes 2002). A few years before this, Kroeber had written a detailed ethnographic report on Greenlandic Inuit in captivity at the Natural History Museum in New York (Harper 2001: 85). While this history is clearly embarrassing, contemporary non-indigenous and indigenous scholars are far from unanimous on what this early social science legacy means today.

The premises underlying much of early anthropological research and practice presupposed an objective standpoint from where it is possible to judge the merits of one way of life over others. Ethnographic and other studies of indigenous peoples in the nineteenth century were 'an extremely subtle and spiritual cognitive imperialism, a power-based monologue, a monologue *about* alien cultures rather than . . . a dialogue with them in terms of sovereignty' (McGrane 1989: 127).

Another dimension of these and similar representations was the insistence on the opposition between culture and nature. Brody (1991/1975: 98) summarizes this: 'The colonialist regards his own society, or societies very like it, as synonymous with culture, and he regards the colonialized as part of nature.' Indigenous cultures were deemed closer to the animal world, and this was underlined in the early ethnographic collections in which indigenous people were hosted and displayed in natural history museums alongside animals, plants and rocks. That indigenous peoples were exhibited in 'human zoos' (Blanchard et al. 2007) meant that they and their material culture had value only insofar as it was a foil to the visible evidence of technological progress achieved by Western society. Across Europe and North America, indigenous artefacts were eagerly collected and displayed in museums as a way of proving this claim. Indigenous peoples were represented as not being contemporaries of Europeans (Fabian 2002/1983), while often being discussed as doomed to extinction in the face of the advancement of a superior civilization (McGregor 1993; Brantlinger 2003; Gigoux 2010). These invidious comparisons and the racial classifications that often informed them were guiding themes of the immensely popular anthropological expositions that occurred up to the mid-twentieth century. The 1931 Colonial Exposition in Paris, for example, attracted more than 33 million paid entries at a time of major economic depression (Conklin 2013: 199). For the audiences, the presentation of indigenous cultures in the controlled settings of the museum or within the boundaries of the exhibition park became sources of authoritative intercultural knowledge widely disseminated in Europe and North America.

Not all aspects of indigenous culture were displayed for scientific and entertainment purposes; some were determined by government officials as so inconsistent with the values of the new settler societies that they ought not to be seen. This shows that the identities of the non-indigenous colonizers were threatened by what they saw as the identities of native peoples. For example, once knowledge of indigenous cultures was circulated among US government officials, some

American Indian practices were regarded as subversive, obscene, dangerous and pagan, and this created political pressure for control and in some cases banning. Concerns about the indigenous identities was so serious in the United States that the state was willing to contravene the rights to freedom of expression and religion.

Consequently, the US Constitution was violated by the government suppression of Native American religious practices under the Courts of Indian Offenses, which was established in 1883. Practices such as the Sun Dance of the Great Plains peoples, the potlatch of the Northwest coast Indians, and a number of different ceremonial dances performed by Pueblo Indians in the Southwest became potentially criminal activities. The Sun Dances, for example, were criticized for the self-harm inflicted upon dancers. They were described by US officials as 'superstitious amusements' at best and 'orgies' at worst (Niezen 2000: 128). As Secretary of Interior Henry Teller remarked in a letter to the Commissioner of Indian Affairs, 'These feasts or dances are not social gatherings for the amusement of these people, but, on the contrary, are intended and calculated to stimulate the warlike passions of the young warriors of the tribe' (Martinez 2011: 101). Teller and other officials believed that indigenous practices were what we might today call religious extremism, and from 1883 onwards they became incorporated into the Indian Religious Crimes Code. This was also part of an attack on what were called 'medicine men', who usually carried out both medical and religious functions and whom Teller believed prevented children from going to school. The coordinated attack on indigenous spiritual practices led to some being abandoned. Referring to the end of the Kiowa Sun Dance in 1887, N. Scott Momaday (1964: 35) tells us: 'The loss of the Sun Dance was the blow that killed the native Kiowa culture. The Kiowa might have endured every privation but that, the desecration of their faith. Without their religion, there was nothing to sustain them.'

Ramnarine (2013: 243) suggests that, in attempting to disconnect indigenous peoples from their histories and cultures, 'colonial projects have involved disparaging the noise of colonized subjects and silencing expressions of language, music, sacred incantation and protest. Sound is also a colonizing agent, influencing the habits of hearing and listening (which are not the same).' This is particularly applicable to the clampdowns on the sacred and secular dances of the American Indians of the Great Plains, most of which involved drumming, whistles, rattles and singing. The prohibition against Native American children singing and dancing at boarding schools is a further measure of this process of cultural erasure (Child 1998; Stout 2012). As we shall discuss further in Chapter 3, indigenous children at boarding schools were prohibited from speaking their languages; these languages were excluded from national curricula and, as a result, they did not find their way into books, thus contributing to the general perception that these languages, and the collective identities to which they were attached, were either unimportant or extinct.

Counter colonial narratives on indigenous identity

Many indigenous scholars have understandably rejected anthropology and evolutionary thinking in general. In part, this is because of their racist legacies, but it is also because an authoritative academic examination of specific beliefs, practices or attributes of indigenous peoples sometimes usurps rights to describe and interpret who they are. While indigenous scholars have drawn extensively from their own backgrounds and worldviews, many have found affinities with theorists of colonialism. These theories assist in articulating identity outside the anthropological construct of what is now called 'indigeneity', often regarded as a tainted artefact of colonialism (Jaimes 1992; Moreton-Robinson 2004: 75–88; Coulthard 2007, 2014; Simpson 2011). As Medak-Saltzman (2015: 12) argues, '"Indigeneity" is all too often invoked as a term – rather than a concept – which reduces it to jargon, removes it from its vital context, and embeds it in writing that otherwise betrays a very limited intellectual and scholarly understanding of Native experiences, issues, and histories.'

Some indigenous writers perceive colonialism as the political process within which indigenous identity must be understood, rather than 'postcolonialism', which often emphasizes indigenous 'agency' within circumstances *after* colonialism (Dunbar-Ortiz 2014: 5). As there has been no decolonization process for them, indigenous peoples clearly live within colonial orders (Yazzie 2000), and as Smith (2012: 24) pointed out, postcolonialism may simply be another way of 'reauthorizing the privileges of non-indigenous academics because the field of "post-colonial" discourse has been defined in ways which can still leave out indigenous peoples, our ways of knowing and our current concerns.' This is a point underlined by Owens (2001), whose scepticism of postcolonial theory extends to its mainstream academic positioning and indifference towards indigenous histories and literatures.

Writers such as Alfred (2005) and Corntassel (Alfred and Corntassel 2005) argue that indigenousness is an identity signalled by prior and enduring occupancy of the land, a point emphasized by older generations of Native American writers such as N. Scott Momaday (1997), who won the Pulitzer Prize for his novel *House Made of Dawn* in 1969. One of the reasons for the inapplicability of postcolonialism in the view of many indigenous commentators is that it normalizes incorporation into the social, political and economic order of nation-states. There are, of course, differences of opinion (see Turner 2006: 96–121), and few indigenous scholars would expunge all non-indigenous postcolonial scholarship from consideration. For example, Ishii (2011) draws on postcolonial theorist Edward Said's ideas about Orientalism to show how many of the voluminous non-indigenous texts on the Hopi are encapsulated within paradigms that make sense principally within a limited and ethnocentric intellectual project. One of the images formed of the Hopi – and this observation could be extended to anthropological studies of many other indigenous groups – is the notion of wholeness, in which the culture is likened to an organism consisting of interacting parts. But, as Ishii observes of the influential work of former BIA director John Collier, this wholeness is contained within a larger whole, which is the United States, 'a cultural island in the stream of modern American life' (quoted by Ishii 2011: 62). The nation-state is assumed to be the container for indigenous identity and culture. The narratives of the Hopi and other Native Americans are quietly, even poetically, folded within it by postcolonial approaches. Therefore, a *decolonial* approach is needed. This does not place intellectual analysis within Western liberal worldviews or academic disciplines, embraces non-Western cosmologies, views neoliberal capitalism as inherently exploitative and advocates alternative economies and polities (see Mignolo 2011). The decolonial model may have been put into words by university professionals, but is put into action by numerous indigenous communities and movements such as the Zapatistas in Mexico and Idle No More in Canada.

The nation-state and indigenous identity

Miller (2011: 27) notes that the idea of indigenousness should not be seen solely as the condition of first occupancy. Rather, she argues, indigenousness is related to the lifeways of those peoples who never adopted a nation-state. This puts indigenous peoples in direct engagement with colonizing groups operating under the umbrella of the nation-state. From the eighteenth century onwards, the transformation of settler societies into independent nation-states can be described as the institutional embodiment of political and economic liberalism into 'an imagined political community'. According to Anderson (1983: 78) these imagined political communities acquired an institutional form through the emergence of 'nation-states, republican institutions, common citizenships, popular sovereignty, national flags and anthems'. In the process, the state promoted and enforced cultural homogeneity in order to guarantee the loyalties of its populations, while also affirming its territorial sovereignty by drawing borders and implementing internal colonization and assimilation policies. The development of a legal framework of citizenship contributed to both the inclusion and the exclusion of ethnic groups and minorities from the state. The ideological motif underpinning these policies was the idea of progress enshrined in individual and property rights and fortified by doctrines of cultural superiority already mentioned.

During the Great Land Rush, indigenous peoples were a problem for the nation-building objectives of cultural homogeneity and sovereignty and, by extension, the idea of progress. On the one hand, their self-defined identities did not mesh well with the various elements of the 'imagined community', while their attachment to their traditional territories posed a challenge to the imposed sovereignty of the state. Such considerations were central to the establishing of settler states like Australia, New Zealand, the United States and Canada. In these countries, indigenous identity came to be attached to official bureaucratic systems of rewards and benefits based on racializing indigenous people through blood quantum laws and similar systems of classification. The prevalence of intermarriage, rape of indigenous women and male-dominated frontier colonization has meant that in settler states people who are considered indigenous in their communities may have had non-indigenous parentage and therefore not be recognized by the state. This led to debates about the role of racial purity in identity. Racial politics is also central to the consideration of indigenous identity in post-independence states, such as those in Africa and Asia that claim that 'everyone is indigenous', and Latin America where ideas of citizenship and conceptions of cultural hybridity (*mestizaje*) have been used to deny distinct indigenous identities. We now turn to some examples of states in which indigenous identities have been the objects of debate, transformation and redefinition.

Australia

After the initial British occupation of Australia by the navy and 736 settler-convicts, the settler society was consolidated between the 1820s and 1860s when British and Irish settlers expanded their territorial control at the expense of Aboriginal peoples, while acquiring increasing levels of self-government (Woollacott 2015: 2–4). Land grabbing was justified by racial ideologies, and these contributed to the genocide of Aboriginal peoples as frontier violence spread through Australia in the nineteenth and early twentieth centuries (Kociumbas 2004: 88–90). The independence of Australia from Britain in 1901, making it a Dominion of the British Empire, did not end the violence, but it did pose questions about the role and identity of Aboriginal peoples in the making of a 'modern' independent Australia. Overall, public policies regarding Aboriginal communities created a system of dependency in which the federal and state governments provided welfare benefits to uprooted Aborigines, while developing strong policies of assimilation in which the forced removal of mixed-race or 'half-caste' children from their families was a cornerstone (Reynolds 2005: 184). Underlying these practices was a complex system of racial criteria of Aboriginal identification based on blood quantum laws that defined, until the 1970s, who was regarded as Aboriginal (Mercer 2003: 430).

This changed in 1981 when the *Report on a Review of the Administration of the Working Definition of Aboriginal and Torres Strait Islanders* proposed a three-part definition of Aboriginal identity based on descent, self-identification and community recognition: 'An Aboriginal or Torres Strait Islander is a person of Aboriginal or Torres Strait Islander descent who identifies as an Aboriginal or Torres Strait Islander and is accepted as such by the community in which he [or she] lives' (Gardiner-Garden 2003: 4). Gardiner-Garden (2003: 6–13) argues that although this definition was an improvement on crude biological categories, its implementation and interpretation proved to be controversial when it came to determining who was and who was not Aboriginal. Individuals, communities and the state often had differing views. In fact, the claims of people seeking Aboriginal status in Tasmania has led to some Aboriginal groups advocating a return to genetic or biological definitions (Mercer 2003: 430).

One of the most profound influences on Aboriginal identity was the forced removal of mixed-descent children from their families and their placement in foster institutions or in adopted non-Aboriginal families. The historian Henry Reynolds (2005: 209) points out that in the 1930s it was assumed that 'full blood' Aboriginals would gradually become extinct, while the mixed-descent Aboriginal would eventually become fully assimilated. In order to help this process, it was necessary to remove mixed-descent children from their families so as to cut them off from their Aboriginal cultural identities. The aim in Australia was therefore to destroy Aboriginal identity altogether. In 1997, the Human Rights and Equal Opportunity Commission (HREOC) released *Bringing them home: Report of the National Inquiry into the Separation of Aboriginal and Torres Strait Islander Children from Their Families*, documenting the dark history behind these policies and the legacies of psychological trauma that these children experienced as a consequence of it. Reynolds (2005: 237), whose book is titled *Nowhere People*, reflects on how his own identity was challenged when he discovered that his father was a mixed-descent Aboriginal who had been removed from his family:

> But what is Aboriginality? It will be clear ... that the evidence is circumstantial and incomplete. But I think we all agree that this was at the core of the hidden history, the obscured identity. Does this make us Aboriginal? There is no easy answer to that question, nor a collective one. And, what is more, you are damned if you identify and damned if you don't.

The United States

The relationship between the US government and Native Americans is built upon the appropriation of Native American lands. The principles that guide recognition are based on some notion of indigenous sovereignty as nations ingrained in the US Constitution, treaties and a complex web of laws and jurisprudence (Wilkins and Lomawaima 2001: 4–11). In 1831, in a landmark case *Cherokee Nation v. Georgia*, Supreme Court Chief Justice John Marshall declared that Indian tribes were 'domestic dependent nations' and that 'their relation to the United States resembles that of a ward to his guardian' (Robertson 2005; Hausbeck 2008: 925–6). However, given the vast geographical expanse of lands claimed by the United States, the different times at which lands were appropriated, and the differences in the reactions of indigenous groups, there are many variations in the structuring of indigenous identity.

As will be described in more detail in Chapter 3, by the 1890s

most Native Americans were confined to federal or state reservations, allotted lands and restricted status lands as they were removed
and displaced from their territories to make way for Euro-American
settlement, agriculture and industry. In the new context of reservations, Native Americans were deprived of much of their economic
base, and the federal government implemented a system of welfare
to assist them, while later allowing for limited self-government. The
delivery of services was the responsibility of the Office for Indian
Affairs (which became the Bureau of Indian Affairs in 1947) and
federal recognition of Native American tribes became a requirement
to determine eligibility for welfare benefits – not as individuals, but
as tribes. Up until the 1970s, however, recognition was 'the result of
a century of . . . desultory and unfocused judicial rulings absent any
cogent or reasonable federal acknowledgment policy' (Quinn 1992:
43). Within the Bureau of Indian Affairs (BIA), the Office of Federal
Acknowledgement (OFA) implemented the *Procedures for Establishing
that an American Indian Group Exists as an Indian Tribe* (CFR 1978).
It provided seven mandatory criteria for federal acknowledgement
and applied to most federally acknowledged groups:

(a) The petitioner has been identified as an American Indian entity
     on a substantially continuous basis since 1900.
(b) A predominant portion of the petitioning group comprises a dis-
     tinct community and has existed as a community from historical
     times until the present.
(c) The petitioner has maintained political influence or authority
     over its members as an autonomous entity from historical times
     until the present.
(d) A copy of the group's present governing document including its
     membership criteria. In the absence of a written document, the
     petitioner must provide a statement describing in full its mem-
     bership criteria and current governing procedures.
(e) The petitioner's membership consists of individuals who descend
     from a historical Indian tribe or from historical Indian tribes
     which combined and functioned as a single autonomous politi-
     cal entity.
(f) The membership of the petitioning group is composed prin-
     cipally of persons who are not members of any acknowledged
     North American Indian tribe.
(g) Neither the petitioner nor its members are the subject of con-
     gressional legislation that has expressly terminated or forbidden
     the Federal relationship. (CFR 1978: Title 25, 83.7)

The burden of proof fell on the indigenous group seeking recognition to petition the state, and it led to the exclusion of many indigenous groups who were not able to meet the requirements listed above, regardless of their self-identification as Native Americans. Miller (2003: 112) suggests that this complex bureaucratic system of recognition is fundamentally unfair as it relies on 'legal precedent, ethnocentric concepts of indigenous life, and nonindigenous forms of evidence and record keeping'. In particular, it largely ignores both the fluidity of Native American groupings and the effects of violence and displacement in altering the composition of these groups. At present, it is the right of each tribe to establish procedures for enrolment of individuals to the tribe. Although they may understand 'blood' differently, many groups use the external racial category of blood quantum as their own criteria for enrolment (Forte 2013: 35). The duty of assistance of the federal government does not emerge from the right of an individual but from the rights of the tribe. Garroute (2003: 6) highlights how this process of recognition has led to conflicts over tribal recognition as well as individual tribal membership.

Canada

The contemporary relationship between the Canadian state and Aboriginal peoples (known variously as First Nations, Inuit and Métis) is a product of similar patterns of settler violence, land grabbing, displacement, poverty, marginality, racism and discrimination that characterized settler colonialism in Australia and the United States.

The question of indigenous identity in Canada has been intrinsically linked to the recognition and exercise of pre-existing indigenous rights over their territories, lands and resources. The Royal Proclamation of 1763 established the general framework by which the British Crown recognized Aboriginal title over their lands, while stipulating that only the Crown could buy these lands if ceded by treaty. What was not ceded by treaty was, in the words of the Proclamation, 'reserved to them' under what became known as Aboriginal Title. Thereafter, various 'numbered treaties' were signed by indigenous groups with the Crown in which extensive tracts of lands were exchanged for monetary and welfare compensations. In international public law, treaties take place between two sovereign nations and so there is an implicit assumption that Aboriginal groups have the status of nations here and elsewhere (Courtoreille 1997:

139). However, no relationship between sovereign equals exists, and Canada has treated Aboriginal peoples as wards of the state, implementing aggressive policies of assimilation and extinguishment of the titles inherited from the Proclamation and affirmed in various Supreme Court decisions.

The Indian Act of 1876 was an attempt to combine all previous legislation related to Aboriginal peoples. It is based on the premise that Aboriginal peoples are not competent to administer their own affairs and that it was necessary to assimilate them into settler society. It establishes the responsibility of the federal government for the education, health and administration of Aboriginal peoples' affairs, including their lands, while defining the legal criteria for recognizing Aboriginal identity. Individuals who met the criteria were recognized as Status Indians, listed on an Indian Registry and provided with an Indian Status Card. The Indian Act was applied to record Indians, Indian bands and Indian reserves. However, this procedure was not applicable for Métis and Inuit. Furi and Wherrett (2003: 2) summarized the main elements of the Indian Act:

> The definition of Indian in the 1876 Act emphasized male lineage. An Indian was defined as any male person of Indian blood reputed to belong to a particular band; any child of such a person; and any woman lawfully married to such a person. If an Indian woman married a non-Indian, she lost her status. The Act and subsequent amendments also continued and furthered the policy of enfranchisement. Various incentives to enfranchise existed, including access to voting rights. Enfranchisement became compulsory in a number of circumstances; for example, it was automatic if an Indian became a doctor, lawyer, Christian minister, or earned a university degree.

Three main implications can be inferred from the Act. First, it is government officials who decide the identity of an indigenous person. Second, blood quantum is central to the definition of indigenous identity, although it severely discriminated against indigenous women who married a non-indigenous man, and thereby lost all of their rights as recognized Indians. This changed only after tireless efforts from Aboriginal women, including Sandra Lovelace, who took her case of gender discrimination to the UN Human Rights Committee in 1981 (McIvor 2004). Only in 1985 were the sexist provisions in the Indian Act removed. Finally, Status Indians could lose registration and become 'enfranchised' by demonstrating knowledge of farming or qualifying as a professional in various occupations.

In 1982 the Canadian government approved the Constitution Act affirming Aboriginal rights (Section 35(1)) in regard to 'Indians, Inuit and Métis peoples of Canada' (Section 35(2)). Although the Act provided constitutional recognition of Aboriginal peoples, it did not solve problems of land claims and demands for self-government, and it remains part of a colonial system that imposes identity upon indigenous peoples: 'self-identification and the open, kinship- and community-based methods of recognizing tribal membership has been, for the most part, superseded by externally imposed, culturally incompatible methods of acknowledging citizenship' (Chabot 2007: 38). The Constitution Act did not derogate the Indian Act of 1876, which, despite a number of amendments, remains the general assimilationist framework for the relationship between Canada and Aboriginal peoples. More importantly, it does not address the major implication for Aboriginal identity that arises from the erosion of land ownership and Aboriginal title. As Alfred (1999: 27) points out:

> The relationship between homeland and identity is critical. Today, our 'Indigenous' identity is rooted too much in the reserve system and *Indian Act* band system. Under this system, there is no opportunity to have a relationship with our traditional lands, and an identity that is founded on this relationship to the land. In our traditional societies, just about every aspect of our traditional identity involved our environment.

Latin America

In Latin America and the Caribbean there are an estimated 826 different indigenous groups made up of close to 45 million people (ECLAC 2014: 36–8). The majority of them live in urban areas, but many are communal farmers, pastoralists and hunter-gatherers in highlands, rainforests and savannahs. The question of indigenous identity in Latin America has to be understood in relation to three broad historical periods: colonial, nation-state formation and globalization.

In Spanish America, *Indios* were regarded as part of the social and economic structure of society rigidly divided according to race: 'a strict racial and class hierarchy operated in colonial New Mexican society, as it did elsewhere in Latin America. Indian peoples occupied the lowest rung in the racial hierarchy, followed by mixed-bloods. Spaniards – those with pure blood – occupied the top rung'

(Brown 2013: 112). This racial hierarchy intersected with the colonial economic system that relied on Indian labour. According to Wade (1997: 28): 'Indio was a specific administrative category – in many ways, a fiscal category, since the typical indigenous person was one who lived in an indigenous community and paid tribute, in labour or goods.' Furthermore, the *Leyes de Indias*, the body of laws that regulated life in colonial Spanish America, provided the legal framework for indigenous peoples. As subjects of the Crown, these laws regulated their labour, tributes, Christian instruction and settlements (pueblos), while granting rights and protections – at least nominally – against abuses and land dispossession. In this context, the recognition of Indian identity was central to their subordinated social and economic status as well as to the recognition of rights.

However, nineteenth-century Creole leaders such as Simón Bolivar, José San Martín and Bernardo O'Higgins, who led the revolutionary movements for independence, were informed by liberal ideas of progress, equality and freedom. In this context, the new republican order sought to eradicate institutions and laws, including the safeguards and limited rights that Indians had during the colonial period, in order to achieve the equality of the Indians. As a result, indigenous peoples were transformed into citizens and, in the process, their indigenous status was abolished. As Earle (2007: 22–9) indicates, the Indian past was transformed into a myth of origin for the newly independent states, while their heirs were transformed into citizens. But as we will discuss in Chapter 2, this was nothing more than a formal recognition, since most indigenous peoples were transformed into landless peasants as they were deprived of their territories and resources.

The new Latin American states looked at the American and French Revolutions for political ideas, to Britain for economic ideas and to the United States for ideas about future colonization. Political elites were eager to exercise their sovereign claims over indigenous territories in order to avoid other nations' claims and also as a way of incorporating indigenous peoples into state economies. In many places, indigenous peoples were regarded as a hindrance to modernization, and they became synonymous with backwardness, drunkenness and laziness. Racial ideas adopted from European social scientific discourses provided justification for the dispossession of indigenous peoples from their lands and resources and, as a result, they became invisible in the official narratives of the state as they were politically, socially and economically marginalized (Langer 2003: xiii–xiv). By the 1930s, state sponsored *indigenista* movements attempted to

establish assimilation policies across the continent and create homogeneous national cultures.

It was not until the 1990s when, in the context of globalization,
multiculturalism, neoliberal policies and indigenous mobilizations,
a new politics of identity began to unfold, and indigenous peoples
became part of new movements to promote their rights as distinct
peoples. The fight against political and social inclusion and the protection of their rights to their territories, lands and resources was
oriented towards constitutional reforms that recognized their identities as part of multicultural nation-states. The recognition of identity
was regarded as a necessary step towards political inclusion and the
recognition of rights. The approval of new political constitutions by
Ecuador in 2008 and Bolivia in 2009 represented significant turning
points in terms of indigenous recognition and the transformation of
indigenous peoples into subjects of rights. The fact that in both countries there are larger numbers of surviving indigenous peoples than in
many other Latin American countries underlines the importance of
this process.

In Ecuador, the election of the left-wing candidate Rafael Correa
in 2006 opened the door for the drafting of a new political constitution. During the negotiations, the Confederation of Indigenous
Nationalities of Ecuador (CONAIE) played a crucial role in pushing
forward the inclusion of indigenous peoples in the constitutional text
and its approval in the national referendum (Becker 2011: 49–53).
The new political constitution starts with Article 1 recognizing the
multicultural nature of the state: 'Ecuador is a constitutional State
of rights and justice, a social, democratic, sovereign, independent,
unitary, intercultural, plurinational and secular State' (Republic of
Ecuador 2008). This political recognition was manifested in the affirmation of collective rights as described by international documents
and human rights frameworks (see Chapter 4, Art. 56–60). However,
this was not straightforward and the very notion of a plurinational
state is open to multiple interpretations. Nonetheless, Ecuador's
new constitution was regarded by many as a way of decolonization
through affirming indigenous identity, political inclusion and the
guaranteeing of collective rights (Becker 2011: 53–5).

In Bolivia, Evo Morales's victory in 2005 not only led to a new
political constitution, but also to the reconceptualization of the state.
Morales, an Aymara, put forward a broad coalition in which indigenous movements played a central role alongside trade unions and
left-wing organizations. Within the coalition, the idea of indigeneity was transformed into a strategy for power and inclusion (Trejos

2013: 47–8). In 2009, a new political constitution was approved, creating the refounded Plurinational State of Bolivia. Indigeneity was transformed into the cornerstone of national identity:

> Art. 1   Bolivia is constituted as a Unitary Social State of Pluri-National Communitarian Law that is free, independent, sovereign, democratic, intercultural, decentralized and with autonomies. Bolivia is founded on plurality and on political, economic, juridical, cultural and linguistic pluralism in the integration process of the country.
> Art. 2   Given the pre-colonial existence of nations and rural native indigenous peoples and their ancestral control of their territories, their free determination, consisting of the right to autonomy, self-government, their culture, recognition of their institutions, and the consolidation of their territorial entities, is guaranteed within the framework of the unity of the State, in accordance with this Constitution and the law.
> Art. 3   The Bolivian nation is formed by all Bolivians, the native indigenous nations and peoples, and the inter-cultural and Afro-Bolivian communities that, together, constitute the Bolivian people. (Republic of Bolivia 2009)

Morales's triumph created a new political paradigm based on indigenous identity, providing new national narratives and symbols and a reconfiguration of state structures (Soruco Sologuren et al. 2014: 175). Indeed, the recognition of indigenous rights within the state also uncovered complexities and contradictions surrounding identity politics. Not all indigenous communities in Bolivia necessarily identify themselves with state sponsored 'indigeneity' even if implemented by indigenous leaders (Canessa 2007: 208–10). Furthermore, indigenous identity in Bolivia reflects tensions springing from identifications people may have with specific ethnic groups and socioeconomic conditions like *campesino* or *pobre*, and the use of these in asserting collective right claims (Albó 2008: 8). These inter-indigenous group relations are themselves structured by prior colonial patterns that promoted racial divisions as a way of control and hegemony.

The largest country in South America, Brazil, offers another variation in the politics of indigenous identity. Here there is a long and complex history of nation building, capitalist economic development and cultural discourses on Brazilian identity. More recently, the question of indigenous identity in Brazil has acquired a global dimension, as the indigenous peoples living in the ecologically fragile Amazonian region have become an international symbol for indigenous rights worldwide, and these include as many as 100 groups that are out of contact with the outside world, and for whose right to

remain uncontacted the NGO Survival International has been cam-
paigning. The identities of these peoples are in many ways unique
in that they are defined externally almost entirely by the fact of their
non-relationship with colonizers.

Like other Latin American states, Brazil was influenced by social
Darwinism, ideas of progress and quests for racial homogeneity.
Although Indians were sometimes depicted in romantic overtones
and nostalgic narratives, they were regarded as a racial problem
(Devine Guzmán 2013). In the 1930s, during the dictatorship of
Getulio Vargas, 'miscegenation' was seen as the way to achieve
national integration through progressive 'whitening':

> [T]he state encouraged the study of Brazil's African and Indian herit-
> age as nationalist folklore while encouraging whitening and repressing
> ethnic diversity through immigration and education policies. At the
> same time, it continued to project the image of Brazil as a socially
> advanced nation that had solved its 'race problem' through miscegena-
> tion and had achieved racial democracy, an area where more powerful
> nations had failed. (Caulfield 2003: 166)

The idea of creating a racially homogeneous state was instrumental to the policy of integrating indigenous peoples into the larger
European-dominated society. In doing this, it was important to
remove them from their territories and resources and appropriate
their labour for the economic base of state building. The Indian
Statute of 1973 established a roadmap for indigenous assimilation
through the creation of restricted indigenous areas and the transformation of the Indians into wards of the state. The Statute provides
a classification of indigenous peoples in relation to their different
levels of integration to society: (a) isolated, (b) in the process of integration, (c) integrated (Estatuto do Índio, Arts. 3 and 4). Through
this scheme, indigenous identity was gradually erased by means of
'paternal guidance' of the state. Albert (2005: 202) explains the
significance of these measures: 'The Indian Statute conferred a
generic identity on autochthonous societies of the country, that of
"indigenous communities," inseparable from their legal status as only
"relatively capable" persons.'

However, indigenous peoples remained defiant in the face of
assimilation policies, while also being exposed to settler and military
violence, invasion of their territories and discrimination. It was in this
context that their identity became politicized. Ramos (1998: 168–78)
distinguishes three stages in the development of ethnopolitics in

Brazil. First, in the 1970s, via the platform provided by the Conselho Indigenista Missionário (CIMI) of the Catholic Church, different indigenous groups began to articulate their demands for justice and rights, while creating a sense of collective identity beyond their individual groups. Second, in the 1980s, the first nationwide indigenous organization was created, União das Nações Indígenas (UNI), where indigenous peoples took the driving seat in the formulation of their demands by appealing to a sense of collective indigenous identity. Finally, a new stage of politicization has seen the emergence of hundreds of indigenous organizations and NGOs that reflect a wider range of indigenous experience and identity politics throughout the country and with related groups across borders.

The recovery of a democratic government in 1985 led to the approval of a new political constitution in 1988 that represented a major breakthrough for indigenous peoples' organizations. The constitution (República Federativa do Brasil 1988) recognized the cultural diversity of Brazil and established a clear framework for the protection of indigenous peoples' rights:

> Art. 231   Indians shall have their social organization, customs, languages, creeds and traditions recognized, as well as their original rights to the lands they traditionally occupy, it being incumbent upon the Union to demarcate them, protect and ensure respect for all of their property.
> Art. 232   The Indians, their communities and organizations have standing under the law to sue to defend their rights and interests, the Public Prosecution intervening in all the procedural acts.

The new constitution represented an overhaul – at least formally – of the assimilationist policies that characterized the relationship between the Brazilian state and indigenous peoples since independence in 1822. Ramos (2003: 413) describes the impact of these reforms for indigenous peoples' sense of identity:

> The new freedom from abusive state control now enjoyed by many – albeit not all – indigenous peoples in Brazil, particularly in the Amazon, is accompanied by a sense of ethnic pride. Indigenous groups that had long been subjected to demoralising methods of submission, such as inculcated shame for being 'ignorant Indians', imposed civil incapacity, and, in some cases, surveillance in tightly controlled reserves, are now celebrating what, on the optimistic side, we may see as an indigenous renaissance. They have learned to objectify their cultures and to appreciate their richness and value as political assets in the interethnic

arenas. They have also purged the derogatory connotations of the term 'Indian' and transformed it into a respectable political category *vis-à-vis*, say, 'White'.

The politics of indigenous identity in Asia

The largest number of indigenous peoples in the world live in Asia. Stretching from India to Southeast Asia, the Philippines and Japan, they continue to preserve and develop their cultural identities against powerful political, economic and cultural threats that challenge their own survival as peoples. The constant pressure of extractive industries and national development policies that seek to exploit natural resources in indigenous territories has led to forced displacements, poverty, violence and environmental degradation. In this context, Asian governments are reluctant to recognize indigenous peoples as distinct from the general population. They often claim that different populations are all indigenous to the country (Kingsbury 2008: 103–7; Erueti 2011: 103–4; Drahos 2014: 24–5). Only people descended from European colonists are seen as non-indigenous. However, a number of states and international organizations, such as the Asian Development Bank, have begun to recognize as indigenous the various ethnic groups whose ways of life and histories often depart markedly from those of the dominant state populations. The examples of Japan, Malaysia and the Philippines will exemplify the broad dynamics of indigenous identity in Asia, but there are of course numerous variations.

The indigenous peoples of the Japanese island of Hokkaidō and the northern parts of Honshu are the Ainu. They are subjects of colonial encroachment by the Japanese, who appropriated their lands some 400 years ago. Further colonial incursions in the nineteenth century coincided with the introduction of Western thought, again including social Darwinism and the concept of race. These radicalized Japanese notions of the self and became incorporated into nationalism (Siddle 1996: 10, 78). Colonization was 'articulated in relation to the advanced industrial military powers of the Western world' (Howell 2005: 156) in which Japanese conventions for understanding difference became grafted onto the idea of progress. The transformation of the Ainu then proceeded by concentrating on details of their customs, personal behaviour and appearance inconsistent with a *Western* concept of civilization. Indeed, the similarities between Japanese and US policies makes sense in light of evidence that Japanese colonizers in Hokkaidō actively sought the views of Americans involved in the assimilation and reservation policies, such as former Indian agent Horace Capron (Medak-Saltzman 2010). In 1899, the Hokkaidō Former Aborigines Protection Act was enacted. In it and its subsequent amendments, an identity was conferred upon Ainu as an inferior people who could obtain land rights only if they cultivated land to the satisfaction of Japanese administrators.

After centuries of discrimination and marginalization, the persistent activism by Ainu organizations from the 1980s onwards, together with the passage of UNDRIP, persuaded members of the Japanese Diet in 2008 to approve formal recognition of the Ainu as an indigenous people (Okada 2012: 7–8). Siddle (1996: 171) describes how Ainu organizations and activists had in the decades before this developed a strategy highlighting cultural identity as a means to claim distinct rights in what he describes as 'ethnopolitics': 'Ainu activists turned ascriptive "racial" categorization on its head. Previously subordinated on the basis of a supposed inherited "racial" inferiority that was reflected in a backward culture, Ainu activists now transformed these same categories of culture and descent into means of positive identification and empowerment.'

Malaysia is another country that has been reluctant to recognize indigenous peoples. The indigenous peoples of Peninsular Malaysia have recently been recognized as Orang Asli. They comprise 18 different groups, which have been blended into one entity by the state. According to Nicholas (2002: 119):

> Orang Asli homogeneity is more of a creation of non-Orang Asli perceptions and ideological impositions than it is self-imposed. Nevertheless, as a result of social stress brought about by the implementation of new development paradigms and new political equations, the various Orang Asli communities quickly adopted the ethnic label – largely as a political tool for more effective negotiation.

Here, different groups found little alternative but to use the concept of indigenous peoples as a way to defend themselves against state threats to their lands and resources and to their self-defined cultural identities as peoples.

In the Philippines, the political constitution has only recently recognized indigenous peoples. The 1997 Indigenous Peoples' Rights Act (IPRA), modelled on the 1994 UN Draft Declaration on Indigenous Peoples' Rights, provides the framework for the relation between the state and indigenous peoples and starts by providing a definition of indigenous peoples:

A group of people or homogeneous societies identified by self ascription and ascription by others, who have continually lived as organized
communities on community-bounded and defined territory, and who
have, under claims of ownership since time immemorial, occupied,
possessed and utilized such territories, sharing common bonds of language, customs, traditions and other distinctive cultural traits, or who
have, through resistance to political, social and cultural inroads of colonization, non-indigenous religions and cultures, become historically
differentiated from the majority of Filipinos.

ICCs/IPs [Indigenous Cultural Communities/indigenous peoples]
shall likewise include peoples who are regarded as indigenous on
account of their descent from populations which inhabited the country,
at the time of conquest or colonization, or at the time of inroads of
non-indigenous religions and cultures, or the establishment of present
state boundaries, who retain some or all of their own social, economic,
cultural and political institutions, but who may have been displaced
from their traditional domains or who may have resettled outside the
ancestral domains. (Republic of the Philippines 1997: Ch. II, sect. 3h)

This definition stresses the major factors included in international declarations on indigenous peoples: historical continuity, self-
identification, self-determination, cultural identity and attachment to
the land. In this sense, IPRA provides an important legal framework
for the promotion and protection of indigenous rights.

The largest number of indigenous peoples in the world are the
Adivasi peoples, who number around 84.3 million in India (IWGIA
2015: 328), 3 million in Bangladesh (IWGIA 2015: 314) and 10
million in Nepal (IWGIA 2015: 321). The Sanskrit word *Adivasi*
means 'original inhabitants', and it was initially used by different
ethnic groups who shared the same struggle against exploitation and
discrimination during British colonial rule (Hardiman 1987: 15–16;
Karlsson 2003: 407). Bhukya (2008: 103–7) explains how during
the century-long British Raj, from 1858 to 1947, anthropologists,
colonial officers and missionaries played a major role in constructing
ethnic identities; the Adivasis – or 'tribal peoples' as they were called
– were represented as primitives, occupying the bottom of the evolutionary ladder that British colonists used to differentiate colonized
populations. Conveniently enough, these categories provided the justifications for anti-Adivasi discrimination and paternal control over
them. The end of British colonial rule led only to further exclusion
from the process of state building as Adivasis became marginalized
because their ways of life, ethnicity, history, language and religion
differed from the dominant groups that inherited the states at the

departure of the British. Both India and Bangladesh refuse to recognize that Adivasis are indigenous peoples, as they argue that all ethnic groups are indigenous to the region (Schendel 2011: 27). In India they refer to the Adivasis as Scheduled Tribes (Das et al. 2012: 205), while in Bangladesh they are recognized as 'tribes', 'minor races', 'ethnic sects and communities' and 'adibashi' (IWGIA 2015: 314).

Nonetheless, the politics of identity is not something external to the Adivasis. Like other indigenous groups, such as the Orang Asli in Malaysia, the idea of using a generic name like Adivasis can be understood as a strategy for recognition of indigenous rights and identity at the international level. Underlining the subversive potential of Adivasi identification, Gupta and Basu (2011: xi) argue that 'the term Adivasi ... contains within itself an expression of self-identification and a rejection of dominant Brahmanical values'. At the same time, the use of the term does reflect ways of life that characterized all these different ethnic groups. Karlsson (2000: 30) explains that the appropriation of Adivasi as a group identifier 'reflects lived experience and a shared collective identity'.

The politics of identity in Africa

Nationalism in post-independence Africa was driven by desires to build separate national cultures under the aegis of the modern state. These states were formed within demarcated colonial borders most of which had little relation to natural demography. New states necessarily brought under their authority disparate peoples with different ways of life and languages to whom national identity was often meaningless. Governments attempted to tackle this in part by promoting policies that made the assertion of ethnic difference a source of conflict. Tribal loyalties and non-modern forms of livelihood were seen as antagonistic to nation building, and, as a result, some states – Tanzania for example – refused to recognize ethnicity as a legitimate category of policy or public discourse (Aminzade 2013: 127). As the history of civil war, coups d'état and genocide in Africa make clear, nation building along European lines has often been catastrophic. Because independent African states were concerned with modernization, the political elites and general public, as in the Americas and Asia, have tended to view indigenous groups such as hunters and pastoralists as backward and in need of tutelage.

The question of specifically indigenous identity, however, emerged only more recently. It has been shaped within human rights frameworks that aim to protect and promote the rights of ethnic groups whose very existence in many parts of Africa has been precarious. Like Asian states, African states have argued that if indigenous identity is understood as aboriginality, then most Africans are indigenous to Africa. More importantly, they have expressed concerns that the use of the term could become internally divisive and threaten the unity of the state, as some groups could claim a right to secession. These concerns were reflected in the discussions of the African Commission on Human and Peoples' Rights (ACHPR) and during the negotiation process of the UNDRIP (Cambou 2015: 144–5; Viljoen 2010: 76; Newman 2010: 149; Tobin 2014: 43).

Despite these concerns, in 2003 the Report of the ACHPR Working Group of Experts on Indigenous Populations/Communities adopted the term 'indigenous peoples' to refer to particular ethnic groups in Africa (Wachira and Karjala 2014: 107–9). Within the human rights framework provided by the African (Banjul) Charter on Human and Peoples' Rights (African Union 1986) the Working Group did not establish a normative definition of indigenous identity, but outlined it by reference to the marginality, discrimination, prejudices and human rights infringements experienced by pastoralists, hunter-gatherers and small-scale farmers.

The Working Group constituted indigenous identities in a number of ways. First, it argued that the notion of indigenous peoples applies to most African peoples, 'The report recognizes that this is a sensitive issue in Africa and acknowledges that, except for a few exceptions involving communities that migrated from other continents or settlers from Europe, Africans can claim to be aboriginal people of the continent and nowhere else' (ACHPR/IWGIA 2005: 12). Second, it established the principle of self-recognition as the main criterion of identity: 'The Working Group then resolved to settle for a socio-psychological description of indigenous people, setting out broad criteria and affirming, as in the United Nations system, the principle of self-definition and recognition of self-identity of peoples' (ACHPR/IWGIA 2005: 12). Finally, it provided the analytical framework for the understanding of indigenous identity:

> The focus should be on the more recent approaches focusing on self-definition as indigenous and distinctly different from other groups within a state; on a special attachment to and use of their traditional land whereby their ancestral land and territory has a fundamental importance for their collective physical and cultural survival as peoples; on an experience of subjugation, marginalization, dispossession, exclu-

sion or discrimination because these peoples have different cultures, ways of life or modes of production than the national hegemonic and dominant model. (ACHPR/IWGIA 2005: 63)

In 2007 the advisory opinion of the ACHPR on the UNDRIP reinforced the principles set by the Working Group and established the three main principles for the recognition of indigenous identity (No. 12, p. 4):

1 Self-identification.
2 A special attachment to and use of their traditional land whereby their ancestral land and territory have a fundamental importance for their collective physical and cultural survival as peoples.
3 A state of subjugation, marginalisation, dispossession, exclusion, or discrimination because these peoples have different cultures, ways of life or mode of production than the national hegemonic and dominant model.

It also made it clear that the adoption of the term 'indigenous peoples' did not threaten the unity of the state:

[T]he ACHPR has interpreted the protection of the rights of Indigenous Populations within the context of a strict respect for the inviolability of borders and of the obligation to preserve the territorial integrity of State Parties, in conformity with the principles and values enshrined in the Constitutive Act of the AU, the African Charter on Human and Peoples' Rights (the African Charter) and the UN Charter. (No. 6)

The recognition and protection of indigenous peoples' rights took a significant step when, in 2011, the Republic of the Congo passed Law No. 5 on the Promotion and Protection of Indigenous Populations. The law recognized as indigenous peoples a number of minority groups, mostly hunter-gatherers, whose ways of life were distinct from the majority Bantu peoples: 'For the Purpose of this Act and without any prejudice to any prior occupation of the national territory, the term indigenous populations means populations who are different from the national population by their cultural identity, lifestyle and extreme vulnerability' (Republic of the Congo 2011: Law 5, Title I, Art. 1). However, the recognition of indigenous peoples by other African states remains a challenge, but steps are being taken – at least on paper – by Kenya, the Democratic Republic of Congo, Burundi and the Central African Republic to protect and promote the cultural, social and economic rights of indigenous peoples.

The politics of indigenous identity in the international system

Indigenous organizations have a long history of advocacy for the recognition of rights within the international system (see Chapter 5). Their main aim has been to promote and protect collective rights to self-determination and the rights to indigenous lands and resources against the colonial institutional structures of states. Although the concept of indigenous peoples is a construct, covering a vast number of people living varied ways of life (Gigoux and Samson 2016: 274), as Smith (2012: 7) points out, 'the term has enabled the collective voices of colonized people to be expressed strategically in the international arena. It has also been an umbrella enabling communities to come together, transcending their own colonized contexts and experiences, in order to learn, share, plan, organize and struggle collectively for self-determination on the global and local stages.' Furthermore, the term is instrumental for social and political mobilizations:

> It is today a term and a global movement fighting for rights and justice for those particular groups who have been left on the margins of development and who are perceived negatively by dominating mainstream development paradigms, whose cultures and ways of life are subject to discrimination and contempt and whose very existence is under threat of extinction. (ACHPR/IWGIA 2005: 87)

Kingsbury (2008: 104) argues that the notion of indigenous peoples could be understood in two possible ways: positivist and constructivist. The former stresses 'a legal category requiring precise definition, so that for particular operational purposes it should be possible to determine, on the basis of the definition, exactly who does or does not have a particular status, enjoy a particular right, or assume a particular responsibility'; the latter is not 'sharply defined by universally applicable criteria, but as embodying a continuous process in which claims and practices in numerous specific cases are abstracted in the wider institutions of international society, then made specific again at the moment of application in the political, legal and social processes of particular cases and societies'. The concept of indigenous peoples is therefore part of the international system overwhelmingly reflecting a constructivist rather than a positivist approach.

The notion of *peoples* is significant because it has been understood as an intermediate entity between the nation-state and the individual, referring to 'all those spheres of community, marked by elements of identity and collective consciousness, within which people's lives unfold – independently of considerations of historical or postulated sovereignty' (Anaya 2004: 103). This conceptualization reinforces the claim for a social constructivist approach to the term 'indigenous peoples', but also stresses the importance for self-definition and diversity. Yellow Bird (1999: 17) argues:

> Any labels used to describe Indigenous Peoples must come from the self-definitions and identities of these groups. Ideally, labels should promote positive social and political interactions between Indigenous and non-Indigenous Peoples. Labels should also promote solidarity among Indigenous Peoples while at the same time recognizing the diversity and sovereignty of each group.

States have implemented a positivist approach in order to define indigenous identity for purposes of administrative control. Additionally, the general positivist framework that underpins the understating of rights requires precise and concise conceptualizations that can be built into normative legal instruments. It is against the insistence by states on this approach that indigenous organizations have refused an overarching authoritative definition of indigenous peoples in international documents, declarations and conventions.

Yet the question remains. Who are indigenous peoples? The answer given by the international community has been in terms of a description rather than a definition. This allows both a certain empirical basis to determine who are the subjects of international law, while preserving the subjective approach based on self-identification. The working definition of indigenous peoples formulated by José Martinez Cobo, the former Special Rapporteur of the Sub-Commission on Prevention of Discrimination and Protection of Minorities, has been highly significant in shaping the debates on indigenous peoples in the UN system. Cobo (1986) provides a broad definition of indigenous peoples:

> Indigenous communities, peoples and nations are those which, having a historical continuity with pre-invasion and pre-colonial societies that developed on their territories, consider themselves distinct from other sectors of the societies now prevailing on those territories, or parts of them. They form at present non-dominant sectors of society and are determined to preserve, develop and transmit to future generations their ancestral territories, and their ethnic identity, as the basis of their continued existence as peoples, in accordance with their own cultural patterns, social institutions and legal system ... On an individual basis, an indigenous person is one who belongs to these indigenous

populations through self-identification as indigenous (group consciousness) and is recognized and accepted by these populations as one of
its members (acceptance by the group). This preserves for these communities the sovereign right and power to decide who belongs to them,
without external interference.

This definition highlights indigenous peoples' (a) historical continuity, (b) longstanding connections to territories, (c) colonized conditions and (d) nondominant status in societies. It also highlights
a subjective dimension by stressing (a) the intention of preserving
indigenous ethnic identity, (b) self-determination and (c) self-
identification. This working definition remains widely used by scholars, international organizations and indigenous peoples themselves as
it gives a general sense of who indigenous peoples are but stops short
of providing a definite conceptualization.

The influence of Martínez Cobo's working definition on the
International Labour Organization (ILO) Indigenous and Tribal
Peoples Convention, No. 169 (1989) is very clear. The Convention
does not provide a definition of indigenous peoples, but it does
provide objective and subjective criteria of identification. Article 1
states:

1. This Convention applies to:
    (a) tribal peoples in independent countries whose social, cultural
    and economic conditions distinguish them from other sections of
    the national community, and whose status is regulated wholly or
    partially by their own customs or traditions or by special laws or
    regulations;
    (b) peoples in independent countries who are regarded as indig-
    enous on account of their descent from the populations which
    inhabited the country, or a geographical region to which the
    country belongs, at the time of conquest or colonisation or the
    establishment of present state boundaries and who, irrespective of
    their legal status, retain some or all of their own social, economic,
    cultural and political institutions.
2. Self-identification as indigenous or tribal shall be regarded as a
    fundamental criterion for determining the groups to which the
    provisions of this Convention apply.

In the process of negotiations leading to the Convention, there were
fundamental disagreements in relation to the use of the term 'indigenous peoples' and its connection to the right of self-determination,
control over natural resources and collective rights. In this sense, the
adoption of the term *peoples* instead of the term *populations*, used in

the previous ILO Convention No. 107 on Indigenous and Tribal Populations (1957), was important, as it led to the wider use of the term in international law and in relation to the principle of self-determination (Morgan 2011: 9–10). A number of states expressed their concerns about the use of 'peoples' and, with it, the implication that self-determination might adversely affect state territorial sovereignty (Morgan 2011: 13–17). Eventually, this point was conceded to the states by the inclusion of a third point in Article 1 that limited the understanding of self-determination in relation to the term *peoples*:

> 3. The use of the term *peoples* in this Convention shall not be construed as having any implications as regards the rights which may attach to the term under international law.

The objective and subjective criteria of identification developed by Martínez Cobo and adopted by the ILO Convention No. 169 would make its way into UNDRIP (ILO & ACHPR 2009: 9–10). UNDRIP does not provide a definition of indigenous peoples, but has emphasized self-identification as the key criterion for indigenous identity. In doing so, it stresses that only indigenous peoples have the power to decide their own identities. A formal definition of indigenous peoples would give states the power to select specific criteria for deciding who is indigenous:

> Article 9
> Indigenous peoples and individuals have the right to belong to an indigenous community or nation, in accordance with the traditions and customs of the community or nation concerned. No discrimination of any kind may arise from the exercise of such a right.

The right of belonging can be interpreted in different ways by different communities and nations, thus highlighting a more dynamic and flexible approach to indigenous identity. Central to self-identification is the recognition of the principle of self-determination from where collective rights spring. The relevance of UNDRIP is that it establishes the foundations for self-determination and self-identity and, at the same time, it supplies a general framework for the protection and advancement of indigenous rights. One thing leads to the other.

2
Colonization

[C]olonialism forces the people it dominates to ask themselves the
question constantly: in reality who am I?

Fanon (1963: 250)

It is impossible to understand the contemporary circumstances of
indigenous peoples in separation from colonialism, the global force to
which the debates in the previous chapter over identity are responding. Hall (1996: 254) argues that colonialism is 'a system of rule,
power and exploitation' and 'a system of knowledge and representation'. As a system of rule, colonial practices are intended to exercise
control over indigenous peoples while appropriating their lands. As a
system of knowledge and representation, colonialism aims to justify
domination over colonized peoples by appealing to specific kinds of
assertions and arguments. European discourses containing various
assumptions about the identities, qualities and rights of different
categories of humanity facilitated the subjugated positions of indigenous groups around the world. As colonial expansion progressed,
it regulated, altered and shaped relations with indigenous peoples
and, by doing so, it also, as Fanon argued, completely distorted how
colonized peoples think of themselves. The vehicles for this were missionary activity, state laws, philosophies and violence.

Missionary discourses and indigenous spirituality

The European Christian states that became colonial powers encountered indigenous groups that had forms of spirituality that differed
and at times conflicted sharply with Christianity. These clashes of

ideas are apparent both at the early contact phase of colonization and as colonialism consolidates itself into nation building. Native North American spirituality, as Deloria (1999) emphasized, is not a specific sphere of life separated out, formalized or inscribed in texts. Rather, spiritual observances were part of everyday life and enveloped in the practices of hunting, gathering, farming, family and community life. Some groups incorporated a full calendar of religious events and these have continued to today. For Pueblo peoples of the US southwest:

> oratories, prayers and songs . . . are not spontaneous outpourings, or outbursts of the troubled heart. They are carefully memorized prayerful requests for an orderly life, rain, good crops, plentiful game, pleasant days, and the protection from violence and the vicissitudes of nature. To appease or pledge their faith to God, they often went on sacrificial retreats, often doing without food or water as penance or cleansing the body and soul for the benefit of man throughout the world. (Sando 1976: 23)

One common feature of indigenous spirituality is that it is based on enduring connections to lands, and is rooted in memories, dreams and experiences. Long-term associations with all animate and inanimate beings are embedded in legends, myths, stories and orature passed down the generations. They are manifested in specific practices and observances. For example, many hunters hold that animals and humans are part of the same *living* conceptual order, and that human well-being is dependent on respect for animals and animal deities. Some groups may adhere to similar beliefs for other living entities, such as trees, rivers and mountains and, for agriculturalists, particular crops such as corn. In such communities, shamans were – and in some cases often are – very important in communicating with animal and other deities and were able to diagnose past misfortunes and discern future events. In contrast to Christianity and other world religions, shamans and other religious figures in hunting societies were not part of a formal hierarchy. Following them and taking their advice was mostly voluntary. Indigenous spirituality in the early colonial contact zones relied on private initiative and practicality, not inherited formulas, liturgical orthodoxy or compulsion (Bowden 1981: 105).

Many aspects of native peoples' spiritual beliefs and practices were at variance with most forms of Christianity that have been and continue to be brought to indigenous peoples. While Christian doctrine and missionary practices varied, the objective of most missionaries was to convert indigenous peoples, regulate activities with them and act as intermediaries to colonial authorities. As such, missionaries were important instigators of social change. Today, the Church leaves one of the most ambivalent legacies of colonialism. As Naomi Adelson (2009: 273) remarks of Northern Canada:

> Despite being just one segment of the colonial enterprise, missionization remains to this day one of the most contentious domains of the history of contact and the key symbolic site of cultural slaughter and disenfranchisement. It is for this reason that, for many indigenous peoples, organized religion is emblematic of the entire enterprise of colonization.

However, as Adelson points out, the legacy is ambivalent in part because many native peoples did not see Christianity and their own spiritual beliefs and practices as totally incommensurate. In many places, indigenous peoples adopted a dual strategy, whereby they adhered to Christian beliefs and symbolism and attended church, but, in parallel, maintained animistic and other non-Christian ideas and practices. In North America, for example, 'many ... Natives have adopted some features of the "ethicized" eschatology of Christianity' (Mills 1994: 18). Many prominent Native American scholars, including the twentieth-century writers Charles Eastman and Vine Deloria, were Christians. Both saw hypocrisies in the actual practice of Christianity, but these and countless other native people from the early contact period onwards perceived affinities between the more visionary and contemplative aspects of Christianity and indigenous spirituality.

Nevertheless, the goal of some missionary activity was not only to instil Christian beliefs, but also to undermine indigenous spirituality, which was a main pillar of an entire social system. This occurred in many places across the Americas and continues to the present day, especially with Protestant evangelizing in the Americas and Africa. In this context, the inroads made by Pentecostal churches into some indigenous communities in Latin America have created new challenges for indigenous cultural identities and spirituality. The strong sense of individualism and religious fundamentalism that characterizes Pentecostalism has led at times to communal conflicts and divisions, but also to new forms of social mobilizations (Brysk 2015; Norget 2015).

For hunting peoples such as the Innu of the Labrador-Quebec peninsula, twentieth-century Roman Catholic missionary activity instilled 'a psychology of fear' (Samson 2003: 32–3, 172–8). As a result, many of the practices associated with the Caribou God and respect for animals have diminished, and some of these have recently been recreated in museums. By destroying the religious organization of the people, the missionaries also destroyed one of the main tools used to deal with many problems faced in the Innu and other indigenous societies. What Ronald Niezen (2000) calls 'spiritual dispossession' involves indigenous peoples' loss of confidence in their own ways of dealing with conflict, suffering and affliction, which were often conceptually inseparable from spirituality.

One of the most dramatic clashes of ideas was between indigenous peoples and Puritanism, the founding creed of English North America. Many settling in what they called 'New England' in the seventeenth century eagerly came to escape religious persecution. In their own view, the Puritans were performing services for the Crown. As instruments of God, they were 'enlarging the kingdom of the Lord Jesus, in the conversion of the poor blind natives' (Masefield 1910: 6). However, many Puritan missions found indigenous conversion to their rigid and judgmental version of Christianity unsuccessful. Given their narrow interpretation of the scriptures, the English became more concerned with eradicating indigenous spirituality altogether than with conversion. Hence, John Eliot, the 'apostle to the Indians', had limited success in inducting 'Red Puritan' natives into self-contained 'praying towns' starting with Natick in Massachusetts Bay Colony. To native peoples used to high levels of freedom and personal autonomy, these towns must have seemed unappealing:

> Customs that conflicted either with the Bible or with English values or prejudices were flatly prohibited. The first law in the Natick code provided a five shilling fine for idleness. The same code forbade husbands to beat their wives, enjoined every man to set up a wigwam 'and not live shifting up and downe to other Wigwams', forbade women to cut their hair short or men to let theirs grow long, and prohibited the killing of lice between the teeth as was customary among New England Algonquians. The code at Concord was even more complete, banning any use of body grease, the playing of traditional games, and numerous other customs. Indians here were also forbidden to tell lies and were required to 'weare their haire comely, as the English do'. For all these offenses, fines would be imposed. (Salisbury 1974: 33)

One of the strongest conceptual differences between the Puritans and indigenous peoples was over the doctrine of predestination: that after death those who were 'the elect' would go to Heaven and others to Hell. This created a stark division between different types of souls. When this doctrine was communicated to indigenous peoples, it was often done so to underscore the severe penalties incurred by anyone straying from Puritan dogma. This began to cause an erosion of indigenous communities, assisting colonists to exert more direct control over them. The effect was to replace indigenous unity with separations between the saved and the sinners, the elect and the non-elect (Bowden 1981: 121). However, only after the bloody Pequot War of the 1630s and the even more violent King Philip's War of the 1670s did native people convert to Christianity in larger numbers, but, by this time, they had lost almost everything. There is evidence, however, that Christianity was not always a divisive force. Sometimes it brought unity to rival indigenous groups and created solidarity. Some groups, like the eastern Pequot, 'have been able to negotiate Christianity in such a way that it does not hamper their Indian identity or sense of indigenous spiritualism' (Burgess 2000: 45).

The process by which indigenous peoples of New England were colonized was not unique. At the same time that colonial theocracy was being established in New England, the Calvinist Afrikaners who shared doctrinal similarities with the Puritans were also fighting a parallel and genocidal holy war against the Khoikhoi pastoralists, Bushmen hunter-gatherers and other natives of Southern Africa (Gall 2002: 51–3). Like the Puritans, the Afrikaners considered themselves 'God's chosen people', and were similarly averse to meaningful inter-cultural dialogue.

A parallel dynamic occurred during the Spanish colonization of New Mexico in the seventeenth century when, after the Pueblo Revolt of 1680, the Spanish concentrated on building churches and convert-ing Pueblo peoples. This was part of a spiritual reconquest in which Roman Catholic friars appointed Pueblo religious leaders. However, the Pueblos cleverly adapted by making the person appointed a token intermediary (the *gobernador*) between them and the Spanish and they thereby retained their own authority structures that were vested in the *caciques*, the spiritual leaders (Silverberg 1970: 49). Thus, they were able to please the Spanish without affecting their own spiritual organization vested in the kiva societies. Pueblo festivals now take place alongside Catholic masses, but each belief system and attached set of practices remains conceptually separate, assisting the Pueblos to maintain spiritual continuity (Sando 1976: 23–4).

French missionaries present another variation. After Samuel de Champlain established a fort at Quebec on the northern shores of the St Lawrence in 1608, in what they called New France, Haudenosaunee (Iroquois), Huron, Algonquin, Cree and Montagnais (Innu) and other indigenous groups were engaged in trading along the Saguenay River and other major rivers flowing into the St Lawrence. Champlain attempted to cultivate the friendship of competing groups of these woodland peoples through both trade and missionary activity. He invited the Jesuits into New France in 1625 and they quickly became the leading religious order for over a century. The indigenous world they encountered was conceived as one urgently needing transformation, beginning with correcting the childrearing methods used by the peoples of these areas. While the French demanded discipline and obedience, missionaries observed that the native peoples favoured tolerance, indulgence and freedom for children. Many illustrations of these contrasts are to be found in *The Jesuit Relations* (Thwaites 1896–1901), the detailed reports of the Fathers sent back to France. Hence, in 1633, after observing the protests when a French boy was about to be physically punished by adults for wounding a native child with a drumstick, the celebrated diarist Father Paul Le Jeune wrote, 'all of the Savage tribes of these quarters . . . cannot chastise a child, nor see one chastised. How much trouble this will give us in carrying out our plans of teaching the young!' (Thwaites 1896–1901: V: 221).

Conversion and, along with it, corrective childrearing instructions and remedial education required the Fathers to undertake the difficult task of learning the indigenous languages. To do this, missionaries had to travel with Indians and adapt to more physically demanding environments (Trudel 1973: 158). According to many reports in the *Jesuit Relations*, the Fathers converted large numbers, although they never achieved complete devotion to the faith or cultural assimilation. Once converted to Christianity, the Jesuits thought that the natives would be more readily accepting of 'reason' and sedentary village societies (Goddard 1998; Blackburn 2000). The obstacles to conversion were thought to include migratory lifestyles, polygamy, lack of self-discipline, the power of shamans, the dearth of vocabulary in native languages for abstraction, and little curiosity about Christianity. But while the Jesuits aimed for spiritual and mental transformation, French interests in the rich Northern fur trade, for example, required indigenous cultural continuity through annual migrations in pursuit of fur bearing mammals. This meant that indigenous spirituality in the forests, river valleys and tundra often survived for longer than elsewhere in North America.

However, even when native people here and elsewhere embraced

Christianity, this was frequently not on the singular and uncondi-
tional terms demanded by the literalist interpretation of faith. Rather,
as Salisbury (2003: 257) has shown, Christian natives had few hesi-
tations about cooperating with non-Christians against colonizers. In
embracing ambiguity, they maintained commitments to the plurality
of truth, as well as to each other:

> What we as scholars have failed to appreciate is the extent to which
> natives could embrace what the Euro-American tradition could and
> can comprehend only as ambiguity. The questions that have concerned
> scholars . . . lose much of their mystery if we think less about Indians
> 'converting,' 'apostatizing,' and 'backsliding' and more about natives
> as understanding and acting out of the many ambiguities surrounding
> their relations with Europeans.

In the seventeenth and eighteenth centuries, a different model of
colonial control was established by the Jesuits in the territories of
Northwest Mexico as well as in the Gran Chaco, Amazonia and
southern regions of Chile. Marzal (2000: 348–9) identifies three
major elements as distinctive to the Jesuit project. First, it established
a physical distance between the missions and colonial settlements
in order to avoid the exposure of the Indians to settler violence and
moral corruption. The missions were built as large villages that could
contain up to 7,000 Indians. Second, they created a socioeconomic
structure that integrated indigenous and European social and economic practices in order to make the mission economically self-
sufficient. Also, the missions were self-governed by the Indians under
the supervision of the Jesuit priests. Third, the system of Christian
instruction incorporated Indian languages and beliefs and practices
that were regarded as compatible with Christianity, while promoting
the celebration of communal festivals and the development of music.

With a few early exceptions, the Jesuits did not use coercion to
bring the Indians to the missions, nor did they rely on the support
of Spanish or Portuguese soldiers. The constant raids against the
Indians by settlers and *bandeirantes* were enough of an incentive
for many indigenous communities to join the missions. In fact,
the Jesuits also encouraged and trained the Indians in the missions
into an effective military force against slave raids led by Portuguese
bandeirantes (Jackson 2015: 55). Once in the missions, they were
free to stay or go, but, if they stayed, they had to adapt to the social
structure and organizations of the mission. The Indians living in the
missions were also exempted from taxation and personal servitude
(López 2005: 38).

Despite these policies, the missions were undoubtedly colonial institutions. The missionaries believed in the need to bring the Indians into Christian life by moving them away from what was depicted as superstition and savage ways of life. The Indians were considered children in need of instruction and protection. The missions had a strong communal orientation towards work and property, but also to discipline. Indians breaching the rules governing the missions or failing to work for the common good could receive corporal punishment, be subject to fines, be tasked with additional work and, in some cases, be expelled from the mission. The missions also played a major role in transforming hunter-gatherers into semi-sedentary peoples, bringing drastic changes to indigenous social organization and spiritual beliefs. Inside the confined and densely populated missions, Indians were exposed to contagious diseases that had catastrophic demographic consequences.

As buffers between indigenous peoples and colonial governments, the Jesuit missions must be credited with shielding some Indians from slavery, protecting indigenous communal lands, preserving some of their languages and cultural identities and creating structures that protected them from the full force of colonial government aims. Nonetheless, the resentment from settlers and colonial authorities against their preferential tax system, their increasing wealth, autonomy and status as safe havens against slave raids led to the expulsion of the Jesuits from Spanish and Portuguese America in 1767, the gradual abandonment of the missions and the appropriation of Jesuit-held lands and economic enterprises by settlers.

Although Christian churches were instruments of colonization, the process is certainly not absent from other dominant religious systems. For example, in the 1960s Buddhist monks were part of a state sponsored effort to convert indigenous peoples in Thailand as a way of assimilating these groups into mainstream Thai society (Schedneck 2015: 162). Similarly, in the 1970s the Malaysian government started a number of social, economic and cultural policies in order to convert the Orang Asli to Islam for the same reasons (Nicholas 2000; Endicott 2016: 21).

Laws and philosophies

An additional means of legitimating the colonial domination of indigenous peoples, perhaps the ultimate source of legitimacy in the colonial world, is the law. Whether it be a monarch or members of a parliamentary assembly, whoever is able to formulate laws by which different groups of people are to be bound within a society has immense power over the future of that society. While missionaries may have attempted to internally transform indigenous peoples through daily contact, laws and philosophies use more abstract, yet ultimately more coercive, means of bringing natives under colonial order.

European colonists came across peoples whose histories, experiences, languages and customs they often found perplexing. As occupation of these peoples' lands grew, colonial powers asserted – mostly to themselves – that they were adhering to a number of laws to regulate their relations with indigenous peoples. Importantly, laws in colonial settings did not derive legitimacy from the same principles invoked in Europe, where, by the seventeenth century, the idea of the voluntary social contract between the government and the populace was held to be the basis for legitimate power. Enlightenment figures like Hobbes, Locke and Rousseau had posited that the social contract with subject populations was the basis for political authority through consent of the governed, yet this principle was not extended to indigenous parties in the course of colonization.

All colonial powers were concerned with proving the legitimacy of their occupation of the New World in particular. The celebrated sixteenth-century political philosopher Francisco de Vitoria formulated a theory of the relationship of Europe to the peoples of the New World centring around the question of how to justify Spanish dominion. His opinions on it led to a rejection of blanket dispossession. Interestingly, although Vitoria considered Indians to be barbarians, he dismissed all monarchical arguments for colonialism based on their non-Christian status and their supposedly inferior psychological or cultural attributes. He did not, however, reject the Aristotelian principle that indigenous peoples' supposedly inferior qualities made them 'natural slaves' and suitable only for being governed (Keal 2003: 70–1). Vitoria argued that the right of dominion came from eight possible 'just titles', a prominent theme among which was wars of conquest that might arise from any hindrance to the Spaniards' right to travel, trade, convert and communicate, all of which he thought were protected by natural law (1991: 278–9; see also Pagden 1995: 61). These principles became enshrined in the Papal Bulls and the Spanish Laws of the Indies, but they did not give unmitigated rights to colonize. Nonetheless, until the nineteenth century, Spain considered most of the Western hemisphere and its peoples a Crown possession.

The English response to the question posed by Vitoria – by what title were 'the barbarians' brought under our rule? – was slightly different. Thomas Hobbes, for example, believed that the sovereign is one man or an assembly of men in whom authority has been invested by a populace in exchange for protection against each other and outsiders. The absolute condition of this social contract arrangement, or 'covenant', is that the subjects concede autonomy and submit completely to the will of the sovereign. Sovereignty can be attained through the establishment of political institutions or by conquest. Either way, covenants are made to bind both subjects and sovereigns (1958/1651: 139–70). For Hobbes, sovereignty was a self-perpetuating power, and English conquest, in theory, would be enough to establish a covenant with the Native Americans. Hobbes's ideas were modified by other philosophers, particularly John Locke as we will see later, to provide auxiliary principles to justify colonization of indigenous lands and peoples.

In the Western hemisphere, European colonizers adhered to sets of formal regulations and informal rules for dealing with each other as nation-states. They brought to the New World established rules of conduct (which became the basis of 'international law') as to how to negotiate and resolve conflicts between themselves and, importantly, as to how to acquire territory. The most important standard was the seventeenth-century Doctrine of Discovery, which consisted of a series of principles to which European imperialists loosely agreed. It held that indigenous people were sovereign nations for the purposes of negotiating only with the 'discoverers', who had the sole right to negotiate for the acquisition of land. As sovereign nations, indigenous people were assumed competent to bind themselves by agreements.

The main instrument to self-legitimate European possession of land in North America flowing from the Doctrine of Discovery was the treaty. Treaties in what became the United States and Canada almost always worked by inducing indigenous parties to extinguish both their pre-existing ownership of the land and their rights as sovereign entities under the Doctrine of Discovery (Deloria 1985; Miller et al. 2010). Given that the settler states had already asserted dominion over territory, treaties were to some extent moot points, and indigenous peoples were relegated to having occupancy or usufruct rights rather than meaningful sovereignty.

While the Doctrine of Discovery served as a broad colonial framework, in practice there were several auxiliary justifications, and these were often overlapping, contradictory and ad hoc. In colonial New England, the ambiguity created by different principles and practices was convenient in assisting colonists to take American Indian land. Although there were some exceptions (most prominently Roger Williams, the founder of Rhode Island), the English made very few attempts to understand how American Indians conceived of the land and what norms and values were important to them. The methods of English appropriation of indigenous lands in North America included (1) royal charters and patents, based on the imposition of an order by the monarch authorizing colonization; (2) a variety of treaties, agreements and exchanges; (3) war and violence; and (4) *terra nullius*, or simply taking possession of the land under the assumption that it was devoid of people possessing meaningful rights to it (Jennings 1975: 106).

In the longer term, more formal agreements were necessary to the English strategy of securing Native American cooperation, especially given that in the early phases of settlement, the English were highly outnumbered. Hence, treaties came into effect as agreements between leaders of the colonists and Native Americans, and these were later adopted by the US and Canadian governments. The early treaties were highly varied arrangements and often haphazard, but in the eighteenth century more formal treaty conferences were organized as settlement expanded away from the Eastern coast. Some of these were developed by the Iroquois Six Nations and applied to both Indians and the English. They involved ceremony, speeches, tobacco smoking and long periods of reflection before anything was decided. The end result was recorded in both wampum belts (shells arranged to record a story) and treaty minutes, which Indians would be asked to sign with a mark. While Native Americans knew what the belts meant, they had to trust the word of the English that what they had heard was what was expressed accurately in the written treaty.

Outside the treaty, some indigenous groups in colonial North America sold their lands when presented with English offers, and these were taken as consent to the drafting of deeds, from which the English could then claim legitimate permanent land ownership. Jennings (1975) calls this 'the deed game', a game in which much of the dealings were fraudulent and involved bribery and alcohol. Native Americans often found the English system of private property incomprehensible. Highly complex and requiring varying degrees of consent, many deed transactions entailed selecting out just one American Indian (or small group of them) to unilaterally consent to removing lands from collective ownership (Baker 1989). Not all those who gave their mark as a signature realized, especially under the hazy, alcohol-laden conditions they sometimes found themselves in, that they were permanently losing their lands. In many instances in colonial North America, native peoples believed the agreements facilitated the simple sharing of land. They only became aware later that settlers had decided to keep lands for themselves in perpetuity, and that this arrangement was set in stone by law (Bowden 1981: 98, 104).

Because the goal in the early colonial period was to obtain possession of land, the law was made to facilitate this purpose and indigenous social and political norms were largely ignored, especially when they presented any impediment to permanent European ownership of their lands (Alfred 2006). Even King George III's Royal Proclamation of 1763, which established that any lands not ceded already to the British Crown were reserved for indigenous peoples under a fiduciary trust relationship, was contradicted by the assertion of 'dominion' and 'sovereignty' over the same peoples and their lands. Interestingly, these assertions were not included in the Indian records, the wampum belts (Borrows 1997). The 'spurious claim', as Anishnabe lawyer John Borrows puts it, established by the limited application of the Doctrine of Discovery was widened in the United States to mean that Europeans who 'discovered' land were sovereign on it, while those indigenous to it were merely 'occupants'. This gave rise 'to a massive displacement of persons and the creation of an entire legal regime', crystallized in the *Johnson v. M'Intosh* US Supreme Court case in 1823 (Robertson 2005: 4). In Canada, the mandate in all treaties to extinguish native ownership to lands and ignore vital parts of the Royal Proclamation likewise derives from an extension of the Doctrine of Discovery and continues in present day land claims agreements (Samson and Cassell 2013). Although many scholars now reject the Doctrine of Discovery – and it has also been repudiated by religious organizations and NGOs – it is implicitly incorporated into the laws of settler states as the basis of non-indigenous ownership rights (Watson 2011; Miller et al. 2010). Whatever principles are invested in the Doctrine of Discovery to protect indigenous peoples, these can easily become redundant through extra-legal actions undertaken to rob them of their lands. Because the settler state largely represents the settler population, it has been in its interests to turn a blind eye to squatting and other forms of illegal dispossession.

Other methods can be and were used when expedient, with some colonists appealing to arbitrary moral principles to legitimate land acquisition. One form of reasoning invoked in colonial New England was that farmers who improved the soil were using nature in a manner consistent with Divine Mandate. Although Puritan ministers

such as John Cotton and John Winthrop had already used these justifications earlier, the real prophet of this argument was John Locke.
His theory of private property had the beauty of being both a priori,
in that it purported to be a natural or Divine principle of action,
and ad hoc, in that it could be (and was) pointed to retrospectively
in North America as a reason for why settlers had an unambiguous
claim to indigenous lands.

Locke believed that private property was one arena that distinguishes the 'state of nature' from 'political society', an advanced
state where people are protected under a social contract with the
state. Individual possession, Locke argued, raises humans above the
state of nature. This process could be observed almost in real time
in North America. 'In the beginning, all the World was America',
Locke famously declared in *The Second Treatise on Government*, and
in claiming this, he made 'America' the zero point from which all
history departed. Locke contended that although they may have had
sovereignty, North American Indians did not have rights to any fixed
property, a prerogative that could only be claimed through 'improvement of the soil' and labour. 'God', Locke tells us, 'who hath given
the World to men in common, hath also given them reason to make
use of it to their advantage and convenience' (1965/1689: 328). To
use it, and follow the exhortation from Genesis to 'go forth and multiply', Christians must apply labour. When people work, they transform nature, and thus transfer it from the communal state of nature
to their private domain. With the growth of private property came the
necessity of money, and political regulation under a social contract
with the sovereign.

Locke regarded indigenous hunting and fishing largely as leisure
activities as they were in England. The only indigenous property
rights were limited to ownership of the animals they killed, since they
used some labour to hunt. If American Indians were all hunters, they
had no rights of land ownership, only usufruct rights (Seed 2001:
52–3). However, Locke's key argument was based on a convenient falsehood that could have been corrected by simply consulting
the records that colonists already had on Indian agriculture. Some
natives were hunters, others were farmers, and many mixed hunting
with farming. Hunters, of course, also 'labour' and make efforts to
manage and conserve the land through mobility, but also through
practices such as fire-setting. Benefiting from this sleight of hand,
English Puritan settlers in North America were then perfectly within
their rights to claim private property, since their farms were evidence
of toiling on the land.

2.1 1664 engraving of Huron women grinding corn from an anonymous artist illustrates the fallacy of John Locke's theory that American Indians were not farmers and therefore had no investment in the soil.

Source: anonymous, Library of Congress Prints and Photographs Division

Lockean principles were later encoded into jurisprudential theories such as those of Hugo Grotius, Samuel von Pufendorf and Emmerich de Vattel, whose *The Law of Nations* of 1758 provided a theoretical justification for Europeans to dispossess those who merely 'roamed'

(Keal 2003: 97–8). This right of private property became an international cover for a Lockean squatter's charter, and from it followed the
idea of *terra nullius* (Buchan and Heath 2006; Samson 2008) used by
colonial powers across the Anglo-Saxon settler world.

From the nineteenth century onwards, global capitalist expansion was facilitated by colonial laws and policies to release collective
indigenous land for private property ownership. Once this was
accomplished, property became fluid, transferable and a basis for the
accumulation of capital. While European peasants, farmers and crafts-
people were brutally dislodged from common lands through enclosures and clearances in the eighteenth century, the same process was
rolled out in the colonies where indigenous groups were similarly dispossessed. Karl Polanyi (1944: 164) explicitly drew attention to these
similarities with the induction of non-Europeans into wage labour:
'Now, what the white man may still occasionally practice in remote
regions today, namely, the smashing up of social structures in order
to extract the element of labor from them, was done in the eighteenth
century to white populations by white men for similar purposes.'

These legal doctrines and intertwined philosophical justifications
for dispossession almost always involved violence. As Roxanne
Dunbar-Ortiz (2014: 8) tells us, 'people do not hand over their land,
resources, children and futures without a fight, and that fight is met
with violence'.

Violence

Setting out from Cadiz and landing on Caribbean islands in 1492
and 1493, Columbus's voyages began a vast expansion of Europe,
a process that brought the Western hemisphere and thousands of
distinct peoples under its domination. Dussel (1995: 26) points out
that the European finding of America was a 'constitutive moment of
Modernity' and the starting point for a world economic system based
on exploitation. Sale (1991: 27) calls it, 'the most important journey
in the history of the human species'. Axtell (2001: 15) remarks that
Columbus's landing 'unwittingly launched the most massive encounter of foreign peoples in human history. More than five centuries
later,' he continues, 'we are still taking stock of that momentous
meeting.' Todorov (1984: 5) tells us that 'we are all direct descendants of Columbus, it is with him that our genealogy begins, insofar
as the word beginning has a meaning'. Todorov is one among many
scholars interested in the significance of Columbus for the present.

The voyages 'began the long process by which a single culture came to dominate as never before all other cultures in the world, to impose its languages in their mouths, its clothes on their backs, its values in their hearts, and to accumulate to itself the power that now enables it to determine nothing less than the destiny of the world' (Sale 1991: 27). This may seem overblown, but certainly the figure of Columbus underpins the US national narrative, furnishing an origin myth for the settler state itself.

Until their organized resistance to the foreigners, the Tainos of Espanola (now Dominican Republic and Haiti) were considered by Columbus and his men to be pliant, friendly and helpful. Indeed, they saved many Spanish lives when one of the ships in the fleet was shipwrecked off the coast. After that they helped build the first Spanish settlement and a fortress called La Natividad. As soon as this was done, Columbus fired a cannonball into the sea to scare the Tainos and make them aware of his power. The 1492 conquest was consolidated by the second all-male voyage of 17 ships, containing priests, soldiers and weaponry. After landing, Indians were rounded up and shipped back to Spain as slaves. Columbus himself returned with 1,600 Tainos (Sale 1991: 138). Women were raped and forced into sexual relations with Spaniards. Summary executions were common. When Columbus discovered that some Indians had taken Spanish property, he ordered their noses and ears clipped, and when he subsequently learned of three more thieves he had them beheaded. Every Spanish fortress rigged up gallows for executing local Indians.

The extent of the carnage here – and what followed on the mainland – was chronicled by the Dominican friar Bartolomé de Las Casas in his *A Short Account of the Destruction of the Indies* (1992/1552). Sale estimates that the original island of Espanola was densely populated with just under eight million Taino people, and this is confirmed by the very detailed calculations of Bacci (2003: 25). Mann (2012: 14) claims that, by the mid-sixteenth century, there were fewer than 500 Tainos. The genocide was a result of violence against Indians perpetuated through the *encomienda* system of slave labour and tutelage, of which Las Casas was a vociferous critic. In a typically evocative passage regarding the establishment of New Spain from 1518 to 1542, he tells us that 'heinous outrages and acts of barbarity have been so vile, the violence so intense, the murders so frequent, the acts of despotism so extreme and the havoc and devastation so widespread throughout the kingdoms of the Mainland that . . . [it] beggars description' (1992/1552: 42).

Most deaths, however, were the result of a different kind of violence resulting from diseases brought by Europeans and to which the Indians had no immunity. Las Casas estimated that the total loss of life in the Caribbean islands and the New Spain colony on the mainland between 1492 and 1542 was 'more than 12 million souls' (1992/1552: 12). 'The first recorded epidemic . . . was in 1493. Smallpox entered terribly, in 1518; it spread to Mexico, swept down Central America, and then continued into Peru, Bolivia, and Chile. Following it came the rest, a pathogenic cavalcade' (Mann 2012: 14).

The loss of indigenous life was astounding, as colonization moved in all directions on the mainland American continent. In 1532, Francisco Pizarro and his soldiers attacked the Inca capital Cuzco and ordered the execution of the King Atahualpa. Military expeditions in search of gold and other riches pushed through Mexico from 1519 onwards, where Hernan Cortés and his men waged war on the Aztec capital Tenochtitlan and shortly after killed the leader Moctezuma and laid waste to the magnificent city. They proceeded into what are now Northern Mexico and the US Southwest. Batalla (1996: 81) calls the mortality in the first century of rule of the colony in Central Mexico 'the most brutal demographic catastrophe in history'.

In the 1580s–90s a series of expeditions by Franciscan friars and soldiers made an effort to colonize territories – which at that time were beyond the Spanish empire – across the Rio Grande and into New Mexico. These expeditions were more organized, involving attempted military occupation and conversion. Large crosses were erected at indigenous pueblos, and each was renamed after a Catholic saint. In 1598, permanent Spanish colonization was entrusted to Juan de Oñate, who obtained a Royal Charter to occupy the land and convert Indians. In each pueblo the Spanish imposed their own authority structures and expected the Indians to abide by them. One incident, however, marked Oñate's control of the territories – a successful revolt at Acoma pueblo dislodged the 30 Spanish soldiers who were demanding food. Among the dead was one of Oñate's nephews. Oñate then vowed a 'war of blood and fire' and sent a huge force to Acoma. Eventually, after several days' combat, 1,000 Indians were dead, the remaining 500 were taken prisoner, and the pueblo was wholly destroyed. The prisoners were tried by a military tribunal, found guilty of rebellion, and Oñate sentenced each man over 25 to have one foot chopped off and endure 20 years of slave labour (Silverberg 1970: 56–7). In between fruitless expeditions in search of gold, other pueblos were routinely raided by the Spanish. When they resisted, Oñate's response was disproportionate military retaliation. In 1601, the pueblo of Quarai was sacked and burned and 900 Indians killed.

The seventeenth century saw increases in the Spanish settler population in New Mexico through a system of land grants, and settlers forced native peoples into a slave labour system under the Spanish Governor Treviño in the third quarter of the seventeenth century. This was the backdrop to the successful Pueblo Revolt of 1680, an event unique to North America in that it occasioned the eviction of European colonists, albeit only for 12 years. At the end of this revolt, the pueblos abandoned almost everything brought by the Spanish, with one exception – the Spanish system of autocratic rule. Popé, the leader of the revolt, made himself something like the Spanish Governor and demanded honours and tributes. Eventually this created disunity, and in 1696 the Spanish regrouped, laying siege to pueblos, and killing hundreds of Indians at each place they reconquered.

The violence of Spanish colonization can be further discerned from the copious records of the colonization of what was called Alta California, now the US state of California. From the first voyage of exploration in 1542 by Juan Rodriguez Cabrillo until the eighteenth century, Spain considered California a way station for its galleons travelling between its colonies in the Philippines and Mexico. But under threat from a spreading Russian fur trading empire along the northern California coast and encroachments from the English – the pirate Sir Francis Drake attempted to claim California for Britain – it moved decisively to occupy these indigenous lands. Beginning in 1769, Spain created small communities and *rancherias* along the coast around Roman Catholic missions run by the Franciscan order. The missions, which were considerably less benign than those run by the Jesuits in South America, employed or sometimes enslaved natives, who became a valuable source of farm labour. These mini-Spanish societies were defended by army garrisons (*presidios*).

At the Los Angeles mission, there were numerous atrocities committed by soldiers, including rape, murders and one battle with Indians that ended with a Chief's decapitated bloody head being placed on a pole outside the soldiers' temporary quarters (Monroy 1993: 28). By the end of the mission period in the 1830s, Indians within a 40 mile radius of the missions had either converted or been killed. Those further inland had suffered from a disruption of food supplies because relations with coastal natives had changed (Cook 1976: 197–249; Monroy 1993: 39). In these circumstances, resistance was difficult because missions destroyed the social and cultural cohesiveness of indigenous societies, and epidemics of fevers, small-pox, measles and dysentery that were incubated and spread by con-fined conditions depleted their numbers.

Extreme violence was not unique to Spanish colonization. War and military conquest became an active element of the English settlement of North America. Violence erupted as soon as the settler population enlarged to the extent that it required lands that Native Americans could not relinquish. In the context of the continual encroachment of the English on Indian lands, the Pequot War of 1636–7 and King Philip's War in 1676 were two early conflicts that resulted in enlarge-ment of colonized territories. In the latter, many thousands of Indians and English lost their lives. According to Lepore (1998: xiii) this was 'the most fatal war in all of American [US] history . . . also one of the most merciless'. Hundreds of Pequot and Narragansett families were killed in a few hours of fighting. Prisoners were sold as slaves and some were sent to Britain's Caribbean colonies. The relative indifference of the English towards the deaths of Native Americans in New England during King Philip's War was justified by 'the idea that Indians were not, in fact, truly human, or else were humans of such a vastly different race as to be considered essentially, and biologically, inferior to Europeans' (Lepore 1998: 167). In colonial contexts, killing is often connected with the idea that others are a lesser kind of human. Axtell (2001: 313) argues that the English colonizers had genocidal intent, which 'was the product not only of the frustrating encounter with Indian warfare but of the extreme ethnocentrism and racism of a people laboring under the illusion that they were chosen by God to wash America "white with the Blood of the Lamb"'.

One of the most notorious episodes of this, and perhaps the first instance of biological warfare, was General Jeffery Amherst's dis-tribution of smallpox-infected blankets to Native Americans after Pontiac's Rebellion in 1763 in the Great Lakes Region. Axtell (2001: 314) calls this, 'the deadliest strain of colonial hatred which had been gestating for over a century and a half'. The violent methods contin-ued after American independence, and these served as levers of dis-possession and relocation across the interior parts of North America, as we shall discuss in the next chapter.

On the other side of the continent, the US annexation of California in 1846 again showed the close links between colonization and extreme violence. The Treaty of Guadalupe Hidalgo that was signed after the US–Mexican war stipulated that American Indians would become citizens of the United States unless they specifically chose to retain Mexican citizenship. However, this and other provisions in the Treaty were disregarded by the newly configured California legislature, which did not recognize Native Americans as citizens and ignored the land rights afforded them by the Treaty (Del Castillo 1990: 173).

The discovery of gold in the foothills of the Sierras and mountains of northwest California in 1848 led to a huge invasion of male settlers into the area. These men had already wreaked havoc on indigenous peoples en route to California. As Richard Grant (2003: 187) put it:

> The 1848 gold-seekers came from all over the civilized world, including its foulest and most disease-ridden slums, and in addition to smallpox, influenza, typhus and whooping cough, they loosed a rampaging epidemic of cholera among the southern plains tribes ... [Indians] were infected at the waterholes, from discarded clothing and blankets strewn along the trails, occasionally from trading with the wagon trains, or looting the shallow graves they left behind. The Cheyennes lost about half their number that summer, and so did the Comanches.

The tragic sequel was to consolidate the new Californian settler society through more violence towards those who stood so visibly as symbols of its origins and contradictions. Immigrants came with overwhelming desires to acquire wealth, and reports show that American Indians in the immediate vicinity of the gold strikes suffered numerous casualties. Miners referred to Maidu Indians in the California Gold Rush areas, and others in Oregon, as 'Diggers' because they were, erroneously, thought only to live on foraging and by digging up roots. However, the term itself often implied something akin to being subhuman (Trafzner and Hyer 1999: 2), which is often a precondition for mass killings. Partly because settlers considered them extremely primitive, an early California law provided that Indians could be indentured to white employers for extended periods of time (Hagan 1998: 193), a situation that lasted from 1850 to 1863 (Madley 2004: 177). Although California was not a slave state, Native Americans were often sold into slavery by miners during the Gold Rush years, and legislation permitted perpetual Native American servitude (Trafzner and Hyer 1999: 18).

The incomers targeted Native women for rape, concubinage and abduction. Livestock stealing and occasional killings of whites were met by colossal retribution, often through extrajudicial executions by settlers. Several massacres of Indian villages occurred in Northern California (Heizer and Almquist 1971: 28–31; Hurtado 1988: 104–6), but death also occurred as a result of starvation on makeshift reservations and of organized vigilante killings (Lindsay

2012: 271–312). Constant encroachments of settlers on the lands of almost all Native American groups led to massive depopulation. For example, the Yuki in the Sierras, who now total only about 100 individuals, numbered around 3,500 in the mid-nineteenth century (Madley 2004: 181). Overall, the population declined from over 300,000 before the advent of the missions to 100,000 by 1834, and by 1913 there were only 17,000 left (Heizer and Almquist 1971; Cook 1976: 258–9, 351). Cook (1976: 351) estimates that the most precipitous decline in the indigenous population occurred in the years after the Gold Rush. The number of American Indians in California in 1880 was only 15 per cent of the 1848 population. There had, Cook argues, been an 85 per cent population decline in 32 years. Even in these circumstances, there was military resistance by some indigenous groups. The most prominent example was in the Modoc War of 1864, in which the Modocs under Captain Jack in Northern California were eventually defeated after being completely outnumbered by US forces (see Murray 1959; Madley 2012).

Missionary activities, laws, philosophies and violence were all central to colonial control of indigenous peoples during the initial contact period in the Americas and in North America, specifically, as we have examined above. Below, we look at how colonial control was implemented in various parts of the world as post-independence states consolidated their power.

Colonial control of indigenous peoples in Latin America

While political discourses on indigenous peoples' cultures play an important role in the way that many Latin American nations represent themselves to the world today, the position of indigenous groups in all these countries remains problematic. In urban areas indigenous peoples face high rates of discrimination, social exclusion and poverty, while those living in their territories are faced with forced displacements, food shortages, epidemics and environmental degradation as a result of armed conflicts, the intrusion of extractive industries, intensive farming and urban expansion. Indigenous peoples of the Amazon basin are particularly exposed to these threats, including those living in voluntary isolation (IACHR 2013).

As elsewhere in the colonial world, the liberal ideology of modernity provided justification for dispossession, control and in some cases extermination of indigenous peoples (Dussel 1995; Stavenhagen 2010). Undoubtedly, the main driving force of colonialism in Latin America has been the quest of all governments to assert sovereignty over indigenous lands. This push led first to the formation of European settler societies and then to independent nation-states controlled in most of Latin America by descendants of Spanish and Portuguese colonists, but also the Dutch and British in the northeast corner of South America, and ex-slave and indentured servant populations in the Caribbean islands. The land of indigenous peoples in French Guiana remains colonized as an overseas department of France.

As we have seen, the initial Spanish and Portuguese invasion of the American continent led to a genocidal demographic decline of indigenous peoples due to war, enslavement, forced labour and epidemic diseases. The colonial powers quickly integrated indigenous peoples that survived the onslaught into the new social and economic orders. Burkholder and Johnson (2010: 135) point out that 'Indians were compelled to participate in the monetized colonial economy, an economy that overlapped but did not totally replace the indigenous one. The methods used to secure labor varied by region and over time. *Encomienda*, *repartimiento/mita*, free wage labor, *yanaconaje*, and slavery were the principal means employed in Spanish America.' Similarly, in Portuguese America, Indians were used as labour on plantations and at mills through slavery or wage work (Schwartz 1987: 81–2). In Amazonia, forced prostitution and the enslavement of Indians continued well into the twentieth century, long after African slavery had been abolished.

A central feature of European colonialism in Latin America was the assertion of Crown ownership of the land. As a consequence of the Doctrine of Discovery, discussed above, the ownership of all land was vested in the Crown and it was at its discretion that limited rights be conferred to settlers or indigenous communities (Peloso 2014: 9). The creation of Indian villages like *pueblos* or *doctrinas de Indios* in Spanish America and *aldeias* in Brazil was an attempt to control indigenous peoples, rationalize Indian labour and facilitate their conversion to Christianity (König 1998: 17). These systems were also designed to provide a certain degree of protection from violence and slavery, re-create indigenous authority in villages and establish nominal protection for indigenous communal lands. However, in most cases the special laws protecting territorial integrity of these villages and indigenous lands were largely ineffective against pressures from colonial administrators and settlers.

The colonial society was a highly stratified order, where the term 'Indian' had a double meaning:

> The process of compressing the great diversity of indigenous cultures
> and social organizations began with the creation of a new identity, that
> of 'Indian', that had not existed before the conquest. Although origi-
> nally employed as a racial description, 'Indian' also became a cultural
> term and for the Spanish Crown, a fiscal category that defined obliga-
> tions for the native population. (Burkholder and Johnson 2010: 213)

Colonialism also facilitated the development of assimilation processes that, on the one hand, led to the disintegration of indigenous
communities as indigenous peoples migrated from their original
homelands or as they were absorbed as a landless *mestizo* working
force in haciendas and ranchos. This proved to be a decisive factor in
the appropriation of indigenous communal land by settlers. In Chile,
for example, Indians living in *pueblos de Indios* in the central valleys
migrated south or were gradually assimilated as landless workers
in the large haciendas, to the point that all distinct communities
disappeared (Bengoa 2004: 67–92). However, in other regions of
Latin America, pueblos and *doctrinas de Indios* formed the basis of
contemporary indigenous communities that, to a certain extent, have
managed to preserve cultural identities and autonomy (Díaz Polanco
1995: 236–7).

Despite the overwhelming Spanish and Portuguese power in
Latin America, not all indigenous groups were always under colo-
nial control. A different story played out in the borderland regions.
For example, indigenous peoples living in the Amazon basin, Mato
Grosso, Patagonia, Tierra del Fuego, the Andes and the northern
border of Mexico, including what became the Southwestern United
States, remained to a large extent independent from colonial control.
At the borderlands, warfare was a constant possibility. When military
violence failed, colonial authorities would sign treaties with specific
groups of Indians as a way of obtaining peace and seeking military
alliances against rival colonial powers, while also promoting trade
and missionary activities (see Bengoa 2004; Hemming 1987; Boccara
2002; Bannon 1974; Blackhawk 2006). Finally, there were also
Indians living in regions away from the borderlands in territories
unseen by European eyes.

The nineteenth-century wars of independence were a significant
turning point in the history of Latin America. While they ended
Spanish and Portuguese rule, colonial control of indigenous people
did not end with the proclamations of independence. It just took a
different form under the Creole elites – people of European ances-
try who had often been excluded from positions of power in the

colonies – who dominated the independence process and the political establishment of the new republics. Upon independence, these elites appropriated the idea of indigeneity by appealing to a mythical indigenous past, providing a symbolic dimension to the fight against European powers. The Aztecs, Incas and Araucanos represented the values of resistance, independence, freedom and dignity in the face of the Spanish and Portuguese oppressor. The Creole elites saw themselves as the natural heirs of these values (Earle 2007: 29–34). However, in real terms indigenous peoples were ignored and marginalized. First, this was because they were often deemed unfit to play any significant role in the newly formed republics. Earle (2007: 175) points out that, although the Indians were formally regarded as equal citizens, they were nonetheless regarded as incapable of exercising citizenship rights: 'If Indians did not feel patriotism, if they were not "sensitive to the revolution of independence", this in itself made them less civilized, since patriotism was one of the markers of a civilized man.' Second, colonial laws that protected indigenous communal lands – and *doctrinas* and *pueblos de Indios* – were largely abolished as ideas of private property and individual rights took hold (Wade 1997: 31). Third, Creole elites conveniently adopted social Darwinist, liberal and positivist ideas that represented the Indian as racially inferior, morally degraded and dangerously savage (Hale 1996; Beardsell 2000).

The new nation-states were eager to claim sovereignty by occupying the most remote regions within what they considered their domain. Conflict with indigenous peoples was therefore inevitable as Indians were regarded as obstacles to progress, orderly settlement and the development of economic enterprises. In this context, the process of westward expansion in North America was a blueprint for colonization to the south. For example, in 1847 the Argentine liberal intellectual and politician Domingo Sarmiento visited the United States, and returned home inspired by its social, economic and political progress, and in particular by the territorial expansion of the Euro-Americans (Zusman 2007: 52–5).

For Sarmiento, the forging of a civilized nation implied the absolute negation of the barbaric colonial past forged by both Spaniard and Indian. To make Argentina anew, he proposed national instruction, the creation of a landowning yeoman farmer class, and European immigration. He also called for the extermination of those who were not educated, especially indigenous peoples of the pampas. He thus emulated the more 'advanced' United States, with its independent farmers and policy warfare toward native populations. (Appelbaum et al. 2003: 5)

These ideas were also echoed in Chile. In the 1850s the Argentine and Chilean governments initiated military campaigns against the Tehuelches and Mapuches living in Patagonia and the Araucanía respectively. In 1879 the Argentine president explained the reasons behind the military expansion to the provinces south of Buenos Aires:

> The old policy of gradual expansion inherited since the conquest has forced national forces to be stretched in a vast area, thus making it sus-ceptible to the incursions of the savages, and has proven to be impotent in order to guarantee the settlers' lives and fortunes as they are under constant threat. It is necessary to abandon such policy and directly confront the Indian in their den in order to subjugate or expel them, and establishing as a border not a handmade trench but the huge and insurmountable barrier of the deep and navigable Rio Negro, navigable in its full extension from the Ocean to the Andes. (Arce 1960: 44)

Echoing the US westward expansion, the Argentine and the Chilean governments viewed colonization of the southern regions as a means of state building. This was a violent process that cost the lives of thousands of Indians and eventually pushed the Tehuelches and the Mapuches off their territories to officially sanctioned *reducciones* as their lands were gradually occupied by settlers. Furthermore, as the colonization process kept pushing south towards the Archipelago of Tierra del Fuego, the genocidal consequences of this process took its dramatic toll over the lives of the Selk'nam, Yagán and Kawésqar peoples (Bengoa 2004: 547–605).

In the 1920s, Latin American intellectuals coined a new term in relation to indigenous peoples: *indigenismo*. On the one hand, it rec-ognized indigenous peoples' cultures as a distinctive value of Latin American societies, but on the other it sought to assimilate them into mainstream society as a way of rescuing them from poverty and social exclusion (Barié 2003: 51–2; Korsbaek and Sámano-Rentería 2007: 201–4). These ideas were built into the first Inter-American Indigenista Congress held in Pátzcuaro, Mexico in 1940. There, Latin American states agreed to the creation of the Instituto Indigenista Inter Americano as a way of tackling the 'indigenous problem' and contributing to state sponsored policies that could improve indigenous socioeconomic status, in particular educational policies (Convención de Pátzcuaro 1940). Again, the United States provided a model. Inspired by the BIA, a number of governments created national offices of indigenous affairs aimed at 'protecting' indigenous peoples through welfare and education policies. Despite the positive sounding rhetoric, *indigenismo* was a paternalistic and assimilationist ideology.

The second half of the twentieth century witnessed the eruption of social and political struggles across Latin America and brought extended colonial control over indigenous peoples and new waves of extreme violence against them. As ruling elites and national security were challenged by political and social movements that incorporated Marxist ideas within the geopolitical context of the cold war, indigenous peoples were often targets of official repression and became targets of counter insurgency policies. For example, the Commission for Historical Clarification set up in Guatemala after the civil war (1960–96) estimated in its report *Guatemala: Memory of Silence* (CEH 1999) that more than 200,000 people, 83 per cent of them Maya, were either killed or disappeared as a consequence of the violence mostly committed by the state (1999: 71–3). In addition, indigenous peoples were often trapped in the fights between powerful drug cartels and armed forces opposing them, particularly in Colombia (Villa and Houghton 2005). However, since the 1980s a process of democratization has swept through the region, opening up a significant space for indigenous peoples' organizations to develop new strategies for claiming their rights and opposing state policies.

The credit for diminishing the violence unleashed in Latin America against indigenous peoples must go to individuals such as Rigoberta Menchú Tum (1992), who won the Nobel Peace Prize for her work on indigenous rights in Guatemala. In her acceptance speech, she stressed the ubiquitous experience of loss of people, community and knowledge:

> I would describe the meaning of this Nobel Peace prize, in the first place, as a tribute to the Indian people who have been sacrificed and have disappeared because they aimed at a more dignified and just life with fraternity and understanding among human beings. To those who are no longer alive to keep up the hope for a change in the situation in respect of poverty and marginalization of the Indians, of those who have been banished, of the helpless in Guatemala as well as in the entire American Continent.

The struggles of indigenous peoples against brute violence across Latin America are ongoing. In 2016, Berta Cáceres, the Lenca leader, winner of the 2015 Goldman Environmental Prize and organizer of opposition to the hydroelectric dam on the Gualcaque River in Honduras, was assassinated by men linked to the company building the dam (Lakhani 2016). Indigenous peoples have also had to contend with a different kind of violence; that entailed in recently implemented neoliberal policies centred on privatization, free trade and the development of an export-oriented economy. These policies have expropriated indigenous non-renewable natural resources and dispossessed them of much of their territories without as much of the overt physical violence evidenced in Guatemala in the 1980s (Escárzaga Nicté 2004; Silva 2009).

Neoliberalism has a direct impact on indigenous communities as states and multinational corporations have easily bypassed environmental concerns and indigenous rights in order to sponsor hydroelectric dams, mines, industrial farming and highways. Environmental degradation, contamination and destruction of the biodiversity used by indigenous peoples was accompanied by state compulsion and violence. One manifestation of this was the North American Free Trade Agreement (NAFTA) between the United States, Mexico and Canada. The same day that NAFTA was launched, the Zapatista rebellion took over much of the Mexican state of Chiapas. One aspect of the protest was the belief that indigenous farmers would no longer be able to sustain themselves through traditional collectively shared and redistributed farming because they would be flooded with cheap subsidized US imports, especially genetically modified corn. As part of the neoliberal economic provisions of NAFTA, indigenous peoples' lands in Mexico were decollectivized and made open to private ownership. This continues to be a major source of social and political unrest in Mexico and Central America because NAFTA opens up land to the highest bidder and makes subsistence agriculture impossible, gradually removing land from the control of indigenous peoples. It then acts as a push factor, driving indigenous peoples to migrate to the United States (González and Fernandez 2002: 53). A 2008 Mexican government report predicted that loss of employment and economic collapse meant that six million Mexicans would emigrate to the United States because of NAFTA (Kaye 2010: 51).

Reactions to the social fallout from neoliberalism were the driving force behind the Zapatista movement, which then became the benchmark for all indigenous resistance (Stahler-Sholk 2007). Other indigenous rebellions have included the 1990 indigenous Inti Raymi uprising in Ecuador (Moreno Yañez and Figueroa 1990) and the widespread indigenous protest movement against the neoliberal policies of the Bolivian state in 2000 (Mayorga and Córdoba 2009).

Colonial violence towards indigenous communities in the form of neoliberal economic expansion continues. Indigenous people are today ravaged by imported infectious diseases, and this is exacerbated with the opening up of their lands to settlement and commercial activities such as agribusiness and resource extraction in the vast Amazonia region. Since the 1980s, Amazonia has witnessed invasions of non-native miners, loggers and fishermen who travel from one indigenous community to another. The accompanying expansion of sea, air and rail links mean that the death toll from imported diseases is an ongoing process. According to the NGO Survival International, the influx of some 45,000 miners or *garimpeiros* in the wake of the 1987 Brazilian Gold Rush had genocidal effects. Survival International's (1990) Yanomami report noted that 13 villages had disappeared over a two-year time period and 15 per cent of the population had died. Even anthropologist Napoleon Chagnon (1992: 211–17), known for his stereotyping the 'fierceness' of the Yanomami, came to similar conclusions, documenting extreme violence, rape, the spread of sickness and the dissolution of Yanomami villages in the wake of this first wave invasion.

Colonial control of indigenous peoples in Africa

Despite the iconic images of Columbus's voyage, his encounter with indigenous peoples is just one antecedent to the contemporary colonial situations of indigenous peoples. It applies to the Western hemisphere, where the divisions between the groups who were native to a locality and those who came later via colonization are clear (Saugestad 2008). The current indigenous rights movement was initiated principally by groups from the Western hemisphere whose historical experiences were somewhat different from those of the groups today considered indigenous in Africa, where new states emerged after decolonization in the mid-twentieth century. However, while the situation of indigenous peoples in Africa – mostly hunters and pastoralists – is not part of the Columbus legacy, it is similarly entwined with the missionary doctrines, laws, philosophies and violence of colonialism and its post-independence aftermath.

By the end of the nineteenth century, emissaries of the expanding states of Europe had colonized the Americas, most of Africa, the Indian subcontinent and other parts of Asia. In fact, the consolidation of a global network of colonial rule was made during the Great Land Rush of that century. Virtually the entire population of

Africa experienced occupation by European powers, especially after the 1894–5 Berlin Conference attended by European governments, the United States and representatives of the Ottoman Empire. The General Act of the conference provided rules for 'effective occupation' of African lands. This was not defined as total rule over each colony, but the eliciting of agreements with local leaders and the establishment of an administrative protectorate. The provisions in this Act are akin to those contained in the Doctrine of Discovery in that both stipulate that agreements with indigenous groups must be obtained on a first come first served basis, and that these agreements provide the legal means by which areas can be settled, occupied and/or commercially exploited. A main aim of the Berlin Conference was to open up imperial trade and possibilities for low-cost resource extraction to enrich companies and the states in which they were based (Stone 1988).

In common with the westward expansion of Europeans across North America, the rules for the establishment of effective occupation and trade in Africa were easy to evade, the enforcement of them virtually non-existent, and the European capacity for violence so great that during the early phases of organized colonization of Africa several instances of genocide occurred. Although focusing specifically on Southern Africa, Olusoga and Erichsen's (2010: 71) points about the common colonial processes are salutary:

> The pattern was the same on every continent. Settlers came in search of land and displaced native populations, leading to the loss of pastures and hunting grounds, and often to famine. Hunger sparked many armed confrontations. The parity of military technology that existed between colonisers and colonised in South-west Africa was a rare exception; elsewhere settlers and soldiers were equipped with far superior weapons to the native tribes who opposed them. Almost always, the musket and later the rifle overcame the spear of the indigenous warrior.

The experience of the various indigenous groups of Khoikhoi, Herero, Nama and San Bushmen in what is today Namibia are valuable examples. The earliest colonization of the Cape of Good Hope in the mid-seventeenth century by the Dutch East India Company and Afrikaner settlers was followed by an aggressive expansion of Calvinist Dutch settlers (Afrikaners) (Gall 2002; Penn 2005). In a process reminiscent of Euro-American miners' responses to indigenous resistance to their intrusion in California, zealous Afrikaners met Khoikhoi and Bushman retaliation for the theft of their lands with overwhelming retribution. The physical violence was complemented by another kind of violence that had the same results. Being pastoralists and hunters, the Khoikhoi and Bushmen needed the freedom to be mobile across large tracts of land in order to survive. The settlers, however, were farmers, and rapidly cordoned off indigenous lands for private property, prohibiting indigenous hunting and grazing. As they grabbed land, the settlers also killed vast numbers of antelope, including the largest African antelope, the eland, and by the 1790s this animal was nearly extinct in Southern Africa (Gall 2002: 79). Other animals hunted by the Bushmen in the area were also depleted by settlers; one, the quagga, a subspecies of zebra, was hunted to extinction by the end of the nineteenth century. This is clearly a parallel to what occurred at the same time on the Great Plains with the destruction of the bison (Hubbard 2014), and the denuding of habitats.

The mass killings of the indigenous peoples of Southern Africa continued as Dutch settlers went further north. The extermination of indigenous groups reached another crescendo after 1884, a year that marked the beginning of German occupation of Southwest Africa, which would last until after the First World War. Indigenous retaliation for land theft was marked by disproportionately violent responses by Kaiser Wilhelm's settlers and military. German conflict with the Herero pastoralists was particularly brutal, with 80,000 Herero driven from their lands in eastern Namibia into Bechuanaland (now Botswana), many dying en route. Other Herero and Nama died in forced labour camps. Gall (2002: 109) argues that by 1911 only half the Nama (9,800 out of 20,000) and a quarter of the Herero (15,000 out of 80,000) survived the German extermination policy. Sarkin (2011: 1) estimated that between 60,000 and 100,000 Herero were killed at the beginning of the twentieth century through a mixture of shootings, induced starvation and drought that stemmed from the sealing of wells and poisoning of water.

Many survivors of this genocide became slaves in the German military. German colonial authorities also introduced the pass laws that became notorious in South Africa under apartheid. The indigenous African population were required to carry badges at all times, and could be arrested and physically punished by any white person for not doing so. Similar to the position of African slaves in the United States, under German policy Africans in the territory could not own any property whatsoever without permission from the governor. African employees on settler operated farms were under an *in loco parentis* system controlled by flogging and physical punishment. Hunting was prohibited (Dieckmann 2007: 73–5), thereby criminalizing the way of life of the San and other peoples. When the British placed Southwest Africa under the control of the apartheid regime in South Africa after the Second World War, generous inducements were given to new white settlers to farm African lands (Dieckmann 2007: 123).

As for Africa as a whole, at the time of decolonization, colonizers often handed state authority over to the larger, more favoured ethnic groups that had been their patrons. This was the method of the British, whose indirect rule system empowered some ethnic groups and marginalized others. Those sidelined were often peoples who, for whatever reason, were able to maintain cultural continuity through hunting and pastoralism. These divisions created the conditions for violent ethnic conflict after independence (Blanton et al. 2001). Where colonists were evicted after political mobilization, the ethnic groups who led the revolts, such as the Ovambo in Namibia and Kikuyu in Kenya, inherited the reins of power. After the transition, hunters and pastoralists such as the San Bushmen, Nama, Hadzabe, Maasai, Batwa and Tuaregs, among many others, became subject to the power of the larger and more strategically placed ethnic groups.

Being subordinated to colonialism exercised by other African groups who inherited European instruments of power and were often under European economic direction, African hunters and pastoralists have recently self-identified as indigenous peoples. Their ways of life were in some ways antagonistic to the political elites under the neocolonial post-independence conditions because they did not share their enthusiasm for Western modernization, industry and culture. In most places modernization was translated into active participation in global capitalism as producers of raw materials. In some new countries, such as Tanzania and Mozambique, where Marxism had been more influential, the orientation was much the same, since both capitalism and socialism shared the goals of industrial economic production. Indigenous groups, on the other hand, either by choice or sometimes simply by their marginalization, had less appetite for industrial labour and more investment in their ancestral lands. Consequently, these groups have often been victims of post-independence conflicts generated by tensions originating from ethnic divisions made during European colonialism. For example, the Rwandan genocide of 1994 took a huge toll on indigenous peoples. According to one estimate, 30 per cent of the Twa pygmies were killed in the genocide and the war that followed it (Lewis 2000: 24).

However, as Li (2010) has argued, the segmentation of colonized populations does not exclusively follow divisions in modes of subsistence. In Africa and Asia, colonists separated out those groups that were deemed suitable as labourers in the market economy. Regardless of their specific way of life, those groups whose lands were needed for commerce were considered as a potential labour force and recipients of individual rights, making their land disposable and fluid. With the imposition of taxes, duties, land, mortgages and the apparatus of finance, it became increasingly easy to lose land, creating landlessness and urbanization. Other groups more remote from the paths of colonial encroachment and commerce were granted communal collective land rights by colonizers, binding them to the land. Hence, the concept of indigeneity co-emerged with the spread of capitalism. The groups in Asia and Africa who today are considered indigenous peoples are, according to this analysis, those that were granted communal title under colonialism, a status that has come under great threat in contemporary African states, which are, in effect, reproducing European colonial practices.

Colonial control of indigenous peoples in Europe and Asia

The forms of colonial control already described for the peoples of the Americas and Africa were direct offshoots of European expansion and occupation, and the process that solidified control over indigenous peoples and their territories was nation building. The same process can occur as a result of monarchs and national political entities simply incorporating territories under their authority.

In the northern areas of Eurasia, including Scandinavia, the reindeer herding peoples and hunters were affected by the fur trade and mining from the eighteenth century onwards, and had been required to pay taxes to tsars and other monarchs (McGhee 2004: 246). But it was the establishment of unitary states that most diminished their autonomy and compromised their ways of life. Following incursions already made under the tsarist regimes, the communist industrial state of the Soviet Union created by the 1917 Russian Revolution expanded west beyond the Urals across the Eurasian steppes and into the boreal forests and tundra of Siberia, colonizing the Nenets, Saami, Evenki, Chukchi and Inuit (Slezkine 1994; McGhee 2004: 246). Colonization of Siberian peoples was often enforced violently, with show trials and sometimes executions of designated tundra *kulaks* (wealthy peasants) (Slezkine 1994: 187–217). Indigenous peoples of the north were considered to be backward on account of their pastoralist economies, superstitious by virtue of shamanism and, worst of all, 'tundra kulaks', because they permitted differences in wealth and status at variance with those arising from within the Bolshevik state (Vitebsky 2005: 187–217).

> [The ideal] new life of the native peoples ... consisted of material proofs of their well-being; there were the Russian-type houses, boarding schools, hospitals, and clubs; there were the usual interiors with bright curtains, typewriters, sewing machines, and well salted Russian meals on 'neatly ironed tablecloths'; there were the well educated and contented people proud of their *kolkhoz*'s [collective farm] productivity, their Russian haircuts, and their imported furniture. (Vitebsky 2005: 353)

A slightly different variant of colonialism appears in the northern Scandinavian areas. Although the Saami reindeer herders had paid taxes to various Swedish and Russian monarchs, as the individual states of Norway, Sweden and Finland affirmed their own national borders from the seventeenth century onwards, the Saami peoples of the coastal and inland northern areas of these territories became state populations. The states that claimed their lands were motivated both by the need to solidify borders against other states, and by the prospects of wealth from mining and settler farming. Within these states, the farming, fishing and reindeer herding Saami became subject to diverging state policies, making Saami unity difficult and also impeding migratory herding because of the Iron Curtain and the erection of a fence along parts of the Finnish border in the 1950s (Kent 2014: 230). The colonial process in Norway rested simply on assertion of authority. As Thuen (1995: 29) remarks, 'the state has "come to regard" itself as the landowner, without any legally binding transference of ownership'. Mere assertion of sovereignty was then formalized by instituting rules making mastery of the Norwegian language a precondition for the ownership of private property in the Saami Finnmark area of northern Norway, and in Sweden introducing aggressive assimilation measures including boarding schools (Lindmark 2013). Throughout the twentieth century, Norwegian state control of the Saami proceeded with the migration of Norwegians and Finns into Saami territories and the imposition of taxation.

In Sweden, the government gave permission for settlers to establish farms on Saami lands from the eighteenth century onwards, thus damaging the highly organized Saami *siida* community structures (Kent 2014: 38). While many Saami were able to stay in their lands in Sweden, others – in Finland and Russia especially – were evicted. After the Russian Revolution, Saami were among the many northern indigenous groups persecuted by the state, and this included not only land and reindeer confiscation, but after 1937 mass executions and massacres of Saami and neighbouring indigenous groups such as the Komi. As Kent (2014: 60) comments: 'An injudicious comment, a conversation at some point in one's life with a Scandinavian or Finn, contact with another accused – all might lead to imprisonment or death.'

Other powers had also colonized lands that were distant from their point of origin. These included the Ottoman Empire, which controlled much of North Africa and the Middle East, carving out territories and leaving subordinated populations of Kurds, Amazigh (Kabyles), Bedouins and Tuareg across these territories (Lazreg 1983; Madani 2003). Japan made incursions into China, and in the fourteenth and fifteenth centuries expanded into what is now the northern island of Hokkaidō, home of the indigenous Ainu (Siddle 1996; Walker 2001). Han Chinese emigrated to Taiwan in various waves over the past four centuries and now control the state, meaning that the indigenous Austronesian Amis, Kavalan and Atayal, among others, are also in a colonial relationship to the state. The Taiwanese Constitution of 1997 includes the concept of indigenous peoples (Simon 2007), while a number of other legal frameworks address issues such as indigenous education, identity and employment (Simon 2011: 27). In this context it is the Executive Yuan that has the power to recognize indigenous tribes; to this day, 16 tribes have been officially recognized. However, the indigenous status of most of the Plains Aborigines (PingPu) is yet to be recognized (Hsieh 2006).

The states that emerged after decolonization from Western powers – such as those on the Indian subcontinent, and the Philippines, Indonesia and Malaysia – principally represented a dominant religious or ethnic group. These groups were often wedded to Western-style modernization, and exerted hegemony over more peripheral religious and ethnic groups such as the semi-nomadic forest dwellers throughout Asia. In the Malaysian peninsula, for example, numerous distinct groups of inland peoples known as Orang Asli have been subjects of a Muslim Malay-dominated state since the independence of Malaysia from Britain in 1957. There is also a very significant Chinese population and a smaller Tamil population, both originally brought to Malaysia by the British for labour on plantations and at mines. The Chinese population now controls much of the private enterprise industrial economy. As the state as a whole is committed to capitalist industrialization, the Orang Asli have increasingly come under pressure to relinquish their lands and politically and culturally assimilate to the mainstream capitalist and Islamic culture of the state (Nicholas 2000).

A similar example is presented in the Chittagong Hill Tracts (CHT) of what is now Bangladesh, where the many indigenous groups, sometimes known as Adivasis, of this vast area were brought under the loose authority of the Mughal Emperors in the eighteenth century. They were subsequently subsumed under the authority of the British East India Company, which annexed the whole of Bengal. The British, however, did not impose direct political authority and allowed the various tribal groups to govern themselves. At the independence of India, the indigenous peoples of Bangladesh became part of the state of Pakistan. Unlike Muslim groups such as the Syllhetis of Assam and the tribal groups of the North West Frontier, the Buddhist, Christian and animist peoples of the CHT were not given any choice over which state they should be incorporated into (Roy 2000: 26). After the violent civil war with Pakistan in 1971, the people of the CHT and their forestlands were simply absorbed into the Muslim-dominated Bangladeshi state. Like many other post-independence states, Bangladesh strongly appeals to a narrative that 'everyone is indigenous', but this occurs, as Alfred and Corntassel (2005: 602) point out, only *after* the state has allowed vast numbers of Bengali settlers to take residence in the CHTs. Since 2014, the CHTs have been under military occupation. Similar dynamics whereby a post-independence religious and/or ethnic group inherited the reins of power from the British and then carried out a programme of modernization apply elsewhere, such as Myanmar (Burma) and Nepal, where ongoing conflicts over indigenous rights remain legacies of this and other forms of colonialism by dominant groups from the region.

Colonial control of indigenous peoples of Australasia

In the islands of the Pacific, indigenous peoples still comprise most of the population, with the exception of New Caledonia, Hawaii, New Zealand, Australia and Guam, where colonial settler populations now dominate (Maclellan 2001: 92). Because of its violent history, large land mass and ancient Aboriginal civilization, Australia features prominently in discussions of colonialism. Aborigines and their descendants have lived for 60,000 years in Australia. They possess 'songlines' that are maps in music and song, each one describing the land, animals, waters, trees and spirits of places familiar to different groups of Aborigines, some of which stretch for thousands of miles across the continent. Their autonomy and cultural continuity was radically altered following the initial British landing at Botany Bay in 1770 by Lieutenant (later Captain) James Cook, who occupies a similar place in Australia's settler narrative to that of Columbus in the United States. The British military and settlers used violence and squatting to usurp the territories of the estimated 300,000 to 1 million Aborigines of 700 distinct groups (Perry 1996: 164) speaking 250 languages (Nugent 2015). According to Lindqvist (2007: 207) 90 per cent of the Aboriginal population was killed by the settler migrations subsequent to the invasion – either from violence or disease.

The British claimed Australia by right of Cook's discovery (Weaver 2003: 169), not, interestingly, through the Doctrine of Discovery. They first established a penal colony in 1788. The 'transportation' of burgeoning numbers of convicts under severe criminal punishments to Australia (along with New World plantations) became a means of the British government to dispose of surplus populations. When they docked in Australia, these men and women became indentured labourers (Perry 1996: 162–3). In a short time, settlers and ex-convicts at the coastal areas gradually fanned out inland, and settlement of Australia was continually increased by the British Poor Laws of the 1830s, which barely made a distinction between poverty and criminality. Thousands of British and Irish paupers and others adjudged to have flaws requiring correction and punishments were shipped to Australia.

For a long time, the dispersal of new arrivals from Britain and freed convicts beyond the coastal penal colony areas was uncontrolled by the Crown. Eventually, 'pastoral leases' were issued to settlers who wanted to establish farms. These were similar to the US Homestead Laws, which enabled settlers to petition the government for title to indigenous lands. Around settler cattle stations and farms, Aborigines became labourers, but violence and continual displacement and forced relocation, including to 'lock hospitals' on isolated islands, spread along the frontier. Land was often taken by force by settlers using their superior arms. Australian history is so littered with massacres that many analysts refer to it as colonial genocide. From 1788 to 1844, about 20,000 Aborigine deaths resulted from murder or from causes associated with the encroachment of Europeans (Short 2008: 32).

In New Zealand, the Treaty of Waitangi was negotiated between

Captain William Hobson and Maori chiefs in 1840. Like the North American treaties, it put into effect a massive land cession which was exchanged for Maori rights in New Zealand under British dominion. In many ways the treaty simply formalized a *fait accompli* because Britain had already made claims to Maori land under the presumed right of discovery (Weaver 2003: 169–71). The process itself was marked by expediency and lack of consent from many chiefs. It took place after settlers had already occupied lands and Maori were stricken with imported diseases. Britain and its settler state of New Zealand have not honoured many aspects of the Treaty.

Elsewhere in the Pacific, in 1883 American Admiral Belknap had remarked of the Hawaiian Islands 2,000 miles from the California coast: 'indeed, it would seem that nature had established that group to be ultimately occupied as an outpost...of the great republic on its Western border, and that the time has now come for the fulfillment of such a design' (Weinberg 1935: 68). After years of European and American settlement of the islands, disruption of the land tenure system and the imposition of huge fruit plantations, the entrepreneurs and settlers (who called themselves 'revolutionists') lobbied for the US military to invade the islands and depose the indigenous Hawaiian monarchy in 1893. Although native Hawaiians opposed this and demanded that their sovereignty be restored, the United States eventually approved an annexation treaty with the revolutionists in 1898 (Parker 1996: 128–31), thus ending any effective indigenous sovereignty over the islands and extending the American colonial frontier far into the Pacific.

3

Land

In the latter half of the nineteenth century, the land of the Ainu people was unilaterally appropriated by the government of Japan under the auspices of a large-scale colonization and development project known as 'Hokkaidō Kaitaku'. We were forced to become ... Japanese nationals. As a result of border negotiations between the Russian and Japanese governments, our traditional territory was carved up and many of our people suffered forced relocation. Moreover, the Japanese government pursued an aggressive policy of assimilation from the very beginning. Under this doctrine of assimilation, the Ainu language was banned, our traditional culture was denied, our economic livelihood was destroyed, and the Ainu people became the object of oppression, exploitation and severe discrimination. We were unable to continue our traditional way of life in our ancestral lands, as fishing became 'Poaching' and cutting wood in the hills was branded as 'theft'. This is an experience common to indigenous peoples everywhere.

Giichi Nomura (1992)

As Giichi Nomura told his audience at the UN General Assembly, changes made to indigenous peoples in the course of colonization were involuntary and most involved some sort of fundamental change to their relationships to their lands. We will proceed by looking at the myriad forms of social change induced by colonial processes of relocation, privatization of lands, sedentarization, forced removal to boarding schools and urbanization. All these involve 'domicide' (Porteous and Smith 2001), the separation of people *en masse* from their homes and the places that formed the bases of their identities. Once they are off their lands, territory is freed up for industry, agriculture, resource extraction, environmental conservation and settlement.

Displacement and enclosures of Native Americans in North America

If there is an archetype for settler colonialism it would be the American westward expansion of the nineteenth century. After the American Revolution, the US Federal government enthusiastically promoted Euro-American settlement on indigenous lands to the west. Before the Revolution, land speculation made settlement of indigenous lands financially lucrative, enriching Thomas Jefferson and George Washington, among other 'founding fathers' (Weaver 2003: 88). Before the break with Britain, the ability of settlers to take indigenous lands was hampered by the Royal Proclamation of 1763, which stipulated:

> And whereas it is just and reasonable, and essential to our Interest, and the Security of our Colonies, that the several Nations or Tribes of Indians with whom We are connected, and who live under our Protection, should not be molested or disturbed in the Possession of such Parts of Our Dominions and Territories as, not having been ceded to or purchased by Us, are reserved to them, or any of them, as their Hunting Grounds. (Quoted in Slattery 2005: 443)

While this Proclamation simply declares that indigenous peoples are under the authority of the Crown, it was a check on the acquisitive zeal of settlers, attempting to maintain the Crown's honour within the framework of colonial occupation. By making it apparent to indigenous peoples that the British government did not approve of unregulated dispossession, while remaining ambiguous on the state of their sovereignty by referring to 'Protection' (Borrows 1997: 161), the Proclamation created the legal conditions to bind indigenous peoples into the colonial order. However, as it was an impediment to land speculation and colonization, the Proclamation held little authority after the American Revolution. Although it still applies more directly in Canada, where there was no break with the Crown, the Proclamation has only relatively recently been invoked to contest the unilateral usurping of indigenous lands in several Supreme Court cases, including *Guerin* in 1984 and *Delgamuukw* in 1997.

With this impediment to squatting indigenous lands removed, settlers poured westward across the United States. Territorial expansion was boosted greatly by the 1803 Louisiana Purchase, by which France sold indigenous territories it claimed west of the Mississippi River.

This opened the continent for American colonists, signalled initially by President Jefferson's commissioning of Captain Meriwether Lewis and Second Lieutenant William Clark to discover an overland route to the Pacific. The mass migration of white settlers that followed provoked violent conflicts, including several massacres of American Indians who rapidly became surrounded and displaced by land-hungry whites after a number of overland trails were established. Some of these conflicts over land escalated into what became known as 'Indian wars', culminating in relocations and then permanent enclosures of American Indians on demarcated reservations.

One of the most dramatic of these displacements was the Trail of Tears of the 1830s. Other forced removals involving the transfer of populations many hundreds of miles from their homelands included the Navajo Long Walk of 1864, the war carried out against the Nez Perce Chief Joseph, and the Modoc War in Northern California, resulting in the removal of Modocs to Oklahoma. Indigenous peoples were further dispossessed by the destructions of biodiversity that enabled their way of life to continue. The willful massacring of the bison of the Great Plains by hide hunters and the US army caused hunger, starvation and forced migration of Native Americans across more than a third of the continent (Hubbard 2014). At the end of the nineteenth century, the reformer and novelist Helen Hunt Jackson (1965/1881) raised the alarm over these atrocities with her popular exposé of US duplicity towards Native Americans in *A Century of Dishonor*.

The century of dishonour could be said to have begun when the state of Georgia unilaterally broke treaties with four American Indian nations (Cherokee, Choctaw, Creek, Seminole) and annexed their land without consent. After they protested, the government 'compromise' to them was that they obtain what turned out to be short-lived legal possession of land across the Mississippi in Oklahoma. When many of them refused to leave their lands, they were escorted at bayonet point. Their lands in Georgia were then expropriated, used for settlement, mining and the importing of African slaves. Alexis de Tocqueville provided a moving eyewitness description of the removal of Choctaws in 1831:

> At the end of the year 1831, while I was on the left bank of the Mississippi, at a place named by Europeans Memphis, there arrived a numerous band of Choctaws ... These savages had left their country and were endeavoring to gain the right bank of the Mississippi, where they hoped to find an asylum that had been promised them by the American government. It was then the middle of winter, and the cold

was unusually severe; the snow had frozen hard upon the ground, and
the river was drifting huge masses of ice. The Indians had their families
with them, and they brought in their train the wounded and the sick,
with children newly born and old men upon the verge of death. They
possessed neither tents nor wagons, but only their arms and some
provisions. I saw them embark to pass the mighty river, and never will
that solemn spectacle fade from my remembrance. No cry, no sob,
was heard among the assembled crowd; all were silent. Their calami-
ties were of ancient date, and they knew them to be irremediable. The
Indians had all stepped into the bark that was to carry them across, but
their dogs remained upon the bank. As soon as these animals perceived
that their masters were finally leaving the shore, they set up a dismal
howl and, plunging all together into the icy waters of the Mississippi,
swam after the boat. (Tocqueville 1945: 351–2)

Most of the people removed in the Trail of Tears went to Oklahoma
with a determination to retain their independence, but within a few
decades the tribal assemblies they established began to lose authority, as white and black squatters gradually outnumbered them (Debo
1940: 29).

By moving them, the Euro-Americans were essentially extin-
guishing unique indigenous identities that were based on close historical connections with specific places. As orated in a letter from
Aitooweyah to John Ross, principal chief of the Cherokees at New
Echota in 1830: 'We, the great mass of the people think only of the
love we have to our land for . . . we do love the land where we were
brought up. We will never let our hold to this land go it will be like
throwing away . . . [our] mother that gave . . . [us] birth' (Woodward
1982: 202–3).

Opportunities for the private appropriation of lands at the heart
of indigenous identity were expanded yet further through the 1887
General Allotment Act. Congressmen started to regard the removal
treaties giving Indians from the Trail of Tears perpetual land title
in Oklahoma as a hindrance to Euro-American settlement and to
the idea of progress itself. Senator Henry Dawes, the author of the
Allotment Act, advised Congress to disregard previous treaties and
abolish tribal status without waiting for consent from native leaders.
The General Allotment Act applied to all American Indians, providing reservations within which each family was allocated a certain
quantity of land. Under the Act, the President was authorized to
negotiate with whatever leaders were identified for a division of tribal
lands, and the 'surplus', initially sold to the federal government, was
made available for new settlers under the Homestead Laws. The BIA

interpreted the Allotment Act as a mandate to American Indians to negotiate division of their lands. Indian agents who were on the scene threatened tribes with dire consequences unless they consented to immediate allotment (Deloria 1985: 6). These new demarcated areas involved a massive reduction of the indigenous land base. In part this was due to the de facto recognition of non-indigenous squatting rights, and also due to the assumption that the only lands needed for the indigenous groups were those under agricultural cultivation, rather than the more extensive land bases used for hunting, gathering and spiritual purposes.

The intention of the allotment process was not only to confine American Indians to smaller areas of land to make room for white settlement, recreation and industrialization, but to destroy the customary system of collective use and occupancy of land practised by almost all indigenous groups, transforming them into individual landowners, farmers and ranchers. Native American territories were reduced from 139 million acres to 48 million acres between 1887 and 1934 (Littlefield 2001: 370), and between 1936 and 1976 another 1.8 million acres of land were removed from indigenous control by the government (Morris 1992: 68).

Native American groups coming under the allotment system were asked to sign treaties, and these were notable for the unequal bargaining position of the two sides and the ethnocentric terms in which they were couched. Kessell's (1981: 261) remarks on the 1868 Navajo Treaty illustrate this:

> The peace commissioners spoke of artificial lines on maps, of parallels and meridians, the Navajos of geographical features, of canyons, mountains, and mesas. The white men talked about ownership and a claim to the land, the Indians about using the land. Moreover, communication between them suffered the unavoidable distortion of translation: from English, a more abstract, mainly noun and adjective-oriented tongue of different sounds and conceptual bases spoken by members of a western, preindustrial society, through Spanish to Navajo, an exceedingly literal verb-oriented language in the minds and mouths of a vastly different people.

Other groups lost lands guaranteed by treaty because of the failure of US authorities to honour the terms or arrangements for a reservation. As meticulously documented by Steven Crum (2011), the 'six miles square' reservation for the Temoake group of Shoshones followed from general provisions in the 1863 Treaty of Ruby Valley, but the land was never demarcated, or, if it was, the precise details were lost, and the government condoned the settlement of Shoshone lands by white ranchers. Within the Shoshone lands more widely, other lands guaranteed by the 1863 treaty have been appropriated for settlement, mining and military testing, including nuclear weapons. The normal remedy for all Native Americans who have lost lands due to the violation of laws and treaties by the United States has been to file a claim through the Indian Claims Commission, which was set up in 1946. Because this does not offer the return of lands, but only monetary compensation, the Western Shoshone have refused to file (Clemmer 2009). However, a contemporary case involving a ruling that questions the jurisdictional boundaries of the Wind River reservation in Wyoming shows that the often dishonest means by which reservations were demarcated can be brought into question by tribes and the courts (MacKinnon 2015: 533–6).

This same process of removal of Native Americans from areas guaranteed by treaty occurred regularly in the nineteenth and twentieth centuries. In all cases, the lands were important to the indigenous peoples, and often, like the Black Hills or *Paha Sapa* of the Lakota guaranteed within the 'Great Sioux Reservation' in the 1868 Treaty of Fort Laramie, the land was the centre of their cosmology. Despite the fact that the US government had already acknowledged that the hills were part of the Sioux lands, it eventually supported white squatters and miners in bids to own their lands. This was one of several acts of humiliation that provoked indigenous resistance through the peaceful Ghost Dance movement. Native Americans at this time were facing disease and starvation, the near extinction of the bison, increasing regulation and control by whites and invasions of miners, land speculators, farmers and squatters. In South Dakota, agents called in the police and military to Sioux territory in November 1890 to deal with followers of the ailing Miniconjou elder Big Foot, who had embraced the Ghost Dance and was seen as resistant to US authority. The people fled into the badlands, but when the last almost starving group returned to the reservation, a detachment of 3,000 soldiers and four Hotchkiss machine guns surrounded them. Suddenly firing began and within minutes more than 300 men, women and children had been killed (Mooney 1965/1896; Wilson 1998: 278–82; Niezen 2000: 130–6). Afterwards, Lakota people were consigned to relatively small reservations in South Dakota.

Although there was somewhat less overt colonial violence in Canada, manipulative techniques of legitimized dispossession occurred there too. As in the United States, indigenous peoples were stripped of property rights and confined to small land bases by means of a system of numbered treaties, which restricted indigenous peoples to fixed land bases called 'reserves'. This process was similarly intended to effect a change of subsistence from migratory hunting to European style farming. Concluded between the Crown and a large number of officially recognized native peoples during the nineteenth and twentieth centuries, the treaties were prepared by Canadian officials ahead of negotiations and simply delivered by agents of the Crown to groups of Aboriginal peoples to affirm. The indigenous groups were configured into 'bands' under 'headmen', who, like many of the leaders who signed treaties in the United States, were wrongly constituted as legitimate representatives of large groups of people. These indigenous leaders or assemblages were made party to treaties that surrendered land to the Crown in perpetuity and, in exchange, the Crown provided monetary compensation, annual annuities for each family and certain specified rights in particular 'reserved' areas. These reserves could be taken collectively or by individual families in severalty at 160 acres per family of five.

While Aboriginal people were domiciled on reserves within the numbered treaty areas, land immediately became free for settlement, industry and use by the government, as it was in the United States. This threatened the perpetuation of indigenous land-based activities, sustenance and culture, and proceeded as the demand for lands extended further north. The effects were as deleterious in the far north because indigenous peoples of these boreal forest and tundra regions rely heavily on animals, fish and wild plants for food. Given that animals migrate, fish swim into large lakes and rivers, and plant seeds scatter across the land, having hunting, fishing and foraging rights in one 'reserve' area is a dubious right (Fumoleau 1974: 235).

Although the numbered treaties contained rights that Canada offered to indigenous peoples, as in the United States, native oral testimony reveals that the negotiations and signing of the treaties were marked by duress, manipulation and a failure of Canada to abide by the terms (Fumoleau 1974; Treaty 7 Elders and Tribal Council et al. 1996: 297–303; Daschuk 2013). Many treaties were negotiated under pressure, including imminent physical extinction from the floods of settlers, miners, gold seekers and land speculators, as well as destruction of the subsistence base. Canadian agents often presented indigenous groups with treaties forfeiting huge tracts of land at the same time that hunger, starvation and infectious disease were widespread and when high death tolls were occurring on the

Plains (Lux 2001; Daschuk 2013). Moreover, this coincided with the disappearance and fragmentation of traditional leadership. As if this were not enough, treaties were signed when heavy drinking had taken root, and Plains groups, under pressure of diminishing food supplies, had started to attack and kill each other (Daschuk 2013: 83). The big attraction of signing was often the immediate pay-off rather than long-term security (Waldram 1993: 33).

Some of the most well-documented twentieth-century displacements of indigenous peoples in the world were those ordered *without treaties* by the Canadian government. In a short period between the 1950s and 1960s, Canada executed some of the most dramatic transfers of populations on the planet. These are remarkable not because they involved huge numbers of people or were motivated explicitly by ethnic cleansing – as was the case, it should be remembered, with population transfers throughout Europe in the mid-twentieth century – but because they involved such profound alterations to the peoples concerned. They were marked by a conviction that indigenous peoples were the property of the state, and were a malleable mass that could be adapted to its needs. The social experiments of this era made indigenous peoples instruments of Canadian state policy, whether that be through standardization of living conditions (village settlements), the cultivation of new economic niches (moving hunters to areas where more fur could be trapped) or as human flagpoles (to claim permanently frozen outlying islands as Canadian territory). Overarching all of this was the need of the state to assert sovereignty over the Arctic regions, where up until relatively recently Inuit people were fairly autonomous and spread over a vast territory. Until the mid-twentieth century, few Inuit understood English and Canadian officials rarely spoke Inuktitut. The state, however, was keen 'to transform Inuit society into a more manageable entity' (Marcus 1995: 32).

Having already initiated some Inuit into commercial fur trapping in the 1930s, the government relocated more southerly Inuit to the far northern Dundas Harbour on Devon Island as a response to the problem of diminishing fur prices. While they fretted about making Inuit part of the money economy, there was relatively little thought for how peoples who were well adapted to one ecological zone might fare in the entirely different and far more arduous High Arctic conditions, where there would be almost no economy. McGrath (2006: 103–4) described the conditions on Ellesmere Island where a group of Inuit from Inukjuak (Port Harrison) on Hudson Bay were relocated as part of the same programme in the early 1950s:

The place was uninhabited and had been since the Little Ice Age thickened its ice caps and grew its glaciers about 350 years ago. There was no evidence that the island would support human habitation. No wildlife surveys had ever been conducted there and it was not known how many fish, marine mammals, birds or land mammals populated the area. What *was* known was that the polar desert conditions did not support anything like the numbers of plant and animal life which flourished around Inukjuak ... temperatures in the High Arctic are on average 15°C lower than those in Inukjuak. In the polar north, temperatures rarely rise much above freezing, even in summer, and in winter they regularly fall below –40°C ... The winds too, are much fiercer, becoming katabatic as they spin along the frozen flats of the Arctic Ocean. The sea around Ellesmere is never wholly free of ice and the navigation season is often as short as four weeks ... On account of its position high above the Arctic Circle, the winter dark period stretches from October to February. For four months of the year it is dark 24 hours a day.

Many relocations such as this one also merged peoples who were entirely distinct and spoke different languages and dialects. This was the case for the Inukjuamiut and Ingluligmiut who were relocated together to Ellesmere Island, but whose communications initially 'were no better than the crude fragmented sign language which served for dialogue between most *qalunaat* [whites] and most Inuit' (McGrath 2006: 130). The three-month dark period and high mountains behind the government village of Grise Fjord made food very hard to obtain in what was probably 'the least productive land in North America' (Marcus 1995: 109). The Canadian government worsened the conditions for the relocated Inuit on Ellesmere Island by reneging on a promise to allow them to return home within two years, compelling the people to live in the 'most isolated gulag in the world' (Wheeler 2010: 123) cut off from their relatives and homelands. Canada continued these experiments into the 1950s, moving and dispersing the Inuit of the northern Labrador coastal areas of Hebron, Nutak and Killiniq to a number of other government or missionary-created Inuit communities further to the south, and in some cases in Quebec. Families were separated, people were cut off from their hunting, fishing and sealing areas, and they were frequently isolated and discriminated against by Euro-Canadian settlers in the new communities.

Other less publicized Arctic relocations by which Inuit became tools to assert national claims to territory were undertaken between the 1920s and 1950s by the Danish government in Greenland, moving people from the south to the north to fend off a Norwegian claim, and in 1926 by the Soviet government, which moved a community of Inuit to Wrangel island off the northern coast of Chukotka in the Arctic Ocean to thwart American territorial claims (McGhee 2004: 109; Marcus 1995: 53).

Dispossession in Eastern and Southern Africa

Paralleling the experience of indigenous peoples in North America, numerous hunters and pastoralists across sub-Saharan Africa were removed from their lands in the late twentieth century. These ongoing removals follow from early to mid-twentieth-century removals by colonial powers that cleared vast areas for extraction, or as in Kenya for European settlers, and thereby created ethnically homogenous geographical zones (Elkins 2006: 18). Given this history, post-independence states often refused to acknowledge any home territories for subpopulations, and declared the population transfers to be for the good of the country itself. At the same time, they often argued that removals were good for the economic development of poor, backward and disadvantaged peoples.

The Hadzabe are a contemporary example of peoples who have suffered removal. They are one of the world's last remaining bow and arrow hunters, and many of this small group of about 10,000 people continue to live by hunting and gathering in lands in Tanzania. However, the ability of the Hadzabe to maintain this way of life is compromised by the seizing of their hunting territories. At the decolonization of Tanganyika in 1961, Hadzabe lands were simply handed over to the new state entity. Early measures implemented by Tanzania were designed to suppress the mobility of the Hadzabe and their neighbours, the Maasai pastoralists, both of whom escaped the British attempts to sedentarize them. As in other new African states that were focusing on nation building and 'modernization', hunting and pastoralism were considered backward and inferior (Marlowe 2002: 267). As a consequence, liberal socialist policies in the 1960s and 1970s under Julius Nyerere's *ujamaa* plan attempted to settle Hadzabe in new villages in Western Tanzania, encouraging them to live in Western style houses, take up agriculture, attend schools and dress in Western attire. Hadzabe were largely averse to these transformations, and many returned to the land to hunt and forage. In the meantime, the government settlements filled up with non-Hadzabe migrants (Ndagala 1985).

To make returning to the land more difficult, in the first decade of the twenty-first century, the government sold Hadzabe lands to developers in the Yaeda Valley for a sports hunting complex to attract wealthy foreign tourists. Any Hadzabe that entered what then became 'private property' was liable to be arrested for hunting in the privatized lands (Barume 2010: 150). Various Hadzabe, as well as independent witnesses, spoke of dehumanizing conditions and deaths of Hadzabe in custody. They have also complained about the degradation of their lands as farmers have inched into their hunting territories (Vinding 2003; IPACC 2007; Barume 2010). Fruit and berry trees and bushes, water flow in the rivers, and the wild animals they depend on for survival have all dwindled with the arrival of farmers. Many Hadzabe turned to cheap alcohol for solace. One report from the Norwegian Council of Churches referred to the Hadzabe living on the 'fringes of survival' (Heggum 2002). As hunting land increasingly is turned over to farmers and set aside by the Tanzanian government for lucrative conservation tourism and sports hunting, the abandonment of the Hadzabe way of life is imperilled, as this testimony asserts:

> We eat bush foods and we are not farmers or pastoralists. Our greatest problem now is land. It has been ours since ancient times. It was bestowed upon us by our grandfathers. In these days a large area of land has been taken away and now the animals have gone away. They have cleared the land and cultivated it. Us Hadzabe have been powerless to stop it. Today some Hadzabe have no land. We live on land taken away from us. Some of us have become drunks begging from tourists. We want to keep the land and protect it. (Kidzali Mahweshi, Hadza hunter, statement given at Conway Hall, London, 16 October 2004)

Equally dramatic is the case of the various groups of Bushmen in Southern Africa. Sedentarization is not, as the Hadzabe example demonstrates, purely a direct result of state policies, but also involves other forces that precipitate the need to change the migratory patterns of life. One factor was the intrusion of missionaries, who were successful in settling groups of Bushmen in South West Africa (Dieckmann 2007: 89). In the mid-twentieth century, South African authorities created 'Native Reserves' where Herero pastoralists and other groups were allocated lands, primarily for the purpose of being accessible labour for nearby European settler farms. Bushmen were initially excluded from this reservation policy, but some of their lands were commandeered for reserves for the Herero and other groups (Dieckmann 2007: 124–5). Throughout the twentieth century, many

Bushmen families existed on the extreme margins of settler society as a kind of underclass or rural proletariat, working when they could on settler farms. With an administrative centre at Tsumkwe, Ju/'hoansi San were granted an area of 'Bushmanland' in South West Africa under the Odendaal Plan of the 1950s during the South African mandate. This eventually became the Nyae Nyae Conservancy.

Around Tsumkwe, provision was made to induct Bushmen into farming and wage labour. However, the Bushmanland area recognized by the state in 1968 was not in lands that they traditionally occupied and was not properly delineated to exclude intruders (Biesele and Hitchcock 2011: 36; Gordon and Douglas 2000: 175–6). Similarly, Hai||om Bushmen were allowed to live in Etosha National Park throughout much of the South African mandate period, but were evicted thereafter to make way for game preservation and tourism in the 1950s. Some Hai||om continued to live and work in the park, but many became labourers on white-owned farms (Dieckmann 2007: 186–96). Today, different groups of Bushmen are dispersed around Namibia, with many living in shantytowns or farms, where they work on white or Herero-owned farms. Namibia has also attempted to create reservations such as that at 'Uitkom' ('Outcome' in Afrikaans) in central Namibia for those Bushmen who have survived the often violent and degrading conditions on farms. As this testimony from Otjinene, one of several Bushmen interviewed by Colin Samson, suggests, conditions here are extremely difficult:

> I was brought up hunting on Herero farms. My first kill was a duiker. It was in *this place*. There was no farm here then. All over here, it was just us. I never saw any whites when I was a child. Back then we never had maize porridge [which was almost the sole source of food at Uitkom], we only had *veld kos* (wild food). Life was totally different. There were some problems in the past. Even though we were hungry in the past, we could cope because we were not doing heavy labour under a white man, who stopped us going out to get wild food. But life today is not good. (Interview at Uitkom, Namibia, 23 June 2012)

After watching a van load of computers donated by German philanthropists being delivered to the school at Uitkom, the translator August Kandaro remarked: 'Our children will now be able to look at computer screens while they're hungry.'

Despite a primordial and close relationship between the San and the Kalahari Desert, in 1997 and 1998, the Botswana government forcibly expelled about 1,700 San from their lands in the Central Kalahari Game Reserve (CKGR) and relocated them to settlement camps where they were expected to remain sedentary (Good 2008: 126–7). At the same time, the government issued licences to multi-nationals for diamond mining, backed by World Bank start up capital (Saugestad 2001; Olmsted 2004). In the process, San were loaded onto trucks and removed from the CKGR, while soldiers destroyed their huts. According to many sources, those who resisted were beaten and tortured, and in 2002, water, food rations and health services were removed from those San who would not leave their lands. As personally witnessed by John Simpson of the BBC, soldiers destroyed water boreholes to hasten the departure of the San, in an attempt to drive them out by thirst (Good 2008: 134). Those who tried to return to their lands were arrested and turned back to the relocation camps, which have now become dominated by poverty, hunger, alcoholism and HIV/AIDS (Ingstad and Fugelli 2006).

In many of the camps, such as New Xade, there are no income generating activities, hygiene is poor due to lack of water, hunting is forbidden, hunger is common and San are often banned from leaving the settlement (Good 2008: 129, 139). As in the United States and Canada, San were also given massive encouragement to switch to farming with individual arable plots and seed distribution (Hitchcock et al. 2011: 79). Although the High Court of Botswana has ruled that the government's actions were illegal, the return of the Bushman to the CKGR has been hampered by Botswana's arbitrary enforcement of its court's ruling, violence, the intrusion of commercial enterprises into Bushman lands and most crucially, a lack of water caused by the closing up of boreholes. In an attempt to starve the Bushmen out of their lands in 2014, President Ian Khama banned hunting, the central activity and mode of survival of the Bushmen (Ontebetse 2014). The removal of indigenous groups such as the San from their lands and the restriction of their movements has been a large part of the agenda for political reform in Africa.

Dispossession in South America

In Latin America the Creole elites considered the colonization of territories as a way of preserving territorial integrity and ensuring economic growth. In the process, indigenous lands and resources were regarded as belonging to the state and therefore open for colonization. The Mapuche case is illustrative in this regard.

During the Spanish colonial era and up to the 1860s, the Mapuche had managed to preserve their independence in the region called the

3.1   Bundles of food are sorted for the monthly food distribution in
New Xade government resettlement camp, Botswana, 2007. Before being
evicted to the camp the Bushmen could feed themselves by hunting and
gathering as they had done for many centuries. In the camp they rely on
government handouts to survive as the government continues to deny
many the right to return to their ancestral land in the Central Kalahari
Game Reserve.

Source: ©Dominick Tyler/Survival International.

Araucanía through a system of treaties with the Spanish Crown and,
despite occasional conflict, this state of affairs continued after Chile
declared independence in 1818. The Mapuche exercised complete
territorial sovereignty and continued to develop their ways of living,
while engaging in trade and commerce with settlers north of the Bío
Bío river (Bengoa 1996: 154).

However, the Creole elites, inspired by the same liberal principles
that informed westward expansion in the United States, were eager
to increase their control over Mapuche territories. From the mid-
1850s these ideas were put into practice and a process of accelerated
colonization took place. The military campaign that supported it was
named the 'Pacification of the Araucanía' and, despite fierce resistance, the Mapuche were defeated and, as a consequence, lost their
self-determination and territorial sovereignty. Bengoa (1996: 173)
highlights the main elements of the colonizing process: (a) the role of
the army in defeating indigenous resistance and guaranteeing control

through a system of forts; (b) the building of private infrastructure and the railroad; and (c) the auction of indigenous lands and a campaign to attract settlers. Thereafter, the encroachment on indigenous territories led to the creation of *reducciones* for the Mapuche and the demarcation of their former territories for settlers, especially European immigrants who were recruited by the government for that purpose.

The state demarcated and registered 5.4 million hectares of Mapuche territory, preserving only 500,000 hectares for their communities (Bengoa 2004: 361). From the late nineteenth century, this dispossession continued through different legal and illegal schemes. The Mapuche communities would continue to lose lands to settlers, haciendas and timber companies. Gradually, the Mapuche were removed to lands that were not suitable for small-scale agricultural and cattle farming. As Lorenzo Colimán, a nineteenth-century Mapuche teacher, sarcastically reflected on the consequences of the colonization process for his people, 'what we have achieved with the civilization that they say we have received is to live tight like wheat in a sack' (quoted in Bengoa 1996: 325).

The process of encroachment on indigenous lands was consolidated further when, in 1973, Augusto Pinochet's military government abolished indigenous communal property and the *reducciones* by dividing all indigenous land and establishing individual rights in place of collective land rights (Bengoa 1996: 416–18). This policy led to further loss of indigenous lands and increased the already high levels of poverty, discrimination and marginality experienced by the Mapuche. To this day the dual process of land dispossession and social and cultural marginality plays a central role in the development of the Mapuche conflict in Chile (Pairican 2014; Rodríguez and Vergara 2015).

Under Portuguese colonization, the ownership of the land in what is now Brazil belonged to the Crown, and the laws protecting indigenous communities implemented were short-lived and ineffective against the pressure of continual influxes of settlers (Johnson 1987: 13). With the independence of Brazil, land was regarded as public property and was transferred 'from the federal to the state and local governments' (Garfield 2001: 89). Agribusiness and military interests in these lands coalesced around liberal ideas of progress. For the Brazilian state, the vast expanses of savannah and rainforests were regarded as economic and political assets. Progress demanded the exploitation of resources for economic wealth and the protection of national sovereignty – especially in the Amazon region

– against competing claims of neighbouring South American states. Post-independence policies therefore opened up indigenous land to further large waves of European immigrants (Ramos 2003: 407).

Nonetheless, indigenous peoples lived in all these territories and the Brazilian governments had to deal with this fact. The basic principle that guided governmental policies towards the Indians was based on the idea of their 'relative incompetence', making them wards of the state. The creation of the Serviço de Proteção ao Indio (SPI) in 1910 embodied this principle by establishing a certain degree of protection to indigenous communities by creating Indian reserves, while implementing a strong assimilationist programme based on education. The long-term aim was to remove indigenous peoples from their territories. Ramos (2003: 409) summarizes this process:

> The legislators fully recognised the Indians' historical rights to their lands, but in order to justify the exceptionality of collective possession – *not* property – of land by indigenous peoples, they placed them in the category of relatively incapable for some civil acts. In other words, the Indians had to be generally acknowledged as legally incapacitated if they were to enjoy the special protection bestowed on them by the state. It was only in this (in)capacity as wards (*tutelados*) that they were eligible to maintain their territories in permanent and exclusive usufruct.

However, indigenous communities were constantly threatened by invasions of their territories, including those living in reserves. In 1967 the SPI was replaced by Fundação Nacional do Indio (FUNAI) whose main mission was to promote and protect indigenous rights, in particular their land rights. Like its predecessor, FUNAI largely operated under the paternalist assumption that indigenous peoples were 'relatively incapable'. In 1973, the Indian Statute was promulgated, and Article 19, among its main provisions, recognized indigenous territories and established an administrative process by which these territories had to be demarcated to protect against illegal invasions. Despite the stated benevolence of this mission, Article 1 of the Statute was explicitly aimed at assimilating indigenous peoples into Brazilian society. A further boost to the protection of indigenous territories came with the approval of a new political constitution in 1988. Article 231 (4) guarantees the 'inalienable and indisposable' right of indigenous peoples to their territories. It also reaffirmed the political responsibility of the state in demarcating these territories. However, in 1996, the Brazilian government, through Decree #1775, opened up indigenous territories for exploitation by allowing third parties to contest these demarcations. Since then, successive Brazilian governments have implemented the demarcation process with more or less success. As of 2015, there were 698 indigenous territories that represent around 13 per cent of the national territory claimed by the state. Over 98 per cent of these territories are located in the Amazon region (PIB 2015).

Although indigenous peoples in Brazil have had their territorial rights recognized on paper, they still face continued dispossession. First, these formal rights have not ended the violence and threats to their communities from illegal invasions by settlers, miners and state sponsored industrial projects. Second, since 2011 the final confirmation of the demarcation process has come to a halt. Only a few demarcation processes have been ratified by successive governments, while many others, although having fulfilled all legal and administrative procedures, have been delayed due to pressure from agribusiness and corporations involved in projects like hydroelectric dams (CIMI 2014: 43). Third, indigenous peoples have challenged the way that the demarcation process takes place as they claim that often it is done without enough consultation and participation of the indigenous communities (Poirier 2013). Finally, the implementation of large development projects 'like the diversion of the São Francisco River in the North-East of Brazil and the Belo Monte dam in the state of Pará although executed outside – and in some cases inside – demarcated areas still had a major impact on indigenous peoples' environment and well-being' (UNHRC 2009: 17).

Continuing physical violence against indigenous peoples in Brazil is directly linked to the huge economic stakes involved in privatizing their lands. Land invasions are enabled by the reluctance of the state to enforce the integrity of demarcated areas. A recent report by the Conselho Indigenista Missionário (CIMI 2014: 17) argues that commercial pressures on indigenous lands comprise the main cause of anti-indigenous violence:

> In summary, we may say that the violations of individual and collective rights operated against the indigenous peoples throughout 2014 are ... linked to a government strategy that favors extractive activities in order to [stimulate] its politics of development. Thus, the exploration of indigenous lands gets promoted mainly by agribusiness in all regions of the country, as well as by the implementation of large scale electric energy projects, with the construction of dams, causing serious impact on the environment and the traditional populations; and by the exploration of timber in the Amazon, especially in Maranhão, Pará, Acre, Rondônia and Mato Grosso.

The same report established that in 2014 there were 135 suicides, 785 infant deaths and 138 murders in indigenous communities in the areas mentioned (CIMI 2014: 16–19). They were all related to the violence unleashed by the failure of demarcation.

In 1980, in concert with international NGOs, the Yanomami peoples filed a petition with the Inter-American Commission on Human Rights (IACHR) against the Brazilian government for not protecting them against the violent consequences of illegal mining in their territories. The IACHR ruled in favour of the Yanomami in 1985 and requested that the Brazilian government take effective measures to protect the Yanomami and demarcate their territories (IACHR 1985). The Brazilian government accepted the ruling and in 1992 finished the demarcation process from which the Yanomami Park was born. This became a high-profile international case that illuminated the threats to indigenous peoples in Brazil as a whole, but the terrorization of the Yanomami was far from over. As recently as August 2015, the Yanomami and other indigenous groups in the state of Roraima mobilized in order to draw attention to the illegal invasion of their territories, despite these territories having acquired the final homologated status (CIMI 2015).

After concluding his visit to Brazil in 2008, James Anaya, the UN Special Rapporteur on Indigenous Peoples, clearly recognized that indigenous self-determination was incomplete, since it was not meaningfully attached to the right to territories. As he remarked: 'Still, it is evident that indigenous peoples lack adequate participation in all decisions that affect their lives and communities, and that they do not adequately control their territories, in many cases, even when lands are demarcated and registered' (UNHRC 2009: 9).

Being colonized by the Dutch and British, Guyana presents another pattern of indigenous dispossession in South America. As elsewhere, the colonists enslaved Africans to produce commodity crops such as sugar cane, rice, cotton and tobacco on indigenous lands. With the ending of the slave trade, they replaced slavery with the indentureship of East Indian labourers who were transported to colonies such as British Guiana (now Guyana), Trinidad and Tobago, Mauritius and Fiji. This created a complex and often fractious configuration of enslaved, indentured, settler and indigenous populations shown in glaring outline in Guyana. Here, a system of 'consolidation' of Amerindians, not dissimilar to the Spanish policy of *reducciones*, concentrated Amerindian populations in small inland tracts of land. This left the path open for the indentured and enslaved groups to work in mining and other forms of resource extraction, while making the formerly dispersed semi-mobile Amerindian way of life almost impossible to maintain or reclaim (Colchester 1997: 133).

Dispossession here was legitimated by the assertion of property rights, first by colonial powers, and second by the Guyanese state. Under the Guyanese Amerindian Act of 1976, about half the Amerindian communities were granted collective ownership of a small portion of their traditional lands. These titles do not include rivers and riverbanks, minerals or subsurface rights. Despite the law, the lands themselves are completely violable, as the state has granted concessions to multinational extractive industries without consultation with indigenous groups who hold the titles. These titles can be revoked or modified if the state deems it to be in the public interest, a concept that it conveniently does not define. Like Native Americans under the Allotment Act, Amerindians in Guyana are also free to sell or transfer their titles (James 2003).

Dispossession of the hunters and herders of Russia and Scandinavia

In the Soviet Union, a society committed to scientific progress and industrialization, similar processes of dispossession were directed at the indigenous reindeer herders, hunters and trappers of the north. Soviet administrators accused northern peoples of being deficient in the qualities required for state organized collectivization of their economic activities and social lives. Indigenous lands were confiscated, often brutally, for 'modernization', because hunters and herders were deemed to have ways of life that were in conflict with the goal of maximum production. As a result, Siberian indigenous people came under strict state authority, which demanded radical changes in their economic organization. Administrative measures were taken to 'correct' their land-based economies and traditional educational methods. Consequently, by the 1950s, 'many nomadic peoples were settled in permanent communities in the interests of providing education and medical services, as well as jobs in industrial ventures' (McGhee 2004: 67). Furthermore, as McGhee points out, 'the removal of children to state-run boarding schools added another incentive to abandon the seasonal migrations that had been part of many groups' yearly rounds for centuries' (2004: 67).

Even though much of their economic activities were already communal, indigenous peoples of Siberia were forced to adopt a rationalistic organization of production and abandon their mixed economies.

They became supervised 'state nomads' with greatly reduced autonomy and land bases to engage in freelance trading, fishing and trapping as they had done previously (Anderson 2000: 37–42).

Soviet administrators attempted to replace the flexibly oriented
collective approach to reindeer herding, trapping and hunting with a
mechanical form of collectivization that made such activities far less
viable. When applied, 'the grand metaphor of universal evolution
and Soviet history leading to a state of mechanized – and increasingly personalized – perfection' was translated into a ferociously
imposed form of economic development (Slezkine 1994: 352). In the
early Stalinist years of the 1920s and 1930s, 'almost every reindeer
in Russia was confiscated and placed collectively in large herds run
by the State as Collective . . . Farms' (Vitebsky 2005: 34). In resistance, local herders hid and occasionally slaughtered their animals to
prevent forced collectivization. McGhee (2004: 66) estimates that as
much as one-third of the Siberian stock of reindeer was lost in the
1930s.

In Scandinavia, the early to mid-twentieth-century extension of
farming further into the north resulted in the seizure of Saami lands.
As McGhee (2004: 249) describes it: 'Pioneer farmers invaded the
reindeer-grazing lands of the Saami, clearing forests that were needed
by reindeer for winter browsing, and shooting reindeer that trampled
their fields, considering them to be wild animals and free sources of
meat.' Like indigenous peoples in many other places, Saami were
also forced into settlements and their children sent to residential
schools, where they were subject to isolation, surveillance and religious indoctrination (Lindmark 2006).

Dispossession of the Ainu in Japan

The promotion of an idea of progress equating state ideologies with
universal history, so common in the United States and the Soviet
Union, was mirrored in Japanese government policies towards the
indigenous Ainu of Hokkaidō. Related to some Siberian peoples, the
Ainu engaged in hunter-gathering and small-scale farming. Their territories also included parts of Sakhalin island and the Kurile islands,
which were the subject of colonial disputes between Japan and Russia.
Exploration, trade and violence all contributed to the transformation of the Ainu and their lands in the seventeenth and eighteenth
centuries, but extensive changes were not made until the nineteenth
century. Although the Japanese considered Ainu barbarous, early

Japanese expansion in Hokkaidō was primarily justified for the imperial well-being and enrichment of the shogunate, rather than the
moral uplift of the Ainu (Walker 2001: 6–10; Howell 2005: 140–50).

More direct steps to transform the Ainu were taken in the late
nineteenth and early twentieth centuries, coinciding with the nationalist Meiji Restoration of 1868, when formal annexation occurred.
Like the North American frontier, Hokkaidō was 'mapped, named
and claimed . . . Order was imposed on the "wilderness" in the form
of grid-like blocks of land divided into plots for agricultural settlement' (Siddle 1996: 57). All this was done under the *Kaitakushi*
(Colonization Commission) in operation from 1869 to 1882. In
the following years, the Ainu language as well as customs such as
tattooing and burning houses of the diseased were banned. Land
was removed from Ainu control, while Japanese from Honshu and
elsewhere moved onto the island. Ainu salmon fishing, which is vital
to their cultural continuity, as well as a variety of hunting practices,
were criminalized. Eventually, intensive schooling and assimilation
programmes were implemented to turn Ainu into rice farmers and
good Japanese citizens. The state also made intensive and eugeni-
cally oriented attempts to encourage intermarriage between Ainu and
Japanese.

At the heart of the dispossession process were the forced relocations
within Hokkaidō and from Sakhalin and Kurile islands to Hokkaidō.
One of the dramatic after-effects of this, including the sedentarization of all Ainu there, was the engineering of a massive depopulation,
from 300,000 in 1800 to about 25,000 at the turn of the twenty-first
century (Porteous and Smith 2001: 77). Many observers believe that
one result of such policies has been the destruction of traditional
Ainu culture; a movement to revitalize the Ainu language and allow
limited salmon fishing only occurred in the last quarter century when
the Ainu New Law was passed by the Diet in 1997 to recognize
the legitimacy of Ainu culture (Cheung 2003). Although this sup-
planted the assimilationist 1899 Aborigine Protection Law, the Ainu
remain petitioners; their rights are subordinated to those of the non-
indigenous majority:

> My father said that fishing salmon is our way of life, so why do we have
> to petition for rights to our culture? My father thought that this was
> not the proper way to do things. Now the only time when we can catch
> salmon is the traditional day of return . . . The government says that
> this is to preserve the resources. But, this is contradictory since others
> [non-Ainu] can fish salmon in the sea. (Shiro Kayano, Ainu leader and

museum curator, interview at Nibutani, Hokkaidō, Japan, 13 January
2008)

Dispossession of the Adivasis of the Indian subcontinent

During the British occupation of India, the Adivasis were compul-
sorily integrated into the colonial economy as 'they were forced to
produce surplus for the feudal landlords and for the British capital-
ists' (Kjosavik 2011: 124). As labourers, they were often displaced
from their lands and transported elsewhere. In the post-independence era, the Adivasis continued to be socially and culturally marginalized, while the relation with the post-independence state – like
the British before – continued to be determined by the drive for
their lands and resources. A steady process of deforestation, land
grabbing and extractive industrial projects have contributed to the
further displacement of the Adivasis, forcing them to migrate and
face the adverse consequences to their well-being and ways of life
(IWGIA 2015: 331–2). Mathur (2003: 179) points to the paradox
that 'many people have even begun to relate their growing impov-
erishment to their productive lands to the phenomenon called the
"resource curse"'.

The Adivasis are one of the poorest groups in India and Bangladesh,
two countries with millions of extremely poor people. Most of this
follows as a consequence of the encroachment on their lands. Their
lives and livelihoods remain under constant threat from extractive
projects and unscrupulous developers and corporations, while at the
same time they are often barred from access to basic state services
available to other citizens. Furthermore, these threats have had particularly negative impacts on Adivasi women. A report prepared by
a number of NGOs in 2014 shows that, like all Adivasi peoples, the
women face discrimination, poverty, violence and displacement, but
they also experience additional oppression because of their gender
(ISAWN/IWFNEI/AIPP 2014: 5).

The prominent case of the armed conflict of indigenous peoples
in the Chittagong Hill Tracts (CHT) against the Bangladesh government highlights the complexities and historical patterns of dispossession surrounding the Adivasis. Bangladeshi state building
entailed imposing a Bengali-dominated cultural and political agenda
on the entire country. The prolonged violent conflict between the
indigenous peoples of the CHT and Bangladesh lasted from 1977
to 1997, and signalled the Adivasis' willingness to fight for territorial

and cultural autonomy (Panday and Jamil 2009: 1054–61). But, 'as soon as armed conflicts began, the Bengali elites began to view the hill communities not only as an obstacle to "national integration" and the creation of the Bangladesh nation-state, but also as a threat to the national security and territorial integrity of the state' (Chakma 2010: 288). The intensely repressive responses of the Bangladeshi army amounted to genocide (Levene 1999) and ethnic cleansing, as thousands of Adivasi were permanently displaced and relocated to settlements (Mey 1984: 7–8). Non-Adivasis have also been forcibly relocated to CHT causing land grabbing and further displacement of Adivasis (Roy 2009: 28).

Despite the peace accord that brought the conflict to an end in 1997, the patterns of dispossession continue to affect the Adivasis in the CHT amidst a militarized environment of intimidation and fear (Panday and Jamil 2009). Amnesty International's 2013 report provided a damning account of the human rights infringements and dispossession that the Adivasi are exposed to. One interviewee told Amnesty International:

> We are now left with no land to do *jum* (farming) and grow crops or forest to go to for collecting fuel wood, and fruits. Life has become very hard as we have the army at very close proximity and I feel very insecure even walking short distances. There are checkpoints by the army we have to cross if we want to travel a bit further in search of fuel. Our home has become an insecure unsafe place to live in. I'm now constantly worried about getting food for my family and security of my children. (Amnesty International 2013: 28)

At the other end of the subcontinent, the original inhabitants of Sri Lanka, the Wanniyala-aetto (or Veddahs), are survivors of a rich forest dwelling way of life, but have over many centuries been encroached upon by Singhalese, Tamil and British colonizers. They have been confined to ever smaller areas of forest, and many of them have given up their way of life and identity. While the Singhalese majority considered Wanniyala-aetto to be primitive jungle dwellers, it was during the British colonial period in the twentieth century when major changes to their ways of life were made:

> The colonial approach was characterized by efforts to transform jungle dwellers into 'civilised beings'. British rule in particular, in the second half of the 20th century, entrusted the civilisation process to missionary stations. The colonial state also claimed land as a principal source of revenue. State authority was imposed through the establishment of

Crown Land, and as a consequence shifting cultivation, hunting and
other *Veddha* activities were restricted. (Lund 2000: 105)

These measures established state authority over the Wanniyala-aetto,
an authority consolidated further with the independence of what was
then Ceylon. Apart from the few who have been able to maintain
the forest-based way of life of hunting, gathering and slash and burn
cultivation, the Wanniyala-aetto have suffered poverty, dispossession
and forced assimilation, and face unemployment, homelessness and
disease (Stegeborn 2004).

The changes made by colonial authorities and post-independence
states to indigenous peoples' connections to their lands had far-
reaching effects on many other dimensions of their lives, including
relations between men and women, family life, the transmission of
knowledge, social organization, spirituality and the inner psychological worlds of people. The remainder of this chapter considers
the broader sociological effects of land dispossession. Parallel effects
to indigenous communities from the use of their lands for resource
extraction specifically will be discussed in Chapter 4.

Embedding patriarchy

Dispossession from land had major impacts on gender relations
within indigenous societies. In some places, the original cause of the
largely deleterious changes to indigenous women can be traced to the
early negotiations, settlements and treaties made between colonizers and indigenous peoples. In a vast number of cases, including, as
Tuhiwai Smith (2012: 48–9) has observed, formal treaties such as the
Treaty of Waitangi between the Maori and English in New Zealand,
the colonizers recognized only male leaders. Thus, even though the
indigenous societies frequently did not permit male-only leadership,
the subsequent land cession negotiations introduced and then embedded male authority in conformity with European patriarchal norms.

Patriarchy was reinforced by colonialism in other spheres, including the transformation of domestic living spaces, especially from
mobile encampments to shacks and houses. For example, within
the Canadian government-built villages in which the mobile Innu of
the Labrador-Quebec peninsula were settled in the mid-twentieth
century, external institutions replaced the economic functions of
the hunting families and imposed male dominance in the economic
sphere (Leacock 1981). Before this, men and women each had active

parts to play in maintaining hunting camps and obtaining food, and children and adolescents also had working roles in camp life. When the constant activity and movement of hunting life was taken from them, the path was open for less coordinated and more fragmented relations between sexes and generations. Missionaries replaced mothers and grandmothers in the socialization of children and transmission of knowledge, and schoolteachers usurped the female educational roles. Sedentarization meant that men and women and the old and young were no longer devoted to common purposes based around Innu norms and values.

Sedentary life initially presupposed a male economic breadwinner through wage labour or through social welfare disbursed to a male 'head of household'. Women were consequently downgraded from their former status, where they could be prime decision-makers with physically active and even strenuous roles in indigenous economies. For the pre-sedentarization Cree of the James Bay area described by Adelson (2008: 321) the largely egalitarian order involved men and women sharing hunting, fishing, trapping and other subsistence activities. Men were more often likely to be hunters and trappers, while women maintained the camp, gathered firewood and collected water, but this division was always permeable. In the government settlements that were imposed in the mid-twentieth century, Adelson found that many women were highly stressed as a result of having to take on a much higher burden of responsibilities associated with the care and maintenance of the household, childcare and even events associated with social and cultural continuity like feasts.

This same process of relegating women occurred among Siberian indigenous groups:

> The Soviet policy towards women in reindeer herding was successful in displacing a majority of Nenets women from the tundra to the villages, from working for one's household to the state economy. Two methods were used to settle women: forced settlement and restrictions, and imbuing younger generations with Soviet values. (Tuisku 2001: 57)

In a similar vein, Lee (1993: 143) noticed that the origins of the subordination of women among the Ju/'hoansi Bushmen could be traced to the advent of a 'household' and the displacement of more varied gender roles in hunting. Sedentary conditions associated with farming and herding created less varied and demanding roles for women, and the advent of migrant labour in South African mines further reduced women to dependants and caused familial instability.

The disempowering of indigenous women occurred because indigenous societies were destabilized when their relationship with their lands was altered. Colonial institutions of tribal governance in vastly reduced areas of land caused many men and women to seek consolation in alcohol and drugs. Their use caused rifts in families and marriages, precipitating domestic violence and child neglect, in which women almost always became victims.

Patterns of gendered social collapse have been documented for many indigenous groups. In many parts of Latin America, for example, women's roles complemented those of men, focusing on food and land. With the removal of indigenous peoples from their farming lands and the influx of cheap manufactured foods, women's status was relegated. Indigenous women in Latin America now face sexual violence and domestic abuse on a large scale, as well as numerous other health problems that are related to induced changes in indigenous societies (Johannesen 2014). In the United States, among the Yakama of Washington state, the local wage labour economy contains more jobs for men, but in the conditions of the reservation, men struggle to access and maintain jobs. This fuels alcohol use and familial breakup. In the past, the Yakama would have had meaningful economic roles for men and women, conditions that promoted family stability. In her study of Yakama cultural revitalization, Jacob (2013: 111) notes that the pattern is replicated across the United States and is indicated by the fact that 21 per cent of American Indian households are headed by women, compared to 12.6 per cent of the general US population, according to the 2010 census.

The high numbers of indigenous women in cities such as Vancouver who are sex workers can also be seen to have emerged from colonial processes of land dispossession. These include the Indian Act and the boarding schools, which precipitated cultural erosion, intracommunal violence, trauma, urbanization and poverty (Farley et al. 2005; Hunt 2013). The lives of Aboriginal sex workers are perilous and they are at risk of violence, HIV/AIDS, ill health, intravenous drug use, alcohol abuse, self-harm and rape. In the same context of cultural dislocation, Aboriginal girls and women from all backgrounds have disappeared and many have been found murdered in very large numbers in Canada. The Native Women of Canada Association (NWAC), Idle No More movement and Amnesty International, among others, have all campaigned for the tragedies that befell the 'Stolen Sisters' to be taken more seriously by the Canadian government and local police forces. NWAC (n.d.) research, which followed up cases of 582 missing Aboriginal women and girls, found that 67 per cent of them had been murdered. These have not been investigated either by the Canadian authorities or by researchers as seriously or as thoroughly as the scale of the tragedies demands (Hunt 2013: 98).

Social and psychological destabilization

New living arrangements, whether they were in villages, reservations or cities, caused massive social and psychological destabilization, of which the embedding of patriarchy in several places was one important dimension. In almost all cases, imposed village, reservation or semi-urban environments became contexts for a very different way of living. The effects of relocations in Northern Canada provide tragically vivid illustrations of this.

The Inuit relocations came under scrutiny in the extensive Royal Commission on Aboriginal Peoples (RCAP 1996: 429–30) report into Canadian government policy. With regard to the Inuit of Labrador relocated from the settlement of Hebron, the report notes:

> Relocation affected all aspects of the relocatees, lives. In Hebron, they had a distinct identity; they lived off the land, and their society was held together by close bonds of kinship, marriage and friendship. These bonds were severed as friends and families were separated and moved. In the new communities they had no claim on resources and they lacked the knowledge needed to live off the land in the new region. Population increases put a strain on resources on the southern coast. Since fewer hunters could hunt, dependence on welfare increased ... With the focus gone from their lives, many Hebronimiut turned to alcohol. Social problems increased as did rates of illness and death.

Similarly, Tester and Kulchyski (1994) described a complex series of relocations involving Inuit in the interior regions to the coastal areas of the Northwest of Hudson Bay. The relocated people had to rapidly adapt to a new terrain and climate; they became increasingly dependent on Euro-Canadian intermediaries and they 'lost control of their own lives' (Tester and Kulchyski 1994: 224). Connected to this was a loss of psychological strength, depression and feelings of hopelessness. McGrath (2006: 176) speaks of the 'schizophrenic quality' of the long dark months that relocated Inuit endured on Ellesmere Island. They 'were no longer able to distinguish what was real and what was not'. The four months of darkness to a people used to light year round 'was a blind drawn across their souls'. Suicide on Ellesmere Island was also very common. McGrath estimated that of all the babies born in Resolute Bay between 1953 and 1962, about one-third had committed suicide by the time of the RCAP inquiry in the early 1990s (McGrath 2006: 276). Elsewhere, the Inuit who moved from different locations around Baffin island to the settlement of Pangnirtung in the early 1960s suffered 'higher rates of substance abuse, depression and violence among males', which they related to the loss of a provider role and a move to a welfare economy (Billson 1990: 207).

A similar type of population transfer occurred in 1956 to the Sayisi Dene. These sub-Arctic caribou hunting people were relocated from their hunting territories to a camp outside the cemetery of the frontier town of Churchill, Manitoba. Narrating her story of the consequences of the movement to 'Camp 10', and subsequent relocation in 1968 to 'Dene Village', Ila Bussidor recalled the young Dene children watching,

> as our parents were destroyed, unable to bear the weight of a way of life that did not belong to them. We witnessed people being beaten, murdered, people of all ages dying in house fires, young women and girls being raped and beaten. Men and women froze to death every winter; there were countless victims of hit and run accident. (Bussidor and Bilgen-Reinart 1997: 5)

Within a couple of years of the relocation, what Bussidor describes as a stable and enduring hunting society had 'collapsed into disorder and despair' (Bussidor and Bilgen-Reinart 1997: 71). Separated from their lands, a whole generation had lost the skills needed to survive as hunters, and all that was offered in replacement was the grinding poverty of a shanty town. During the 1956–77 period of relocation, nearly half the Sayisi Dene who died did so 'violently, from alcohol-related causes or as a result of living conditions at Camp 10 or Dene Village' (Bussidor and Bilgen-Reinart 1997: 146).

Within a few years of the agglomeration of Inuit at Salluit close to Hudson Strait on Ungava Bay in the 1960s, social chaos broke out and Inuit started behaving in ways that were previously unknown. With the introduction of migrant wage labour in mining:

> Many families started making it [home-brew] and drunkenness became rife, with unhappy results . . . card games grew more serious and fights broke out. There was more and more extramarital sexual activity . . . Some people 'lost their senses' and ran around in the snow without clothes; one of these people nearly died. One girl is said to have given birth to her father's child. (Graburn 1969: 186–7)

When communal activity through travelling, seasonal hunting, fishing, summer gatherings and festivals started to disappear, so did the sense of meaning and purpose that bound people together. Activities that would have been antithetical to the values of the small indigenous groupings filled the void. The loss of permanent mobility meant a parallel loss of numerous sources of communal solidarity and removed the independence of action and decision making that was essential to hunter-gatherer societies (Graburn 1969: 182).

Not far south of Salluit, the Canadian government built shacks for the Innu in the 1960s in two settlements in northern Labrador. A prime rationale for the move was for the Innu to obtain health and welfare services. It was born of a conviction that Innu children ought to learn English to prepare themselves for what was envisaged as a booming resource extraction economy, which has yet to materialize. Government administrators used compulsion to bind Innu to the settlements by threatening to take away social welfare if families vacated the village to resume hunting activities (Samson 2003: 32–3). Not surprisingly, Innu people experienced life in the settlements of Utshimassits (Davis Inlet) and Sheshatshiu in Labrador, as well as 12 other villages in Quebec, as very harsh, especially compared to the life they were accustomed to as hunters in the forests and tundra of the interior. Alcohol, drugs, sexual abuse, suicide, gambling addictions and marital breakups all disrupted social stability, and the legacies remain. The prospects for those who survive to become future generations also look bleak. According to a 2004 study, 35 per cent of Innu youth display learning difficulties associated with Foetal Alcohol Syndrome (Philpott et al. 2004). Suicide clusters remain a problem, with five young people taking their lives in the villages of Uashat and Maliotenam, Quebec in 2015 (Montreal Gazette 2016), and three teenagers in three months at Kuujjaaq, which has a suicide rate 25 times the Canadian average, a neighbouring Inuit community on the Ungava peninsula (Curtis 2016; Siver Times 2016).

After one generation in the Labrador villages, the Innu Nation took stock of their experiences through a gathering of voices oral history project (Innu Nation and Mushuau Innu Band Council 1993: 33). The following sentiments from two Innu women were typical:

The bad thing about the past is that they moved people here and the whites told us lies about what our houses would look like. I sometimes think that the person who moved us here was crazy and he didn't know that the Innu had rights. (Penash, Utshimassiu woman)

I think they changed our whole way of living, our values, spiritual life, language and our physical well-being. We are not as strong in mind, body and spirit as we once were. I think the changes are helpful in some ways but not much. They are very damaging in other ways. (Enen Antane, Sheshatshiu woman)

Very poor housing and overcrowded multigenerational occupancy of single family dwellings are the contexts for the massive downturn in northern indigenous peoples' well-being. Similar types of destabilization occurred when the Ju/'hoansi Bushmen of Namibia and Botswana were being settled around small towns such as Tsumkwe, where vast numbers of the occupants of Bushmanland gravitated. With insufficient means to pursue hunter-gathering and the failure of agriculture, the population of Tsumkwe mushroomed and men started migrating to the mines of South Africa in the 1960s. The cash proceeds of their labour led to the opening of stores around hunting camps. With some cash to spend, consumer goods became more prevalent, and the maintenance of this type of consumption required continuous wage labour. As Lee (1993: 144–6) reports, sugar purchased at the stores was used to make homebrew alcohol, which in turn precipitated quarrels, jealousies, violence and even death in the larger Bushman settlements. A dysfunctional social order became more entrenched after the 1970s as more Bushmen became sedentary, and Tsumkwe is 'characterized by overcrowding, conflict and a host of other social problems like alcoholism, malnutrition, exceptionally high infant-mortality rates, apathy and general alienation' (Gordon and Douglas 2000: 176).

The decline of indigenous medicine and spirituality exacerbated the effects of these self-destructive activities. The resources that indigenous people would have used to deal with social and psychological dysfunction as well as physical illness were either unable to address the new afflictions or they were displaced by Western medicine. Biomedically trained doctors, nurses and social workers assumed control over indigenous health almost everywhere except the most remote locations.

The eradication of indigenous culture through schooling

In many places, coerced formal schooling modelled on European classrooms was introduced immediately after people were cleared from their lands. This acted as an important additional source of cultural and psychological collapse, cementing the loss of meaning and purpose incurred by removal of indigenous peoples from their lands. Schools shift the transmission of knowledge to colonial institutional settings divorced from the land-based experiential context that forms the basis of most indigenous knowledge. Schools, and those who teach in them, determine what counts as knowledge, and how it is presented and acquired. Achievement at school came to embody official notions of success, and the professional teacher became the expert charged with inculcating non-indigenous knowledge, shaping how indigenous people were perceived and what opportunities they could access outside their own communities.

Formal education in colonial contexts attempts to go even further by replacing and eradicating indigenous cosmologies. The concepts of being, time and the self, and the relationship of humans to the land and to animals among indigenous peoples are often very different from what is found in European cosmologies, as well as in the world-views adopted by modernizing post-independence states. Indigenous cultural concepts are embedded in their languages, but the language of the dominant ethnicity within states became the lingua franca. In formal educational settings, teachers and administrators regarded the colonial languages as superior to the extent that indigenous children in many locations were physically punished for speaking their own language. When students returned to their families, they were often unable to communicate with their parents, grandparents and siblings. To minimize what was seen as contamination of children by native worldviews and languages, boarding schools for indigenous children were frequently located far from their home. Native worldviews were depicted by policymakers and educationalists as backward, unenlightened and, if they persisted, likely to imperil the futures of those who stuck to them. Teachers and other intermediaries, generally white women, as Jacobs (2009) has pointed out in her detailed study of child removals in Australia and the United States, taught what they interpreted to be Christian principles and the individualistic values of modern settler society.

In the Anglo-Saxon settler states, the push to 'educate' indigenous peoples was to some extent driven by social Darwinism. In the early twentieth century, policies in Australia, the United States and Canada became influenced increasingly by racial science. In the eyes of the British authorities in Australia, mixed-race children should be exposed to boarding school education, so that the backward Aboriginal element in their inheritance could be diminished and, with luck, eliminated. A succession of Australian administrators advocated

eugenics, and laws, such as the 1905 Aborigine Act, regulated almost
every aspect of an Aborigine's life. The Chief Protector of Aborigines
in Western Australia from 1915 to 1940, Auber Octavius Neville,
was one of the most influential policymakers to embrace the racism
embodied in these policies. 'Half-caste' and 'quadroon' Aborigines,
in Neville's opinion, should not only be schooled in European values,
but should marry whites so that the Aboriginal race would eventually
die out (Buti 2005). At these schools, 'the children were taught to
despise their own language and culture. All ties with parents, relatives and friends were severed' (Lindqvist 2007: 101). James Isdell,
Travelling Inspector and Aboriginal Protector, articulated the justification for the kidnapping of indigenous children in Australia in 1909:

> I am convinced from my own experience and knowledge that the
> short-lived grief of the parent is of little consequence compared with
> the future of the children. The half-caste is intellectually above the abo-
> rigine, and it is the duty of the State that they be given a chance to lead
> a better life than their mothers. I would not hesitate for one moment
> to separate any half-caste from its aboriginal mother, no matter how
> frantic her momentary grief might be at the time. They soon forget their
> offspring. (Haebich 2000: 235)

As well as assuming that indigenous peoples have shallow emotions
with regard to their kin, and undercutting the essential relationships between parents and children necessary for socialization, this
policy attempted to alter childrearing patterns. As Lindqvist (2007)
observes, Aborigine children grew up with great freedom and were
loved and cherished rather than beaten and disciplined, a fact that
appalled the colonial authorities.

The ordinance authorizing the abduction of Aboriginal children
remained in force until 1957. It has been estimated that in New
South Wales, one in six were removed from their parents before the
law was changed, and that 100,000 people of Aboriginal descent
there do not know anything about their birth families or communities
(MacDonald 1995: xiv). Only in 1995 were the Stolen Generations
inquiry and the *Bringing Them Home* (HREOC 1997) report established to shed light on a policy that has had ongoing effects on
Aboriginal peoples. The report argued that, 'when a child was forcibly removed that child's entire community lost, often permanently,
its chance to perpetuate itself in that child. The Inquiry has concluded that this was a primary objective of forcible removals and is
the reason they amount to genocide.' When children are denied the
right of meaningful transmission of the beliefs, practices and world-

views of their parents and communities, their culture will die. The effects on the individuals taken away from their families, and on the family members and the wider aboriginal communities, are equally devastating. Many of the testimonies heard at the inquiry speak to the multigenerational trauma caused by forced family breakups.

The stories are no less disturbing in Canada where, over time, the Roman Catholic, Anglican and other churches assumed control of the education of indigenous children. The Canadian state began funding church-run schools and by 1896 there were 45 such schools in operation (Fournier and Crey 2006: 147). In the late nineteenth century, recruitment for these schools occurred as settlers encroached upon indigenous lands, destroyed animal habitats and made survival precarious. Disease and starvation were often a context for the removal of Aboriginal children from their families.

Canadian schools were notorious not only for the deliberate efforts to destroy indigenous cultures and languages, but also for the trauma inflicted upon the children, their families and whole communities. Recruitment into these schools was extensive, with autumn round-ups of children to coincide with the beginning of the school year (Smith 2009: 7). In some communities, all children between the ages of 5 and 18 were separated from their families (Funk-Unrau and Snyder 2007). Like the Stolen Generations of Australia, Aboriginal children in Canada also experienced forced removal, cultural indoctrination, extreme physical and mental punishments and sexual abuse. Many indigenous children died in these schools. In the *Where Are the Children? Healing the Legacy of the Residential Schools* travelling exhibition, which was installed at many venues across Canada between 2002 and 2003, numerous survivor stories were on display – such as the following from Melvin Jack:

Q. Are there other experiences, things that happened to you that really stand out that you can share today?
A. Yes. I was abused by the supervisor. I believe I was 6 or 7 years old at the time. I didn't know what was going on. His reward to me was a chocolate bar. Unfortunately I talked about it after. I talked to one of the boys and it got back to him. We were in the Dormitory and he gathered everybody up and he called me up. He didn't speak. He didn't explain to anybody why he was punishing me. He just told me I shouldn't have talked about it. He laid me over a desk and he had a fibreglass fishing rod and started to whip me, to the point where I lost control of my bladder and I was screaming. Every time I screamed he told me to shut up. That sealed my lips for it seemed like an eternity. (Legacy of Hope Foundation n.d.)

Although indigenous children in North America were normally taken for several years – rather than permanently, as in Australia – after about 130 years of residential schooling spanning seven generations, the effects were long term. Smith (2009: 8) remarks that 'from the mid-1800s to the 1970s, about one third of Aboriginal children were confined to schools for the majority of their childhoods'. New Zealand also established special native schools for Maori. These too were premised on assimilation, but were not renowned for the brutality of the schools in Australia and Canada.

There have been tens of thousands of individual court cases involving sexual abuse of native children in Canadian boarding schools. Several Anglican and Catholic dioceses have gone into bankruptcy as a result of the claims, and, in 2000, the Anglican Church of Canada announced that it was on the verge of bankruptcy. In November 2002, the Canadian government announced that it would give the church $25 million to pay for outstanding damages. The Roman Catholic Church in Canada has filed for bankruptcy protection, but, unlike the Anglicans, is contesting every single case. The Baxter National Class Action suit against the Canadian government, which involves 90,000 former students of boarding schools, was initiated in October 2002. In 2014, the Catholic Church was accused by the Canadian government of withholding millions of dollars in compensation from victims (CBC 2014).

These schools have been the subject of a number of national inquiries and official reports, including an entire chapter of the influential Royal Commission on Aboriginal Peoples report of 1996. Led by Justice Murray Sinclair, the much-anticipated Truth and Reconciliation Committee in 2015 reported the conclusions of its investigations of the residential school system, determining that it was a form of genocide, violating the UN Convention on Genocide by the forcible transfer of children from their families and physical destruction of people (Truth and Reconciliation Commission of Canada 2015).

Although there were precedents going back to the Jeffersonian era in the United States, boarding school programmes there intensified in tandem with the allotment process, as Native Americans were increasingly being confined on reservations (Jacobs 2009: 27). The archetype of the US boarding school was the Carlisle Indian Industrial School established in 1879 by Captain Henry Pratt in Pennsylvania as the first off-reservation school for Native Americans. Its mission was to catapult natives 'from savagery to civilization'. Carlisle was modelled on Fort Marion prison in Florida, an institution that Pratt had developed for holding American Indian prisoners of war, which included among its inmates the famous Apache leader Geronimo.

Native American children were often removed far from their homes and away from parental influence. Others were taken to schools built on reservations. Sometimes parents gave up children voluntarily, but, as in Australia and Canada, they were often either coerced or taken in by federal agents who persuaded them to collaborate, especially at times when indigenous communities found it difficult to procure sufficient means to support their children. For example, Don Taleyesva records in his memoir details of life in the early days of the Hopi reservation in Arizona:

> A few years before my birth the United States Government had built a boarding school at the Keams Canyon Agency. At first our Chief, Lolulomai, had not wanted to send Oraibi children, but chiefs from other villages came and persuaded him to accept clothes, tools and other supplies [probably used as bribes], and to let them go. Most of the people disliked this and refused to cooperate. Troops came to Oraibi several times to take children by force and carry them off in wagons. The people said it was a terrible sight to see Negro soldiers come and tear children from their parents. Some boys later escaped from Keams Canyon and returned home on foot, a distance of forty miles. (Simmons 1942: 89)

So painful was the relinquishing of children that the Hopi cut a deal by surrendering a group of men to the military to serve time in Alcatraz prison in exchange for keeping the children with their families (Child 1998: 13). At school, the boys' hair was cut, English was imposed as the only legitimate language and Euro-American culture, ideals and religion were taught. These boarding schools operated on a military style regime, in which children were often forced to undertake physical labour, both to subsidize the institution and to inculcate them with the virtues of hard work, their natural state, according to many Euro-Americans, being one of indolence and sloth.

As elsewhere, the pedagogical methods used caused immense personal, communal and intergenerational harm to Native Americans. Beatings, neglect, malnutrition, forced heavy labour and sexual abuse, often on a massive scale, were just some of the legacies of US boarding schools (Smith 2009: 6–7). It is important to keep in mind, however, that indoctrination was never total. Students resisted and creatively adapted to institutions, and sporadic congressional

3.2   Tom Torlino, Navajo (Diné), before and after his time at Carlisle
Indian Industrial School, PA, *circa* 1882.

Source: The Richard Henry Pratt Papers, Yale University

funding meant that the more totalitarian version of education could
not always be implemented as many authorities desired. By 1943
there were 34,000 American Indians in government schools, but, by
this time, boarding schools were being phased out in favour of more
broadly focused public day schools (Noriega 1992: 379, 383).

These methods were replicated elsewhere. The Soviet programme
of residential school education, for example, was part of a wider
policy of assimilation to move Siberian indigenous groups into industrial labour. In setting up residential and village schools, the Soviets
collectivized childrearing practices, replacing indigenous traditions
based on the extended family. As elsewhere, state institutions took
over from parents and grandparents as conveyors of knowledge.
Shamanic religious practices were heavily discouraged and ridiculed
as primitive. Russification of herders, hunters and pastoralists was
an important aim of the Soviet state during the twentieth century.
Younger generations of Evenk reindeer herders, for example, were
inculcated with the ideals of Soviet modernization (Bloch 2004:
103). Similarly, boarding schools were imposed across the Saami ter-

ritories of northern Scandinavia. This followed Lutheran missionary activities designed to discourage non-Christian beliefs and nomadic lifestyles. In Norway, under Norwegianization mandates, children were not allowed to speak Saami in schools until 1959. Although these culturally and personally destructive policies have been abandoned in Scandinavia, their legacies remain (Smith 2009: 18–19). The trauma and pain is apparent among Saami who both resisted and attempted to adapt to the Norwegianization programme (Minde 2003).

Although the experiences of the children varied because the actual arrangements were diverse, the reasons for removing children were the same everywhere. Migratory groups of hunters, pastoralists and herders, as well as diverse groups of minorities within states, have often been subject to similar policies in parts of Central Asia, China, Indonesia, India, the Middle East and Africa (Smith 2009). These were also part of nation building exercises to create cultural homogeneity following land expropriation. They were motivated by similar ideologies that smaller peoples were backward and inferior and would benefit from becoming more like the dominant ethnic groups.

4

Environment

But the white people are other than us. They probably find themselves very clever to be able to constantly produce a multitude of goods. They were tired of walking and wanted to go faster, so they invented the bicycle. Then eventually they found it too slow. Next they built motorcycles then cars. Then they found that all that was still not fast enough, and they created airplanes. Now they possess a great many machines and factories. Yet that still isn't enough for them. Their thought remains constantly attached to their merchandise ... I fear that this euphoria for merchandise will have no end and they will entangle themselves with it to the point of chaos. They are constantly killing each other for money in their cities and fighting other people for minerals and oil they take from the ground. But they do not seem concerned that they are making us all perish...

Kopenewa and Aubert (2013: 338)

Commenting on the fatal fixation with haste and material possessions, the Yanomami shaman and activist Davi Kopenewa identifies the motivations behind the European idea of progress. Most indigenous peoples have maintained their lands without viewing nature as a rigidly bounded political territory or as the source of rapidly marketable commodities. Instead, they have emphasized the inseparability of humans from other living things. They have often held to nonmaterialist philosophies that do not separate the world into nature and culture, viewing features of the landscape as sentient and significant beings. Rather than understanding the environment as an object, it is treated as a dimension of society and culture, all of which are living.

Hunters, for example, have deep bonds to the animals they hunt, the fish they catch, and the trees, plants, waters, deserts, moun-

4.1 Davi Kopenawa Yanomami signs copies of his book *The Falling Sky* at the launch organized by Survival International in London (September 2014).

Source: Survival International

tains and tundra that form their environments. The act of hunting closely intertwines human and animal societies, as outsiders who have worked with indigenous hunters have suggested (Ingold 2000; Brody 2001). Referring to Siberian hunters, but broadly generalizable (Weir 2008), Anderson (2000) has called this process of mutual engagement in the world, 'sentient ecology'. According to indigenous legends, these relationships represent long-term associations extending back millennia. For example, in Innu cosmology, the bonds between animals and humans stretch back to times when they spoke the same language and when mammoths roamed the northern lands not covered by ice (Samson 2013: 100). Native American legends commonly tell of transformations and communications between humans and animals, and these show affinities and interdependence between different life forms. Similar observations could be made of indigenous farmers such as the Pueblos of the US Southwest, or fishing peoples such as the many groups of the US Northwest and British Columbia (Samson 2013: 106).

Private property and capitalism

Sentient ecology, however, did not wash with those who colonized indigenous peoples. One of the most important justifications for inducing the environmental transformation of indigenous peoples was that their beliefs about nature were irrational and unproductive. In settler states such as those in North America and Australia, indigenous peoples were initially regarded as wasting God's bounties. Brody (2001: 61) associates the command in Genesis to 'go forth and multiply' (which is reinforced in the King James translation of the Bible) with the adoption of farming by Christians. Farming requires constant manipulation of the environment and fulfils the 'farmer's destiny' to subdue and manipulate nature. A long line of secular Western thought, state policy and law builds on these foundations. One of the most influential figures in the development of English Common Law, William Blackstone, embedded these assumptions in the law in his *Commentaries on the Laws of England* published between 1765 and 1769. He justified the idea that nature is intended to be the general property of humans by regarding the earth and everything on it as the immediate gift of the Creator. Ownership of property procured from the land makes productive use of it, and at the same time introduces capital accumulation.

Seeing peoples who did not claim nature as property and who therefore lacked capital, colonizers during the Great Land Rush observed that indigenous peoples did not have economies with the dynamic power to promote the growth of material wealth. Conveniently, they also believed that history had a preordained way of unfolding, and this followed a particular *economic* logic. During the Great Land Rush, capitalist economic theory from Adam Smith onwards constituted the accumulation of capital as the preordained direction of history. At a high point in the chauvinism expressed in capitalism, the notion of a singular path to economic well-being was given voice by W. W. Rostow, who published in 1960 his 'non-communist manifesto', *The Stages of Economic Growth*. Rostow argued that all economic progress moves through five stages. These stages were those traversed by the Western capitalist countries of his day; concluding that all future economic growth would have to follow this blueprint, Rostow argued that nature must be capable of being privately owned and appropriated for economic success.

The idea of a singular path to prosperity continued with neoliberal economic doctrines. These were espoused from the 1960s to the 1980s by economists such as Milton Friedman, whose writings were a great influence on right-wing leaders such as Ronald Reagan and Margaret Thatcher, as well as authoritarian client states in Latin America and Africa. In simplified form, neoliberalism holds that a flourishing economy and social harmony are dependent on continued high profits for businesses. The businesses are the 'supply side' of the economy and all prosperity is dependent on the availability of goods and services from them. This means, above all, controlling labour costs and public expenditure, privatizing public services, lowering taxes and facilitating means for corporations to pay very low or, in many cases, no taxes.

While there were permutations set out in Western economic thought, one constant was the almost mystical belief in the universal validity of one economic system. Underpinning this was the representation of humans as innately egoistic, thus making human nature consistent with the theory of progressive social change towards a market economy. Adam Smith's assertion of a natural tendency to 'truck, barter and exchange' – and hence adopt capitalist markets – implied a wired-in trajectory of capitalist development. In the age of development discourses, the *belief* in a universal process made possible by innate human qualities was a powerful impetus compelling Western states to demand changes in non-Europeans and to bring about in Europe massive social and economic transformation. Hence, state intervention to support capitalism, which underwrites infrastructure costs for business at home and abroad, became a feature of neoliberalism (Harvey 2005; Ong 2006).

The rise of global industrial capitalism coincided with an induced change from more communal approaches to production and egalitarian distribution to economies predicated upon individualized wage labour delivering the proceeds of labour to owners and shareholders. As companies took possession of indigenous lands for the minerals, timber and agricultural products to manufacture and sell as consumer goods, indigenous landscapes became denuded of animals, minerals and indeed anything saleable. Towards the close of the nineteenth century, about 12,000 African elephants were slaughtered every year just to make billiard balls for the British market (MacKenzie 1988/1997: 148). Similarly, the North American fur trade, operated by British and French companies, fed the insatiable demand of Europeans for a variety of felted beaver fur hats that were a mark of luxury and political allegiance (Wolf 1982: 159). This depleted the fur bearing mammals on which Native Americans depended. The near extinction of the beaver also upset the complex ecological system upon which other plants and animals depend (Cronon

1983). Similar processes occurred in South America, where sea lions
and chinchilla were commercially hunted to the brink of extinction
(Iriarte and Jaksić 1986).

Since the Great Land Rush, regions that were far removed from
industrial capitalism have become easily accessible. In settler states,
the right to privately owned land was made dependent on state
authorized titles, treaties or land claims, and these often duplicitous
land cessions legalized non-indigenous private property acquisition. At the same time, they provided few meaningful protections
to unilateral confiscation of collective indigenous lands, as we have
seen. The process also involved transforming egalitarian indigenous
societies into more individualistic and atomized communities. This
occurred through the introduction of monetary exchanges, as, for
example, in the North American fur trade, or of livestock, in colonial and post-independence attempts in Africa to make independent farmers of groups like the San Bushman (Gall 2002: 81). As a
result, possibilities emerged for the accumulation of private property
and, with this, private wealth. One of the most powerful forces that
encouraged these changes is the complement to neoliberal economics, the development mandate.

Development mandates

The contemporary emphasis by states, corporations, international
financial institutions and philanthropic foundations, such as the Bill
and Melinda Gates Foundation (McGoey 2015) and Tony Blair's
Africa Governance Initiative for economic development, build upon
nineteenth-century appeals to progress as a justification for imperialism. The development blueprints were formulated in the eighteenth
century and embellished by the theories of utilitarian philosophers,
many of whom had formative experiences combining Empire with
commerce. Some of the most notable include John Stuart Mill
and his father James Mill, who worked for the British East India
Company, and Sir Henry Maine, who was a legal member of the
viceroy's council in India. Although there were some prominent
sceptics who questioned the means by which supposedly beneficial
change was implemented in colonies, and even those who satirized
the singular notions of truth and reason, including some of the
leading figures in the Scottish Enlightenment (Rist 1997: 38), these
never gained political ascendancy.

Dominion over nature was thought to bring economic progress, while slavish devotion to nature, or survival within it, as the practice of non-Europeans was often depicted (McCarthy 2009), brought poverty, disadvantage and suffering. From these premises, it followed that the need to fashion the physical world in the image of the industrializing countries was urgent. Colonizing nations brought in select crews of merchants or skilled labourers to help exploit whatever wealth they deemed to be held within the lands and waters they occupied. Businessmen pioneered much of this expansion in nineteenth- and early twentieth-century Africa. The 'scramble for Africa' was led by figures such as entrepreneur and mining magnate Cecil Rhodes, who saw the African peoples as no obstacle to his own enrichment; he even dreamed of annexing the stars and planets. Colonialism became almost inseparable from wealth creation, which in turn was often trumpeted by plunderers as the apex of human achievement.

With the ending of formal colonialism after the Second World War, the racial theories that had been such a great blessing to colonial entrepreneurs were replaced by preaching the virtues of bootstrap capitalism as a first step for non-European peoples. A series of largely technocratic cures for 'underdevelopment' was then launched by the Western powers. US President Harry S. Truman's 1949 inaugural address, stressing the urgent need to spread industrial and scientific progress to the poorer peoples of the world, was one of the clarion calls for induced change across the globe. His 'bold new program . . . for the improvement . . . of underdeveloped areas' had a wide appeal among Western governments and launched the age of development (Binns 2014: 100).

Post-independence African politicians inherited and often championed colonial assumptions that indigenous peoples were backward, and many crudely embraced the development discourse. Speaking in terms that would have made social Darwinists blush, in 1996, Festus Mogae, then Vice-President of Botswana, remarked: 'How can you have a stone-age creature continuing to exist in the time of computers? If the Bushmen want to survive, they must change, otherwise, like the dodo they will perish' (quoted in Nettleton et al. 2007: 72). Emissaries of Botswana's patron states such as Britain have echoed these sentiments, with Baroness Jenny Tonge (2006) proclaiming the urgency of indigenous modernization because the San were suffering from 'underdevelopment', mired in the 'stone age' or the 'Mesolithic era'. In a review of sub-Saharan African sedentarization policies, Campbell (2004: 19) concludes that development policies, far from improving the lives of hunters and pastoralists, 'have turned self-reliant people into vulnerable clients'.

The same fervent claim to good intentions animates contemporary state and corporate programmes for the building of dams, clearing of forests and mining of indigenous lands. The proponents of the industrialization of indigenous lands often appeal to images of growth, improvement and progress to harmonize the goals of profit making with wider social goals. Contemporary examples of this abound in the discussions of the dramatic changes to indigenous social organization entailed in industrialization and energy production. Canada, a state that has aggressively pursued a resource extraction-based economy, presents a good example. Some recent academic and political discussions there argue that resource extraction on indigenous lands points to different and often improved forms of indigenous engagements with the land (Samson 2016). Slowey (2008: x) presents capitalist resource extraction as a form of liberation, arguing that 'neoliberal globalization may be a remedy to First Nations dispossession, marginalization, and desperation because it opens up space for First Nations self-determination'. Rapid industrial transformations, which represent a kind of accelerated version of those undertaken over many decades in industrialized countries, are viewed as rectifying Aboriginal social disadvantage. Indeed, Canada's information on outstanding Aboriginal land claims depicts the resolution of claims as largely a means to bootstrap capitalism (Aboriginal Affairs and Northern Development Canada 2003). Many indigenous lands across Asia, Africa and Latin America have been likewise targeted for neoliberal industrial transformation. In these places, international organizations such as the World Bank and International Monetary Fund heavily support private industrial activities on indigenous lands, in part because they help repay national debts and may also be presented as a means to alleviate material poverty and low living standards.

To legitimate such changes, many governments openly express exasperation with peoples who exist outside the main industrial, export oriented economy. Modernity is equated with being sedentary, schooled and living from monies procured by wage labour. In many countries, the world's remaining pastoralists and hunters are objects of stigmatization and ridicule by the dominant populations (Brody 1981). Politicians, some academics and large sections of public opinion regard their activities as an embarrassing anachronism, fuelling resentment of indigenous occupancy of lands that could be used for industrial development. Mobile occupancy of large and often highly biodiverse territories is a threat to both the control needed by states over populations and capitalist economic development. Because 'nomads' are depicted by governments as in need of remedial help, the strategic use of the development mandate has a wide appeal, not least to Western donors.

Wage labour is a vital aspect of the ideology of development because it serves as a transition point to economic progress. Even though the profits of backbreaking industrial labour accrue largely to owners of companies, the enthusiasm with which labour is touted as a vehicle for economic improvement and social mobility has been undimmed. With the lands of migratory groups commandeered for industrialization, indigenous groups are being forced into the main-stream economy, but principally as subproletariats or, frequently, 'unemployed' living in shantytowns or cities. In Siberia, for example, influxes of immigrants and prisoners from European Russia helped to reduce indigenous peoples to minorities as towns and cities were created as outposts of industrialization, resource extraction and pun-ishment. Indigenous Siberian pasturelands were destroyed by cities like Noril'sk, which spawned 'hydroelectric reservoirs and transpor-tation routes' with 'plumes of toxic vapours . . . downwind from the smelters' (McGhee 2004: 247).

At the same time, many Western countries have reduced, and in some cases almost entirely abandoned, extractive industry in favour of green technology production, services and finance. Industrial production activities, with all the associated environmental costs, hazardous working conditions and conflicts over land, are thereby outsourced to the global South or to indigenous lands such as those in northern Canada, the western United States, Siberia, Greenland, Brazil and Australia. Extractive industries can benefit from this arrangement with cheap labour, low social costs and immense profits, which have grown exponentially in recent years. For example, profits in metal exploration increased by 1,000 per cent between 1998 and 2011 in Guatemala alone (Dougherty 2011). The new global resource rush involves complex changes in transnational forms of property ownership (Borras and Franco 2012). China, for example, has huge investments in lands in resource-rich countries such as Australia, Brazil and Russia (Salidjanova 2011).

Land grabbing and bootstrap capitalism

The frenzy for the world's remaining fossil fuels and energy supplies now shapes how nations are conducting foreign and domestic policy. This 'new colonialism' (Liberti 2013) also involves wealthy states acquiring or leasing lands in debt-ridden poorer countries almost exclusively for the mass plantation, greenhouse and polytunnel production of agricultural products for industrialized countries that either have urbanized their lands or, like the fossil fuel producing Gulf states, are situated on lands unsuitable for agriculture. Lands in Latin America, Africa and large swathes of Asia, in addition to indigenous lands in industrialized countries such as Canada, are also used for dams and hydroelectric projects both for internal energy consumption and export.

A stark, but typical example of these processes predating the current discussions of land grabbing is the Kariba dam project on the Zambesi river in what is now Zambia. With World Bank financial backing, the colonial authorities in British Central Africa dammed the Zambesi river at the Kariba gorge in 1955. This precipitated an involuntary resettlement of some 57,000 people in total (World Commission on Dams 2000: 124), including the Gwembe Tonga farmers and hunters. Their homes, gardens, burial sites and areas of spiritual and cultural significance lie within the fertile Zambesi River valley that was flooded. The Gwembe Tonga lost all rights to their land – already eroded by British colonial authorities that granted them only usufruct rights – and they were subsequently partitioned into two groups reset- tled long distances from one another in Zambia and Zimbabwe. The project, which had only negligible benefits to Africans, was carried out by the British authorities with virtually no prior consideration for the indigenous inhabitants (Tischler 2013: 59–60).

Colson's (1971) early study of the effects of the hurried resettle- ment of the Gwembe Tonga uncovered numerous adversities arising from the displacement, including a rise in factionalism, a breakdown in communal activities, a shift in gender roles as women assumed a greater workload, and an undercutting of indigenous forms of gov- ernance and leadership. Already the British colonial authorities had effected a change in women's rights by refusing to recognize tradi- tional female ownership in favour of male-only property rights, which were then transferred to the relocation communities (Colson 1971: 114). The health of the Gwembe Tonga also suffered from a 'marked increase in drunkenness' (1971: 27) in the years immediately after resettlement. The more recent World Commission on Dams report on the Kariba dam supports Colson's findings, noting that the Tonga had no say whatsoever in either the resettlement itself or the condi- tions of it. Over time, Colson's (1971: 70) bleak observation that the Tonga had a 'fear of extinction of their humanity' has been borne out in the elimination of the native language and epidemics of measles

Most of the Tonga tribesmen whose Northern Rhodesian villages will be inundated when the Kariba Gorge is flooded will have been resettled in other areas of the Zambezi valley by the end of November.

An African dressed in a G string is pictured as he watched the unloading of possessions that include a dog from a six-wheeled lorry at the site of his new village.

4.2 British government documentation of the relocation of the Gwembe Tonga.

Source: The National Archives Image Library

and cholera, along with malaria, dysentery, hunger and HIV/AIDS. Similar upsurges in problems such as pervasive alcoholism parallel the erosion of indigenous livelihoods in parts of North and South America where dams have been built (Weist 1995; González-Parra and Simon 2008: 1777). In fact, the social and psychological problems associated with development-induced 'internal displacement' are remarkably similar to those caused by the displacement subsequent to wars and armed conflict (Muggah 2003).

The usurpation of Adivasi lands in India to make way for extractive industry had similar effects on women as those recorded above for the Gwembe Tonga. The expansion and operation of mining and extractive industries in all the Adivasi territories, and the building of large dams such as those in the tribal areas of North East India, 'created massive displacements of Adivasi and tribal villages, resulting in food insecurity, poverty, violence and abuse especially amongst indigenous women and girls. This has increased their vulnerability to trafficking and sexual exploitation as they look for means to survive and earn income' (ISAWN/IWFNEI/AIPP 2014: 6).

Brazil is at the epicentre of land grabbing. Monocrop plantations of soya for animal feed and oil have been established across the province of Mato Grosso do Sul. Throughout Brazil, this occurs with little regard to the existing laws to protect the rights of indigenous peoples, and this is enabled by the Brazilian Congress being dominated by large agricultural and mining lobbies (Watson 2013). President Dilma Rouseff has been firmly wedded to Brazil's Program for Accelerated Growth initiated by her predecessor Ignacio Lula de Silva. Often, land grabbing is legalized through state sponsored energy development and food production projects (Pedlowski 2013) such as the massive factory-like projects in Mato Grosso do Sul, which are pushing further westwards into Guaraní lands and now completely surround the 3,500-hectare Guaraní reserve where 11,000 people live. Most Guaraní are no longer able to support themselves through their own agroforestry economies, but work principally as wage labourers on the plantations (Liberti 2013: 144–5). Since the 1970s, Guaraní on the Paraguayan side of the frontier were subjected to a similar disconnection as roads were built into their forests and appropriated for cotton, soya and wheat production, both by corporations and by impoverished Paraguayan settlers. Robbins (2006: 155) estimates that, at the current rate, 'the Paraguayan forests will be gone by the year 2025', and 'with the rainforest went the way of life of the Guaraní'. They now live on a reserve with a small forest surrounded by vast plantations.

Elsewhere in Brazil, Watson (2013) reports that land grabbing is also facilitated by the failure to enforce the demarcation of indigenous territories, and has now reached formerly uncontacted peoples:

Even where land is recognised, loggers and settlers invade with impunity. The Awá, one of the last nomadic hunter-gatherer tribes in Brazil, who number just 450, have lost an astounding 31% of their forest heartland. About 100 Awá are uncontacted and on the run in a desperate attempt to evade the chainsaws and guns.

In other parts of South America and Africa, and parts of Asia such as Malaysia and Indonesia, the confiscation of indigenous peoples' lands for agrofuels is gathering pace. Plantation farmed products such as ethanol from sugarcane, biodiesel from palm oil and jatropha for automobile fuel, seen as one solution to the impending exhaustion of crude oil, are now grown on lands previously used for low carbon lifestyles (McMichael 2009; Liberti 2013).

Many post-independence states have few laws to protect indigenous land rights, and often ignore the laws that they do have. For example, Guyana, run since independence by either non-indigenous Indo-Guyanese or Afro-Guyanese political parties, inherited a state apparatus from the departing British. During the regime of Forbes Burnham, placed in power in 1964 by British manipulation of electoral rules, and surviving until 1985, the socialist government commissioned a vast number of foreign financed 'modernization' projects with virtually no environmental oversight. These were located on Amerindian territories of the interior. Under Guyana's laws, Amerindians are given title only to villages, not to lands, which are *terra nullius*. Mineral rights and resource development are rights that the state reserves for itself (Forte and Melville 1989: 5). Mining, dams, roads and logging, much of which was supported by IMF and World Bank backing, have eroded habitats for subsistence farming, hunting, gathering and fishing and made such livelihoods virtually impossible. Guyanese police have harassed and beaten Amerindians who object to the mining on their lands (Colchester et al. 2002). Because of state corruption and also the incredible inducements being offered to free up indigenous lands, signed Amerindian titles and agreements have provided little protection against land grabbing. The ongoing effects of this and its clear violations of both state and international law are well documented in a recent report from the Amerindian Peoples Association in Guyana (Dooley and Griffiths 2014).

It is rarely referred to as land grabbing, but in the Western settler states a number of political processes legitimate the confiscation of indigenous lands by corporations, and this is occurring with increasing regularity. States such as Canada and Australia combine negotiation with indigenous peoples over land with bureaucratic compulsion to surrender it. In Canada, after the *Calder* Supreme Court case of 1973, the state established a 'comprehensive land claims' system to adjudicate between the competing claims of Canadian sovereignty and underlying indigenous ownership of land not extinguished by treaty. The comprehensive land claims process demands extinguishment of indigenous land title and requires huge diminutions of indigenous territory and rights in exchange for some self-government rights and cash compensation. Some current land claims agreements are additionally made contingent upon Aboriginal participation in large-scale and frequently environmentally damaging resource extraction or energy production, such as the massive Muskrat Falls hydroelectric project in Labrador on the most important river on the territory of the Innu peoples of Labrador-Quebec (Samson and Cassell 2013; Samson 2016).

However, settler states do not rely solely on their legal systems to engineer the reduction of collectively owned indigenous lands. In the United States, for example, indigenous groups are adopting 'corporate strategies' in order to preserve some measure of their ways of life on the reduced land bases (Fixico 1998: x). One example of this, and parallel to the Canadian land claims process, is the 1971 Alaska Native Claims Settlement Act (ANCSA), which 'rejected all claims to original ownership of land by the indigenous population in exchange for a sum of $926.5 million . . . and packages of land that amounted to 44 million acres' (Sale and Potapov 2010: 78). The funds were distributed through 13 native corporations, but about half of the compensation monies accrued through revenue sharing with oil companies already embarked upon their operations. Indigenous survival on less land in Alaska was therefore heavily linked to oil and gas exploitation, mining and clearcutting old-growth forests (Strohmeyer 1993: 186–9).

Indeed, what Rata (2003) observes of 'neotribal capitalism' among Maori in New Zealand may apply more broadly, as some leaders appeal to tradition and indigenous independence to enrich themselves along with non-indigenous professionals who help nego-tiate joint venture and other resource extraction deals. The financial rewards may sometimes be so great that indigenous leaders are able to cut deals with investors for fabulous payouts for themselves, and often little redistribution to other members of their communities. This was the subject of a recent investigation of Tex Hall, Tribal Chairman of the Fort Berthold reservation in North Dakota. Hall allegedly was involved in several business partnerships with oil companies and various intermediaries, while also being empow-ered to sign away collective tribal lands for oil drilling (Sontag and MacDonald 2014). Even where there may be no corruption, benefits are often short-term booms followed by bust. For example, after ANCSA:

economists who have analyzed Native capitalism find that the majority of the regional corporations are in real trouble. Besides bad investments, much of their money has been dissipated on legal fees, often by fighting one another. Endless lawsuits over sharing of revenues derived from the sale of natural resources, over grievances filed by dissident stock-holders, and over challenges to subsistence rights have enriched Alaska's lawyers. One corporation officer estimates that lawyers have skimmed off at least $100 million in fees from the original $962 million claims settlement. (Strohmeyer 1993: 186)

Predictions about economic progress from bootstrap capitalism are, of course, often proved wrong. Given that many indigenous people worldwide lack the educational and other qualifications for skilled labour or management and executive positions, opportunities in the new extractive industrial sectors are overwhelmingly in manual labour positions with subcontractors on relatively short-term building projects. Indigenous communities dependent on resource extraction labour face massive public health problems and disruption of communal activities (Goldenberg et al. 2010); promises of economic progress that were made following land claims agreements, such as Nunavut in Canada, have proved to be false (Légaré 2008).

Environmental racism: resistance and coercion in the sacrifice of indigenous lands

Environmental racism is the common practice of situating industries that emit hazardous wastes and cause general ecosystem degradation in close proximity to lands occupied by poor, minority and indigenous populations. Such practices mean that the burden of ill health and the expense of avoidance activities such as staying indoors at certain times or refraining from land-based activities fall upon populations that are already disadvantaged. In the places where indigenous peoples have not already been displaced, their marginalization is often a reason to make lands available for commercially lucrative, yet toxic, industrial activities. Indigenous lands are being sacrificed in Australia, where there is a vast amount of uranium mining; in Canada, home of the world's single largest most environmentally destructive project, the Alberta tar sands; in India and China, where there is deforestation, damming and the devastation of river systems; and in Brazil, with constant industrial encroachment into the Amazon rainforest.

In North America, the fact that tribal authorities have some self-government rights paradoxically makes their lands appealing to extractive industries because there are often lower levels of environmental and other regulatory oversight. Tribal authorities are often in a relatively powerless position to resist the entreaties of corporations, and this has been shown to be the case with regard to toxic waste disposal in particular. For example, the closing of a phosphorus plant on the Fort Hall Shoshone-Bannock reservation in Idaho resulted in members of the tribe agreeing to a $40 million payout to absolve the FMC Corporation from its promise to remove the hazardous waste when it closed the plant, as per the original agreement. This meant capping 123 acres of the hazardous waste in ponds with liners that are known to leak after 25 years. In his account of this situation, Lacey (2003: 414) spells out the health hazards:

> The ponds contained elemental phosphorus, cadmium, chromium, zinc, and lead, as well as radionuclides, the evaporation of which significantly contributed to the overall air emissions from the plant. At their peak, the ponds emitted up to 224 pounds per day of phosphine and 611 pounds of hydrogen cyanide into the air, both gases known to attack the nervous system or cause death when inhaled in sufficient quantities.

In neighbouring Wyoming, fracking on the Wind River reservation has already produced groundwater contamination, but 'federal environmental laws currently exempt operators in Indian Country from disclosing many of the chemicals used in produced water [wastewater from fracking], as well as their associated health and safety risks' (Williams and Hoffman 2015: 453). In this case, discharged waste water is emptied onto tribal pastures and grazing lands. Contamination has already been found in domestic tap water, and all this is perfectly within US federal law through a loophole applied exclusively to Indian lands.

Under pressure from corporations, high-level nuclear waste storage was proposed by leaders at the Utah Goshute Skull Valley reservation in association with a consortium of nuclear utility companies. The project was depicted as a means of assisting with 'hopelessness, alcoholism, migration, and language loss' and 'a bottom-line tool for cultural survival' (Lewis 2007: 321). Although the tribal leadership approved the deal, the BIA and the Department of Interior voided it on appeal. If it had gone ahead, the Goshutes' land would have been a store for thousands of nuclear fuel assemblies, each containing ten times the long-term radioactivity released by the Hiroshima bomb over a 30-year period and weighing in total 44,000 tons (Davis 2002: 59). While the Goshute, Wind River and Shoshone-Bannock cases indicate that there was some level of agreement, the insecure positions in which indigenous peoples have been placed in North America mean that many are not making entirely free choices over the adulteration of their own lands.

In parts of the US Southwest, indigenous lands have been given over as 'national sacrifice areas' by the federal government. The term arose in the 1990s out of the perceived necessity of designating certain environments as expendable to maintain US living standards and to protect other areas. It was used relatively recently by various resource extraction companies and the Department of Defense (Hooks and Smith 2004). The idea is that for the well-being of the public, certain areas need to be subjected to permanent degradation, and often made uninhabitable. One of the most important 'sacrifice' activities is hardrock mining, ubiquitous in the Four Corners area of the Southwest, which employs numerous toxic chemicals to extract minerals, and dumps these in large tailing ponds. Equally vital is military testing of the sort carried out at the Nevada Test Site on Western Shoshone lands. Test bombing presents extreme health hazards from the contamination of lands and waters caused by spent ammunition, fuel spills and radiation.

Hydroelectric projects are also major enterprises in the arid Southwest. These require dams that cause flooding and can have a devastating effect on forests, soils, fish, wildlife and people close to them. The Hoover dam in Arizona, for example, spawned numerous other dams, and a dramatic degradation of the landscape that affected the peoples of Northern Arizona, and especially the Mojave, Chemehuevi, Hopi and Navajo. The dam became a monument to the Western claim to greatness by dominating nature, with Secretary of the Interior Harold Ickes announcing at the dedication of the dam in 1935: 'Pridefully, man acclaims his conquest over nature' (Leslie 2007: 4). It is not surprising that indigenous groups within the region have been beset with the fallout from conquests over nature. The adjacent Shoshone lands are used for cyanide leach gold mining in Nevada (Fishel 2006/2007). Navajo lands were plagued by the largest radioactive leak in US history from uranium mining (Grinde and Johansen 1995: 3; Brugge et al. 2006), and the Navajo population now suffers from a range of cancers associated with the mining.

The adverse health consequences of industrial activities on indigenous populations are well documented across the world, where numerous places are de facto national sacrifice areas. One of the most notorious cases is methyl-mercury poisoning of indigenous peoples in Canada and Brazil (Boischio and Henshel 2000). Such poisoning affected the Ojibwa people of Asubpeechoseewagong (until recently commonly known as Grassy Narrows), Ontario, Canada. This was caused by the Dryden Chemical Company dumping 20,000 pounds of mercury into the Wabigoon-English river system and poisoning the fish caught and consumed by the Ojibwa. It resulted in neurological and other symptoms associated with Minamata disease (Harada et al. 2005). Fearing that a plan to clearcut adjacent forests could induce more mercury poisoning of the local rivers, the community of 1,500 petitioned for an environmental impact assessment. At the end of 2014, their petition was rejected by the provincial government despite a Supreme Court decision earlier in 2014 which decided that clearcutting could go ahead subject to its duty to consult (Porter 2014). Problems continued in 2015 when the community called a state of emergency over the presence of potentially cancer-causing disinfectant by-products in their water supply (Porter 2015).

Other examples include the PCB (polychlorinated biphenyl) and mercury contamination of the seals and fish eaten by the Inuit in the High Arctic (Cone 2005). PCB, which is used in a wide variety of industrial products, such as electrical appliances and wiring, coolants, flame-retardants, paints and pesticides, is implicated in cancer among Inuit. Dioxins and other persistent organic pollutants from iron plants, copper smelters, cement kilns, pesticides and municipal waste plants are transported by currents and also in plankton, fish and larger marine mammals to indigenous lands and waters of the far north. Inuit who have been tested in Northern Quebec have extremely high levels of dioxins in their bodies, and the passing of carcinogens from Inuit mothers to babies in breast milk is the subject of artist Roz Mortimer's (2007) film *Invisible*.

In Canada alone, there is a veritable gold rush in northern British Columbia, extensive hydroelectric, mining and logging activities envisioned by Plan Nord in northern Quebec, and mining and drilling across other aboriginal regions of northern Canada. The Alberta tar sands development is an extreme example of the environmental, health and social damage that accompanies extractive industrial activities on indigenous lands today. It consists of a complex of lands, which have been cordoned off for oil exploration and extraction by corporations including Shell, Chevron, BP, Exxon, numerous smaller Canadian companies and subsidiaries of the China National Petroleum Corporation, all excited by an estimated 1.7 trillion barrels

4.3 Tanya Tagaq in costume on Baffin Island in the film, *Invisible*.
Dressed in red, Tanya represented the toxins imported from industrial sites
now shown to have been found in Inuit mothers' breast milk.

Source: Film still, © Roz Mortimer 2006

of oil. The substance they are looking for is solid bitumen embedded in sand. Extracting it involves first clearing forests of virgin spruce and pine and scraping off the sandy topsoil. In this process, four tons of sand is displaced to produce one barrel of oil (Klare 2012: 102). The bitumen is then released by a form of open pit mining or by injecting steam into the deep buried tar sands, heating vast quantities of sand to release the bitumen oil. Klare (2012: 102) describes the area, which is adjacent to the lands of four groups of Dene and Cree, as 'a blackened moonscape, with enormous man-made craters sitting alongside vast piles of discarded rock and pools of poisonous wastewater'. These communities face what Huseman and Short (2012) call a 'slow industrial genocide'. It is – or was – home to a rich ecosystem containing migratory ducks and geese, numerous species of fish and large but declining herds of woodland caribou and wolf packs, all of which are at risk of not being able to reproduce themselves as their habitat becomes lost. Caribou extinction in the vicinity is widely predicted (Schneider et al. 2010).

The industrial processes at the tar sands also result in the leaching of toxins into lakes, rivers and human water supplies, the disposal of millions of tons of petroleum coke sludge waste, and air pollution so bad that Canada withdrew from the Kyoto protocol on climate change in 2011. The tar sands are seen as so vital to the national economy that Canada deliberately misled the UN in its report to the international body on climate change. It did this by omitting data showing a 20 per cent increase in pollution from the megaproject (De Souza 2011). Furthermore, the transportation of tar sands oil via the $7 billion Keystone XL pipeline to ports on the Gulf of Mexico risks environmental and health damage to other indigenous lands. Indigenous groups, including the local Mikisew Cree, and environmental organizations have been active in drawing attention to the enormous health and environmental risks posed by the tar sands (Tenenbaum 2009). Regarding the tar sands, the Mikisew Cree Chief George Poitras (2009) remarked:

> My people are dying, and we believe British companies are responsible. My community, Fort Chipewyan in Alberta, Canada, is situated at the heart of the vast toxic moonscape that is the tar sands development. We live in a beautiful area, but unfortunately, we find ourselves upstream from the largest fossil fuel development on earth. UK oil companies like BP, and banks like RBS [Royal Bank of Scotland], are extracting the dirtiest form of oil from our traditional lands, and we fear it is killing us.

The Keystone XL and tar sands have been the subject of widespread and well-organized indigenous protest in Canada, especially through the Idle No More movement, which has appealed to the 2007 UNDRIP (Ornelas 2014). Celebrities such as Neil Young and Willie Nelson have added their voices of opposition to the pipeline. In November 2015, President Obama rejected the pipeline as a signal of efforts to fight climate change, but this could be reversed if Republicans win the 2016 US presidential election.

Because they strip out biodiversity, these dramatic alterations of the landscape deter and often prevent indigenous peoples from practising land-based activities. A 2013 spill of 9.5 million litres of toxic waste in Alberta on lands used by the Dene Tha resulted in every tree and plant dying over some 42 hectares (Vanderklippe 2013). Looking at indigenous peoples' relationships to land, Global Health Watch (2005: 169–70) concluded that environmental degradation, pollution and biopiracy were all serious sources of both disconnection from land and health problems resulting from the poisoning of local ecologies, which prevents people from using the land as a source of animal, plant and spiritual sustenance.

These destructive industrial activities are present elsewhere, but often the corporations in question are European- and North American-based. The involvement of corporations in indigenous territories often precipitates internal as well as external conflicts. Major and often violent battles have occurred since the early 2000s between indigenous peoples and governments over resource extraction in the United States, Botswana, Brazil, Paraguay, Peru, Canada, Colombia, Congo, Guatemala, Indonesia, Kenya, Nigeria, Philippines and West Papua (Vidal 2009). Indigenous social movements have mounted opposition to mining, hydroelectric power generation, logging, agribusiness and biofuel production. People such as the Achuar of the Amazonia region of Peru are filing suits in American courts against US oil company Occidental. They are telling stories 'of poisoned rivers, contaminated fish and oil-soaked earth, of sick children and parents' (Los Angeles Times 2008). In Guatemala, Mayan groups have garnered international support, including that of the UN Special Rapporteur on Indigenous Populations, James Anaya, in opposing the activities of the Canadian company Goldcorp that set up gold mining operations at the Marlin mine on their lands without consultations (Law 2008; Barnett 2010). Elsewhere in Guatemala, security guards working for Canadian company Tahoe Resources shot indigenous protesters at the Escobal mine in 2013, and in 2014, a youth activist was shot and killed at the same location. Hearings for a lawsuit related to these incidents began in a British Columbia court in 2015. This adds to a growing number of similar court cases against Canadian companies operating on indigenous lands in Guatemala (Molyneaux and Imai 2014). The NGO Cultural Survival (Sanders 2015) has argued that Canadian extractive companies are the worst violators of indigenous peoples' rights worldwide:

> Despite the reputation held by Canada for its comparatively respectful human rights practices, the country's recent actions in Indigenous territories both at home and abroad has caused Vancouver businesses to gain notoriety in Latin America as the worst in the extractive industry. Both in terms of environmental degradation and human rights violations, the Canadian government has failed to prevent the corrupt behaviors of its extractive industries – the result of lacking policy standards and enforcement on the part of the Canadian government.

According to the World Bank's Corrupt Companies Blacklist, a list of firms banned from doing business with the World Bank due to their chronic malpractice, Canada is the reigning offender, providing 117 businesses out of the 600 listed. Efforts by the Canadian government to address such transgressions on indigenous lands have been particularly poor, even after communities, UN bodies and environmental reports have called for its attention.

Not all industrial activities on indigenous lands are undertaken by Western corporations. In Chile, the privatized power company ENDESA is building six hydroelectric dams on the powerful Bío Bío river, which flows from the Andes to the Pacific. With the initial construction of the first dam in 1992, the other dams are going ahead over the objections of the Pehuenche peoples, several hundred of whom will be displaced from their lands (Latta 2007). In 1997 the more ambitious $600 million Ralco dam project was approved by the Chilean government. Ralco impacted two Pehuenche communities, Ralco Lepoy and Quepuca Ralco, and flooded the cemetery of Quepuca Ralco as well as several sacred places of the Pehuenche. The dam and subsequent inundation of lands displaced 93 families, who were removed to resettlement villages built by the private power company (González-Parra and Simon 2008).

The most devastating effect of industrialism is global warming, which is measured by higher average temperatures and is manifest in less ice coverage in the North, drought in the South, hotter summers, colder winters and more extreme and unpredictable weather. In a review of the human rights implications of the impacts of climate change on indigenous peoples, Havemann (2009) argues that, in most places, indigenous peoples are far more vulnerable to the effects of climate change than other populations, because of both their marginalization and their commitments to land-based practices. In central Australia, Aboriginal communities 'face the largest projected temperature increases and the least climate-proofed public infrastructure, services and housing', while coastal Aborigines face damage to the coral reefs, along with more flooding, erosion and cyclones (Havemann 2009: 4). In sub-Saharan Africa, desertification is diminishing the lands available to the San Bushman and other hunter-gatherers. Across Asia, temperature increases and decreased rainfall are leading to the collapse of forest ecosystems and pressures on forest-based peoples, while coastal peoples are facing flooding. Havemann (2009: 5–6) summarizes the impact of climate change on indigenous peoples:

> Climate change is likely to increase the vulnerability of Indigenous peoples to continuing poverty and poor health. In an increasingly competitive environment, Indigenous peoples' lack of political and economic power seems likely to continue to limit their ability to assert and defend their land tenure, to maintain access rights to natural resources and to sustain diversified traditional livelihoods.

Because the ecosystem in the Arctic depends on its low temperatures to maintain the habitats of the animals, fish and plants, the preservation of these areas is highly precarious. In some parts of Alaska, permafrost is rapidly thawing and releasing carbon and also methane into the atmosphere, creating a continuous warming loop. Furthermore, Alaska, Northern Canada, Siberia and especially Greenland, which is 'mega-industrializing' (Sejersen 2015: 64–106), are simultaneously victims and sources of fossil fuel generated global warming.

Average temperatures in the Arctic have risen by between two and four degrees Celsius since 1900 (Wright 2014: 221). This is also affecting settlements and causing some coastal Inuit to relocate (Cone 2005; Kolbert 2006). The melting of sea ice affects polar bears, seals, bacteria and plants that the Arctic peoples ultimately depend upon. The lowest minimum Arctic sea ice since satellite records began was registered in 2012. It was 50 per cent lower than the 1979–2000 average. By 2030 most of the Arctic could be free of ice, imperilling the hunting of sea mammals and making travel on waters previously under solid ice more precarious. There are disturbing indications that Northern peoples' relationships to their environments are dramatically and deleteriously changing, and their extensive knowledge of the weather patterns and ability to predict weather is becoming irrelevant. With more treacherous and unpredictable conditions for both humans and animals, global warming threatens indigenous peoples' ability to procure healthy wild foods such as caribou, ducks, geese and seals.

Unfortunately, the national priorities of states claiming territories within the Arctic Circle may only make these problems worse. As symbolized by the Russian planting of a flag under the Arctic Ocean in 2001, states are starting to solidify maritime boundaries in order to exploit vast mineral deposits and onshore and offshore oil. Accidents associated with this may become more common as the ice rapidly vanishes and exploration is made increasingly feasible (Borgerson 2008). As the 1989 Exxon Valdez accident showed, the Arctic ecosystem is particularly vulnerable to oil spills, and these have devastating effects on all life in the areas, killing almost everything in the marine food chain. Additionally, drilling scares away whales and interferes with their sonar communication with each other. Some marine mammals suffer hearing loss posing a threat to their ability to communicate, and whales have beached and died in the vicinities of seismic surveys and drilling operations (Griffin 2012). This in turn impedes the food supply and cultural continuity of groups like the Iñupiat who live close to oil drilling sites (Abdalla 2012). The effect of these losses to biodiversity incurs subsequent losses of subsistence livelihoods, precipitating upsurges in mental health problems including Post Traumatic Stress Disorder (PTSD) – for example, in Inuit communities near the Exxon Valdez spill (Oliver-Smith 1996). Nevertheless, Royal Dutch Shell and BP, the big players in oil exploration in the Arctic, have paid billions in legal fees to secure their rights to appropriate sites.

The industrialization of indigenous lands has, of course, been challenged. In fact, there are countless international, national and local NGOs working to fight powerful corporations, and even small groups of indigenous peoples mobilize every day against environmentally damaging fossil fuel extraction projects. In the United States, the Turtle Mountain Chippewa and Eastern Cherokee have banned fracking in recent years (Indian Country Today 2011, 2014). Resistance by indigenous groups, including those organized under the Idle No More movement, has involved protests, civil disobedience and the use of social media to oppose environmental degradation and the state's financial powers over indigenous groups (Tupper 2014; Barker 2015). Of particular concern are oil pipelines, including the massive Enbridge, Northern Gateway and Keystone XL, hydroelectric power plants, fracking, nuclear waste storage and mines on or adjacent to indigenous lands. Idle No More and other critics argue that these developments were pushed through either against the spirit of existing treaties or after insufficient consultation with indigenous groups.

Civil disobedience can often be a turning point in the recognition of indigenous rights. At the very least, it can be a marker of the visibility of indigenous groups within states. A forerunner of some of the more recent development conflicts was the battle between Saami and the Norwegian state over the building of the Alta hydroelectric project and dam. A campaign of protest and civil disobedience by the Saami and environmental NGOs to prevent the flooding of land that would have inundated the Saami settlement of Masi in Finnmark was successful. Although the Saami activism did not stop the building of the dam itself, it was an important statement of an indigenous Saami identity within Norway (Thuen 1995; Sand 2014). In 1989, a Saami Parliament opened with considerable powers to enable the cultural continuity of the Saami peoples. If it were not for the activism over Alta, the Parliament may well not have come into existence. However, where there are minerals known to be in the ground, extractive industries often do not take no for an answer, returning repeatedly to petition states and cut deals with indigenous leaders. More recently, the Saami lands have been targeted for intensive mining of uranium, iron ore, nickel, phosphorus and valuable rare earth minerals. One-eighth of Finland has been set aside for mining,

4.4   Saami activist Mikkel Eira at 'Point Zero' during demonstrations
against the Alta Dam, 1979.

Source: courtesy of the World Heritage Rock Art Centre, Alta, Norway

and the Swedish government has already planned relocations of villages in the Arctic regions, which are also home to populations of
lynx, bear, wolverines and wolves (Vidal 2014).

The ability to resist varies enormously depending on the integrity
of environmental regulations and the vulnerability of groups to political and economic pressure and, in some cases, violence. In much of
Latin America, resistance depends on the recognition and honouring of indigenous land rights, and particularly the integrity through
which the demarcation of indigenous territories is undertaken. In
many places, there are long delays in accepting indigenous claims
for demarcations, lax enforcement of them, and rival non-indigenous
and corporate claims to indigenous lands. Reviewing the experiences
of four countries in Latin America, Stocks (2005: 97) concludes that
'the forward movement in regard to indigenous lands is in real danger
of being contested so sharply and powerfully that it will effectively
be extinguished'. While there are some protections for indigenous
peoples wanting to maintain their lands and ways of life, institutions
such as the World Bank have been resolutely pro-development. The
Forest Peoples Programme (2014), an NGO that is known for the
thoroughness of its research, reported 'in an unprecedented move,

the World Bank will be proposing that governments could "opt-out" of requirements designed to protect indigenous peoples from unintended and negative consequences from development activities funded by the multilateral lender'.

Against this, the threats to indigenous peoples from extractive industries have generated indigenous cooperation across borders. In 2014, more than 60 representatives of indigenous and other forest communities from Africa, Asia and Latin America came together with various NGOs at the International Workshop on Deforestation and the Rights of Forest Peoples, in Palangka Raya, Indonesia, 'to share experiences and seek solutions to the unrelenting destruction of forests around the world and the risks to forest peoples' rights, well-being, forest territories and cultural heritage' (Litvinoff and Griffiths 2014). The extensively documented report produced by the workshop criticizes the top-down methods of imposing deforestation and the threats to customary uses of forests by indigenous peoples in Indonesia, Malaysia, Cameroon, the Democratic Republic of the Congo, Guyana, Peru, Colombia, Paraguay and Liberia.

Conservation mandates

Not surprisingly, states and corporations have realized that continued unchecked industrial expansion will result in the eventual elimination of the resources needed for capitalism to continue. While the burning of fossil fuels promotes consumption, economic growth and living standards, the alarming and largely conservative predictions about global warming fatally undermine the ability of people to enjoy the supposed benefits of industrial activity. Given this conflict, 'sustainability' has often been interpreted to mean that environmental protection need not imperil economic growth. By adopting green technologies and environmental impact assessments, and by setting aside lands for conservation, those who use the language of sustainability often hold that the negative environmental effects of extractive industries and fossil fuel dependence can be offset.

Conservation is a prominent measure of sustainability that can have adverse effects on indigenous peoples because they use and inhabit many of the tropical forests, animal-rich plains, river valleys, canyons, deserts and other areas of scenic beauty that have been earmarked for protection. Although there are many different models of conservation, much of it has become a means of enabling market-based development measures. This can be seen through National

Park initiatives, where indigenous peoples worldwide have been evicted and prohibited from carrying out traditional activities within park boundaries (Poirier and Ostergren 2002), leaving the areas themselves open for commercial tourism. This broad pattern was apparent in the early establishment of Game Reserves in Africa. These were set up in reaction to the massive declines in wild animal populations that resulted from the destruction of habitats from commercial farming and especially game hunting under colonial rule (Mackenzie 1988/1997: 201). Environmental depletion became visible as settlers established farms further into the lands of hunter-gatherers in Southern Africa. Zealous overhunting by the settlers was a reason for the establishment of parks such as the Etosha National Park in German South West Africa where, by the end of the nineteenth century, lions were scarce, white rhinos had disappeared and the last elephant herd had been killed (Dieckmann 2007: 74–7).

Conservation continued to act as a lever of expropriation of indigenous peoples in post-independence African countries without any appreciable settler populations. Lewis's (2000) report on the Batwa pygmies of the Great Lakes region of Central Africa describes how the Batwa of the various countries in which their lands lie were expelled from their lands, sometimes violently as in the 1960s in what is now the Democratic Republic of the Congo at the hands of the state conservation authority. In Uganda, Batwa suffered from the twin forces of encroachment into their forests by farmers, who necessarily felled trees, and conservationists who supported the creation of National Parks, thus curtailing hunting and gathering rights. The upshot of these forces was to make the subsistence economy impossible, and, as a consequence, Batwa became 'badly paid low-status casual labourers or porters and many rely on demand sharing (begging) to support their families' (Lewis 2000: 20).

With millions of indigenous peoples removed from their lands for conservation projects, and up to 600,000 displaced tribal peoples in India alone (Chatty and Colchester 2002: 2), this pattern is undoubtedly global. The compendium of studies by Chatty and Colchester (2002) show these processes in fine detail across a wide spectrum of locations. In Sri Lanka, the Wanniyala-aetto were expelled from their lands in the eastern side of the country to the new settlement of Henanigala South, which lacked the resources, the almost 5,000 people who were evicted from their lands to make way for the Maduru Oya Park (Lund 2000: 106). According to the NGO Survival International several Wanniyala-aetto with permits to be in the park have been shot and killed by park guards (Survival International n.d.).

As Dowie (2009) demonstrates, sustainable indigenous engagements with the land have been replaced by poverty-stricken livelihoods
as bottom-rung wage labourers in tourism and park conservation,
with high levels of social and psychological dysfunction occurring in
adjacent indigenous communities. Others have been displaced and
evicted as a result of state conservation measures with little regard to
their welfare, minimal consultation, and a simple expectation that the
indigenous groups live in the same unequal and precarious manner
as other subaltern populations. A side attraction of some conservation projects in Africa is the commodification of indigenous cultures,
making the living display of local costumes and customs part of the
tourist experience (Witz et al. 2001; West et al. 2006).

Although the numbers of indigenous peoples affected are smaller
than in Africa, a similar combination of conservation and development themes were bundled into the establishment and operation of
the US National Parks. Indigenous lands at Yellowstone, Yosemite,
Glacier and the Grand Canyon, as well as many national monuments
and other lesser-known sites, were set aside for ecological preservation. Soon after opening Yellowstone, the US government built rail
connections to get people there, then opened entertainment venues
such as dance halls, movies, bear pit shows, baseball and golfing. Not
long afterwards, roads for cars were built to allow mass tourism, and
gradually petrol stations, gift shops and hotels were added. The first
head of the National Park Service (NPS) in 1916 saw no problem in
'making a business of scenery' (quoted in Opie 1998: 377). Close to
four million tourists visit Yellowstone per year.

Undoubtedly, the setting aside of lands of outstanding beauty for
preservation in the United States has slowed industrialization and
Euro-American settlement. But only after indigenous lands had
been requisitioned and many Native Americans displaced did the
NPS enlist the cooperation of indigenous leaderships in the management of the parks. Since the 1980s, the confiscation of indigenous
lands at these sites, including the Grand Canyon, has been reduced
on account of legislation respecting Native American cultural and
religious freedoms, which include practices associated with specific
landmarks (Moorhouse 1996: 122).

Urbanization mandates

Before colonization, some indigenous groups lived together in large
numbers in urban-like settings, such as Cahokia, the centre of the

'Mississippian culture' along the eastern side of the Mississippi river (Pauketat and Emerson 1997). In Central and South America, the vast living complexes of the Aztec, Maya and Inca civilizations are well known. The classic Mayan sites contain living quarters for hundreds of people, ceremonial centres, ball-courts, temple-pyramids, structures for administration and leaders' residences, and vast plazas (Culbert 1974: 61). The populations of these sites had either disappeared by the time of European colonization, as in the case of Cahokia and many of the Mayan sites, or their cities were destroyed and dismantled by the Spanish, as with many large civilizations from Mexico southwards.

The urbanization of indigenous peoples today, however, is caused by desires by states and corporations to use their lands. Any indigenous group that has some natural resource on their lands is vulnerable to displacement. As Fixico (1998: 191) remarks of the United States: 'The competition for Indian resources may very well be the last era of Indian–white confrontation, for, when all is said and done, the tribes will have nothing left that white society wants [except casinos].'

The antecedent of the more recent resource motivated displacements occurred directly in some parts of the United States in the mid-twentieth century as many federally recognized tribes were terminated. Driven partly by Native American soldiers' experiences of living and fighting with non-indigenous men in the Second World War, the government encouraged the relocation of vast numbers of reservation dwellers to cities. After various inquiries and Senate hearings, 109 Indian nations were dissolved between 1945 and 1960. Advocates of the scheme in Congress argued on the basis of human rights and universality, with Senator Watkins of Utah likening the 1953 Termination Act to the Emancipation Proclamation (Wilson 1998: 354).

This policy either abrogated or proposed a renegotiation of treaties that had already entailed surrender of millions of acres of land – often prime timber and farm lands – to the United States in exchange for particular guarantees about rights, protections and aids. Termination affected 12,000 Native Americans and almost 1.4 million acres of their lands (Fixico 1986: 183). They were told, in effect, that many of the treaty guarantees that had previously been exchanged for their lands were now null and void. Termination dramatically reduced tribal lands still further, as tribal members were given a choice of either holding on to their allotments, managed for them by a private trustee, or receiving cash compensation for them. Many decided to take cash, and the windfalls were often spent immediately.

Termination abolished federal responsibilities to tribes, including the fiduciary trust relationship through which the financing of reservations was administered. It also destroyed the pre-existing social and economic organization of the reservations, undermining all tribal authority, and indigenous groups also lost government services, schools and health facilities on the reservations. Eventually, through tireless efforts and lobbying of congressional representatives, lawyers and the Native American Rights Fund, some groups were able to reverse the Termination Act, restoring their status as federally recognized Indians with treaty and other federal rights.

At the same time as funds to reservations were withdrawn, money for relocation to cities was informally channelled through the BIA, beginning in the early 1950s. These efforts culminated in the Relocation Act of 1956, after which thousands of American Indians moved to cities. The first centres were in Denver, Los Angeles and Chicago. The BIA recruited candidates for relocation, paid the cost of removal, placed them in jobs and helped them in housing and other adjustments, consciously trying to 'separate relocated Indians from their tribal associations' (Debo 1970: 377).

Over time, more cities were designated for relocation and more funds put into the programme. The experiences of natives in cities were often traumatic, although some did succeed in employment and other aspects of city life (Fixico 2000: 19). After adverse experiences, many returned to their reservations, which were more tolerant, communal and friendly than cities. Those who stayed in the cities often ended up in slums. Over time, many horror stories, involving Native American alcoholism, divorce, and suicide, started to emerge (Fixico 2000: 18). Between 1951 and 1973 more than 100,000 Native Americans were relocated to cities.

Parallel trends towards urbanization of indigenous people were apparent in Canada in the 1950s and 1960s. Inducing people to abandon their lands and communities caused disruption to cultural continuity, compounded by residential schools, as well as to economic development and local government initiatives. According to the Mohawk political commentator Russell Diabo (2013) and Idle No More (2014), the Stephen Harper government intended the contemporary comprehensive land claims policy to be the vehicle to resuscitate the termination of collective rights to land to enable resource extraction projects on what would become fee simple lands. The most powerful means of termination are mandatory provisions in contemporary land claims agreements that require that Aboriginal signatories either extinguish or agree not to assert their collective ownership or

Aboriginal title rights (Samson and Cassell 2013; Samson 2016). With indigenous land bases shrinking through these processes, subsistence livelihoods become less viable, and the urbanization of Aboriginals in Canada that is already well under way seems set to increase.

North American policies are similar to Chinese state directed 'termination' policies towards herders on the Tibetan plateau, which force migratory peoples to move to semi-urban settlements (Lafitte 2013: 90–1). As Foggin (2008: 50) relates it:

> There are two main rationales invoked to support this policy, one environmental and one development-oriented. Either way, a potential major social consequence is the creation of inner city-type problems even in small rural towns. Such problems include the concentration of poverty, high levels of unemployment, and increased dependency on the state for subsistence. Some resettlement villages already are being called 'theft schools'. The first argument in support of urbanization under the 'ecological migration' plan is that herders are assumed to have played a major role, through over-grazing, in the recent degradation of the natural environment. Secondly, there is an apparent bias toward farming and towns, as opposed to pastoralism and rural living, that seems to have led many decision-makers to address the development matter of providing social services (especially health care and education) by focusing effort mainly on the process of urbanization, with an implicit assumption that there will then be a direct consequent improvement for all people, including new residents, irrespective of their success at adapting to new living conditions and economic opportunities. However, what has already been reported indicates that the social consequences of urbanization may outweigh the hoped-for benefits. Additionally, the prior history of such relocation/migration ventures – as seen for example in native American reservations in the USA, First Nations in Canada and aboriginal reservations in Australia – gives clear cause for concern.

The author here makes an explicit comparison between Chinese policies and previous negative experiences in North America.

In a follow-up to its 2007 report on Tibetan herder relocation programmes, Human Rights Watch documents the vast scale of urbanization of Tibetan herders since 2000 as part of the government's 'Great Development of the West' policy (HRW 2013a). It was estimated that, by the end of 2013, 90 per cent of the herder population, about 413,000 people, would have been urbanized, mostly against their will. Many herders have already been relocated and housed in purpose-built towns far from their lands. Others have had their villages 'remodelled', traditional houses bulldozed and new dwellings built

4.5 In a residential compound recently completed, but yet waiting for its inhabitants, a Tibetan herder has brought his livestock, sheep and horses to graze in the rubble. The government campaign to move Tibetan herders to urban areas and curtail pastoralism has put the nomads' traditional lifestyle and livelihood at risk. The environmental rationale behind this policy is questioned by human rights groups and scientists alike.

Source: Gilles Sabrie, 'Last Nomads'

to conform with a 'New Socialist' design for identical multi-storey apartment blocks. The HRW report also documents shoddy housing construction, a lack of sanitation and water, and the emergence of a number of social problems in the new towns. In effect, whole herder communities have been forcibly transferred in less than a decade from pastoralism to alternating between unemployment and wage labour.

Whilst the Chinese government justifies these policies by appealing to a development strategy of boosting an underprivileged population and protecting a fragile ecosystem from overgrazing, it has opened up Tibetan indigenous lands to industrialization through energy production and mining. There is little room for the mobile land-based pastoralist economy of the Tibetans when raw materials for the world's factories promise more rapid enrichment (Lafitte 2013). HRW (2013a: 22) notes that similar observations about deteriorating social conditions have been made by Chinese language studies of these forms of coerced urbanization. Testimonies taken for the HRW report documented the means of coercion, the punishments meted out, including imprisonment for anyone who refused, and the loss of livelihoods and meaning coinciding with the moves to the apartment blocks. For example, Tenzin Gyaltso, a Tibetan herder who was interviewed for the report, stated,

> People are so desperate; they're going to lose everything. My family is rich by local standards, we have yaks, horses, sheep, and goats, and over 20 *mu* [1 *mu* is 1/15th of a hectare] of land. We never lacked food. My family home was built at great cost using the best material: the best timber, the best stones, everything. We had spent 50,000 Yuan building this house. And now we have to relocate to the new houses built by government [at the other end of the valley.] Besides, we have not been allowed to take any of our herds to the new place – we had over 100 yaks, 15 horses, and close to 200 sheep and goats. But we have to sell everything. Thankfully my family could arrange to send the yaks to some relatives living elsewhere, but this is a disaster, we're losing everything. People in the village are desperate. They don't have any skills, and don't have any herds or land worth speaking of anymore. How is the next generation going to survive?

Although long superseded by China, the pre-eminent model of authoritarian industrialization is that of the Soviet Union. It too dispatched many indigenous groups to urban areas, and made strenuous efforts to compel them to embrace manual labour and materialistic collectivism as incarnated in the Soviet state ideology. All this was attempted in the Stalinist period, but much of it was not realized until the 1970s. After forced collectivization and sedentarization, 'in the late 1980s every other native northerner died as a result of injury, murder or suicide. Most of these deaths were alcohol-related' (Slezkine 1994: 375). More recently, the privatization policies that have succeeded sedentarization in the Inner Mongolia area of China have given rise to 'widespread social anomie . . . a rapid rise in alcoholism, theft and brigandage' (Humphrey and Sneath 1999: 8) in the towns where pastoralists were forced to move.

A final contemporary illustration of this process is the current urban relocation and sedentarization of Palestinian Bedouin populations by Israel. Echoing China's policies towards Tibetan herders, in 2014 it was revealed that the state plans to move 12,500 Bedouins from their encampments in south Hebron in the Occupied Palestinian Territories to one new city to be built for them in the Jordan Valley. The encampments are scheduled for demolition and, with that, the history, experiences and way of life of the Bedouins. Shulman (2014) refers to this as 'culturecide'. This policy in the Occupied Palestinian Territories builds on processes beginning at the formation of the Jewish state of Israel in 1948. At that time, around 80 per cent of Palestinian Bedouins were expelled to neighbouring territories (Abu-Saad 2008: 1725). Bedouin owned and cultivated lands in the Negev desert were declared *terra nullius*, and to be, by fiat, Israeli state land. Israeli courts have determined that, as nomads, Bedouin have no property rights. Palestinian Bedouins of the Negev who survived within Israel were then moved to 'restricted areas', and eventually to seven planned towns between the 1960s and the late 1980s (Abu-Saad 2008: 1733). Some 100,000 Palestinian Bedouins have refused to move and are attempting to preserve their ways of life. But these settlements are, according to Abu-Saad (2008: 1736), by state design the most deprived and marginalized in Israel. Refusal to move to new planned urban settlements, however, is becoming less of an option as demolitions are creating 'facts on the ground' and pastoralist Bedouin are being evicted as callously as were the San Bushmen in Botswana, mentioned in Chapter 3. The NGO B'Tselem (2015) reported on demolitions of Palestinian Bedouin villages in 'Area C' of the North Jordan valley, which took place in early 2015:

> These demolitions are part of the Israeli authorities' longstanding policy designed to expel thousands of Palestinians from dozens of communities throughout Area C from their homes on various pretenses. Israeli officials have repeatedly declared an intention to take over land in Area C in order to create 'facts on the ground' that will facilitate annexation to Israel in a future peace agreement and, until then, de facto annexation. In recent years, the Civil Administration has been planning a permanent site for Bedouin communities from the Ma'ale Adumim area and from the Jericho area in the Jordan Valley, to be called 'Ramat Nu'eimah'. The plan is being drawn up with no input from the residents themselves, who oppose it.

Land grabbing, industrialization, displacement and urbanization are all means by which indigenous peoples have become disconnected from their lands. This occurs also among other peoples as well and is known as 'the extinction of experience' (Nabhan and Antoine 1993). The effects of disconnection may be more acute in indigenous societies because they had little or no internal compulsion towards industrialism and urbanization. Rather, indigenous societies have evolved spiritual beliefs, ceremonial traditions, sacred designations and worldviews that are embedded in historical and ongoing relationships with their lands. For many indigenous groups, both personal and cultural identities are intertwined with the physical landscape and nature as a whole. The languages they speak are intimately connected to the landscapes in which they have dwelt for millennia (Basso 1996; Cruikshank 1998). Away from their homelands, the preservation of indigenous cultural identity becomes a significant challenge. Displaced indigenous people often become atomized, and disconnected city dwellers are faced with exploitation and ethnic discrimination. However, at the same time, an increasing body of literature examining the effects of urban migration on indigenous peoples' identities has shown that some are also reconstructing and revitalizing their cultures in these and other contexts (see Anderson 2013; Escárcega and Varese 2004; Imilán 2010; Lawrence 2004; Peters and Andersen 2013; Watson 2014; Andersen 2015).

5

Rights

After all, our rights as sovereign nations were not granted by the Constitution. They existed before there was a Constitution.

Cladoosby (2015)

One of the most significant milestones in the expansion of human rights since the 1980s is the passage of the 2007 United Nations Declaration on the Rights of Indigenous Peoples (UNDRIP). The Declaration is broadly characterized by two central features: it is the outcome of activism through which indigenous peoples' organizations involved themselves in its formulation and adoption, and it recognizes indigenous collective cultural, social and economic rights beyond a Western legal framework focused on individual rights. Significantly, this declaration and other human rights protocols were formulated in response to ongoing colonial domination of indigenous peoples and build on almost a century of indigenous resistance through international institutions.

Indigenous peoples and rights

The relationship between indigenous peoples and rights today has to be understood in the context of the resurgence of interest in colonial policies. As discussed in Chapter 2, European occupation of indigenous lands was justified through the Doctrine of Discovery and often, by default, through *terra nullius*. In British settler states, these two principles established legal foundations of colonial rule. Although treaties and other agreements followed later in most places, except Australia, the underlying assumption was that the colonial power, or Crown, had meaningful sovereignty over the colonized territories, while indigenous peoples' sovereignty resided in their mere usage of lands. Indigenous customary law, traditions and government were disregarded as sources of rights. Rights were meaningless unless granted by colonial authorities through their laws or the treaties they drafted. However, as we have seen, the legalities were often imposed under duress and were violated and ignored by the states that created them, paving the way for assortments of indigenous rights that were always violable merely by the assertion of sovereignty.

The social contract theorists of the European Enlightenment cemented a conception of rights as being principally individual rights. In law, these individual rights could be exercised through rights to private property. In fact, the jurist William Blackstone made private property the central guarantee of government, and the existence of a state the basis for people in 'civilized' societies, who alone could be accorded these rights (Keal 2003: 102–7). The expansion of individual and private property rights was made possible by the dual political and economic revolutions in France and Britain that led to 'the triumph of a bourgeois-liberal capitalism' (Hobsbawm 1964: 2). These were reinforced further by the US Declaration of Independence and Constitution.

Because concepts such as sovereignty and lawmaking institutions of state were imposed upon them, many indigenous people quickly came to distrust the law and see it as a form of manipulation. In the colonial order, indigenous peoples had no rights other than those that were conferred upon them by the state, which was (and is) the sole source and arbiter of rights. As the European settlement of indigenous lands proceeded in the Americas, Australia, New Zealand and parts of Asia and Africa, it was through the 'state-centred legal structures' based on absolute notions of state sovereignty that these rights were exclusively granted (Anaya 2004: 7; Samson and Short 2006: 169).

The modern nation-state confers rights through citizenship, but in relation to indigenous peoples two problems arise. First, these rights are individual rights and, as Morris (2006: 13) indicates, it is questionable whether cultural rights, or indigenous rights in this case, can be achieved 'within the liberal, individualistic framework that has traditionally underpinned guarantees of universal human rights'. Second, many states simply maintained the colonial relations with indigenous peoples from former colonial powers. Indigenous peoples face the state not as citizens, but as objects of control; not as subjects of rights, but as peoples whose own autonomy had been severely truncated.

Crucially, the emancipatory potential of liberalism was not extended to indigenous peoples, but rather they became a symbol of the hypocrisy of the great boast of the 'rights of man' and 'inalienable rights'. Significantly, the Western realization of this hypocrisy was not made in light of the appalling slaughter occasioned by African slavery, Columbus's 'black legend', westward expansion in North America or the scramble for Africa, but in response only to the bloodbaths in twentieth-century Europe. After the Second World War, the 30 articles of the Universal Declaration of Human Rights (UDHR), adopted by the UN in 1948, established a framework of civil and political rights for all human beings. Under this, *all* peoples 'are equal before the law and are entitled without any discrimination to equal protection of the law' (Article 7). However, indigenous peoples have not been able to enjoy the right to equality before the laws. Stavenhagen (2008: 259) argues that this is due to a combination of factors: (1) inefficient implementation of a human rights framework; (2) inadequate state policies in relation to human rights; (3) obstacles that indigenous peoples face as a consequence of persistent discrimination. Furthermore, the liberal framework of the UDHR does not accommodate the collective rights of indigenous peoples for self-determination, territorial rights and cultural identity.

One of the impediments to the recognition of indigenous rights, ironically, was decolonization. Following the UDHR, continuing colonial violence and the 1955 Bandung conference of nonaligned and newly independent countries, it became evident that colonialism was inconsistent with universal human rights. In 1960 the UN reacted through Resolution 1514(XV) (Quane 1998: 548), which followed the UN Declaration on the Granting of Independence to Colonial Countries and Peoples. The Resolution reaffirmed that 'all peoples have the rights to self-determination'. It specifically referred to territories that were either Trust territories or not self-governing. However, under the pre-existing blue water or salt water convention in international law, a colonized people must be at least 30 miles distant from the colonial state to qualify for decolonization (Lam 1992: 616). Because of this important caveat, indigenous groups in settler societies did not qualify for decolonization, nor did other groups whose territories happened to fall within new independent states.

Nonetheless, the UDHR did provide a model of discourse on human rights that could help indigenous peoples appeal to an authority outside the state and gain access to the specialized forums of the UN (Niezen 2003; Xanthaki 2007; Morgan 2011). Furthermore, the discussion of human rights in the UDHR provided a moral ground from which to put pressure on states to recognize and protect particular indigenous rights. For indigenous peoples' organizations, the language of rights represented an opportunity to engage with the nation-state from a different standpoint:

> Indigenous peoples' claims to existence as societies differentiated from mainstream national societies are taken nowadays as valid arguments in the dialogues with the states ... In this sense, it can be said that Indigenous peoples participate today in an argumentation community together with the agencies of national states ... the state does not have the monopoly of valid arguments anymore. (Oliveira 2009: 13)

At the same time, there are those who are sceptical about adopting the politics of rights, and believe that this could lead to further assimilation and legitimization of colonial structures (Niezen 2005). In relation to Canada, but applying the argument more widely, Alfred (2009: 176) writes:

> To enlist the intellectual force of rights-based arguments is to concede nationhood in the truest sense. 'Aboriginal rights' are in fact the benefits accrued by indigenous peoples who have agreed to abandon their autonomy in order to enter the legal and political framework of the state. After a while, indigenous freedoms become circumscribed and indigenous rights get defined not with respect to what exists in the minds and cultures of the Native people, but in relation to the demands, interests, and opinions of the millions of other people who are also members of that single-sovereign community, to which our leaders will have pledged allegiance.

Despite the embedding of rights within nation-states and the transformative cultural and social impacts that claiming rights can have upon indigenous peoples, many indigenous groups have turned to the international legal arena as a way of advancing their rights and affirming their distinctive identities. In some ways, the international engagement is at least of a different order than participation in state processes in which liberal 'recognition' is all too often a form of colonial incorporation (Echo-Hawk 2013; Coulthard 2014).

Indigenous rights as sites of contestation

Up until very recently, the regime of rights governing indigenous peoples has been explicitly 'domestic'. Although shaped by different historical and political circumstances, indigenous peoples face similar challenges especially in relation to political recognition, land rights and self-determination. A few examples from around the world illustrate variations in the *internal* politics of indigenous rights, which in all cases still provide some space for contestation and resistance.

In Australia, two issues have been at the forefront of aboriginal claims for rights: the recognition of Native Titles to the land and the Stolen Generations. First, the *Mabo v Queensland No 2* (HCA 1992) resolution of the Australian High Court acknowledged Native Title as a legitimate source of land rights for Aboriginal peoples, and that this predated colonization. *Mabo* invalidated the principle of *terra nullius* by which Aboriginal peoples were historically denied any rights to their lands. Second, the publication of the HREOC report, *Bringing Them Home*, in 1997 addressed the social and cultural impacts of federal, state and territorial policies of abducting and forcibly schooling Aboriginal and Torres Strait Islanders' children. In both cases, indigenous peoples were not only claiming rights but also challenging state sovereignty over them as groups and as individuals.

In the United States, the federal government holds trusteeship over Native American lands and affairs despite the latter being recognized by its own Supreme Court as sovereign nations. Without their consent, contrary to what might be supposed from the Enlightenment tradition of the social contract, Native Americans were pronounced to be 'dependent domestic nations' under the Marshall decisions of the 1820s and 1830s (Robertson 2005). UN Special Rapporteur James Anaya summarizes this central contradiction in US law regarding the rights of indigenous peoples:

> Looking beyond the constitutional text to historical practice, the colonial era law of nations and reason, the United States Supreme Court established, in a series of early 19th century cases, foundational principles about the rights and status of Indian tribes that largely endure today. Supreme Court doctrine recognizes that Indian tribes are inherently sovereign with powers of self-government; indeed they are 'nations' with original rights over their ancestral lands. Within this same body of doctrine, however, the sovereignty and original land rights of tribes are deemed necessarily diminished and subordinated to the power of United States, as a result of discovery or conquest by the European colonial powers or the successor United States. (UNHRC 2012: No. 14)

Native Americans are constituted as being sovereign, yet this is obviously only in a subordinate form, construed as 'self-determination' under the overall authority of the United States. In turn, this self-determination is often limited or highly regulated through the trusteeship status (Cladoosby 2015). While the use of the words 'sovereignty' and 'nation' as applied to Native Americans stretches their meaning to breaking point, and the very ambiguity of these terms provides grounds for the state to impose its hegemony on federally recognized groupings of 'nations', it also provides space for contestation over rights.

In 2008 the Japanese government officially recognized the Ainu of Hokkaidō as indigenous peoples, despite longstanding policies to promote national homogeneity. Ainu organizations had actively campaigned for their recognition as indigenous peoples to claim specific social, political and cultural rights. As Siddle (1996: 170) indicates, 'one of the main motivations for the construction of a counter-narrative of Ainu nationhood was precisely the denial of Ainu existence that historical amnesia and the master-narrative of homogeneity made possible'. In this sense, cultural politics became a strategic site for the affirmation of identity. In 1997, the Ainu won a landmark case as they challenged the legality of the expropriation of their lands for the construction of the Nibutani dam. In its decision, the Sapporo District Court ruled that the Ainu constituted a distinctive ethnic minority with specific rights in Japan (Levin 1999).

In the Philippines, the 1997 Indigenous People's Rights Act (IPRA) established the legal framework that regulates indigenous peoples' issues and their relation with the state. However, the effective implementation of these rights has been undermined by the development of an export-oriented economy that relies on extractive industries. As Molintas (2004: 273) points out:

> in the 1970s pressure upon indigenous communities' land base intensified as the national economy became increasingly foreign-dominated and export-oriented. Because they occupy areas rich in natural resources, indigenous communities have been besieged by a growing number of foreign and local corporations engaged in mining, logging, plantations, and other export industries.

In this context, the Philippine Mining Act of 1995 made it easier for extractive industries to appropriate large extensions of indigenous peoples' lands. As a consequence, indigenous peoples have been displaced from their traditional lands, and their leaders and communities have been exposed to various forms of violence. It is against this background that indigenous peoples' organizations have

5.1 Nibutani Dam on the Saru River, Hokkaido, Japan. Ainu activism
against the building of the dam led to the recognition of the Ainu as
indigenous peoples in Japan in 1997.

Source: Carlos Gigoux

actively campaigned for the recognition of their right to free, prior
and informed consent (FPIC) which was granted by the IPRA. The
honouring of FPIC, however, has been weakened by the conflict-
ing interests surrounding resource extraction and restrictive judicial interpretations of the Act (Gilbert 2006: 113–14; Holden and
Ingelson 2007).

In Africa, although the very notion of indigenous peoples is contested by most states, hunter-gatherers and pastoralists who constitute distinct groups have claimed their right to be recognized and
protected as indigenous peoples as they are exposed to violence,
discrimination and displacement from their traditional territories.
Indigenous peoples' rights across Africa serve to protect cultural
identities and lands:

> The types of human rights protection which groups such as the San,
> Pygmies, Ogiek, Maasai, Barabaig, Tuareg, Hadzabe etc. are seeking
> are, of course, individual human rights protection, just like other indi-

viduals the world over. However, it goes beyond this. These groups seek recognition as peoples, and protection of their cultures and particular ways of life. A major issue for these groups is the protection of collective rights and access to their traditional land and the natural resources upon which the upholding of their way of life depends. (ACHPR/IWGIA 2006: 14)

In Latin America, indigenous peoples have focused their rights claims on a number of areas: (1) constitutional recognition, (2) self-determination, (3) political representation, (4) land rights, and (5) cultural rights. According to the report published by the Economic Commission for Latin America and the Caribbean (ECLAC 2014), the main challenge for indigenous peoples in the region is to ensure that their indigenous rights are included in the process of policymaking and that they are considered when it comes to the approval of extractive industrial and intensive farming projects on their lands. The export-based economy that characterizes most Latin American states has put great pressure on the exploitation of natural resources on traditional indigenous territories, with detrimental impacts on their well-being, security, health and environments (ECLAC 2014: 11–18).

Internationalizing indigenous rights

Indigenous peoples' appeals to international frameworks of rights expose states to a supranational set of laws. Ironically, these embody the liberal principles through which most states legitimate themselves. It is strategic, then, that indigenous peoples' organizations have appropriated the liberal principles and framed their claims within the international human rights discourse. In this sense, Morgan (2009: 122) points out that 'the case of the development of a global framework addressing indigenous peoples' rights presents a compelling illustration of the dynamism and inherently flexible character of rights'. Thus, indigenous groups have used international human rights laws to take states and private companies to highly visible sites, such as international courts, for the discussion and determination of rights. The paradox, however, is that, in the current international system, rights are ultimately enforced only by the same states that may be guilty of failing to recognize these very rights. There are considerable tensions also between collective rights articulated in international legal instruments and the bias towards individual rights favoured by states.

While indigenous peoples situated themselves as actors in international political encounters through their oratories, ceremonies and treaties with colonizers, the presence of indigenous peoples in formal international legal forums goes back to the League of Nations. In 1923 the Haudenosaunee Chief Deskaheh and in 1925 the Maori leader T. W. Ratana travelled to Geneva in order to request the recognition of their cultural and land rights in Canada and New Zealand, respectively (Hunter et al. 2012: 451). Although, in both cases, they were denied the right to speak at the League of Nations, their presence signalled the intention of indigenous peoples to use international settings as a way of discussing and promoting their rights as peoples. Here, indigenous peoples became 'legitimate subjects of international law with rights to exist as distinct peoples' (Morgan 2011: 5), and the global indigenous movement has been a salient force in the UN system.

The first international document regarding indigenous peoples' rights was the International Labour Organization Convention No. 107 concerning the 'protection and integration of indigenous and other tribal and semi-tribal populations in independent countries' (ILO 1957). The ILO was at this time concerned about the living and working conditions of indigenous and what were called 'tribal' populations. However, its underlying objective was assimilation, arguing that, to improve these conditions, it was necessary to integrate indigenous peoples into mainstream societies. In part because of indigenous rejection of assimilation through active mobilizations around the world, indigenous peoples began attending meetings at the UN and these led its Economic and Social Council to establish in 1982 the Working Group on Indigenous Populations (WGIP). WGIP provided a space for indigenous peoples' representatives to work alongside experts on human rights, thus setting the scene for more concerted advocacy of indigenous rights. Parallel to WGIP, in 1989, the ILO published Convention No. 109, concerning 'indigenous and tribal peoples in independent countries' (ILO 1989). This set an international standard from which indigenous rights would be considered, and established the definition of indigenous peoples as inhabitants of a country or region prior to conquest, colonization or the assertion of state sovereignty. Convention 169 gave new life to Article 27 of the International Covenant on Civil and Political Rights, which had been in force since 1976, stipulating that: 'In those States in which ethnic, religious or linguistic minorities exist, persons belonging to such minorities shall not be denied the right, in community with the other members of their group, to enjoy their own culture, to profess and practise their own religion, or to use their own language.'

From these bases, a number of initiatives were launched to promote international awareness of indigenous human rights, living standards, education, land rights and health. The UN General Assembly proclaimed 1993 the International Year for the World's Indigenous People, 1995–2005 as the first International Decade of the World's Indigenous People and 2005–14 as the second International Decade of the World's Indigenous People.

In 1994 the UN Sub-Commission on the Promotion and Protection of Human Rights adopted the Draft Declaration on the Rights of Indigenous Peoples submitted by WGIP in 1993. The Draft was sent to the Commission on Human Rights, which established a working group to study it alongside indigenous and state representatives. In 1993 the idea of establishing a forum for this was recommended at the World Conference on Human Rights in Vienna. This resulted in the UN Permanent Forum on Indigenous Issues (UNPFII) being established by the UN's Economic and Social Council in 2000, with the first session taking place in 2002 (García-Alix 2003). UNPFII created a space for indigenous representatives, advocacy groups, independent researchers and experts to meet and discuss a whole range of issues that complemented the work carried out at WGIP.

Finally, in 2007 the UN Declaration on the Rights of Indigenous Peoples was adopted by the General Assembly. This was the culmination of years of work by indigenous peoples' organizations at the UN, as well as sustained pressure on states and transnational companies through social and political mobilizations and litigation in national and international courts. Victoria Tauli-Corpuz (2007) recalls the centrality of indigenous involvement in the making of UNDRIP: 'I hail representatives of Indigenous Peoples who patiently exerted extraordinary efforts for more than two decades to draft and negotiate the Declaration. This Declaration has the distinction of being the only Declaration in the UN which was drafted with the rights-holders, themselves, the Indigenous Peoples.'

In addition to participating in international forums and social and political mobilizations, indigenous peoples also developed national and international networks. These provide greater visibility, human and material resources for advocacy and research, and, although some of them are compromised by governmental funding, have built political platforms to deal with states. The names of some of these organizations give a sense of their variety: the Confederación Nacional Indígena de Ecuador (CONAIE), the Asian Indigenous

5.2   Victoria Tauli-Corpuz, Chair of the United Nations Permanent
Forum on Indigenous Issues, addresses the United Nations General
Assembly after the adoption of the Declaration on the Rights of Indigenous
Peoples, at UN Headquarters in New York (13 September 2007).

Source: United Nations

Women's Network (AIWN), the Indigenous Peoples of Africa
Coordinating Committee (IPACC), the First Peoples of the Kalahari,
the International Indian Treaty Council (IITC), the Amerindian
Peoples Association in Guyana, the Innu Council of Nitassinan,
the Mohawk Nation of Kahnawake, the Cordillera Peoples Alliance
in the Philippines (CPA), the International Indigenous Women's
Forum (FIMI: Foro Internacional de Mujeres Indígenas), the Saami
Council, the Organización Nacional Indígena de Colombia (ONIC),
the National Congress of American Indians (NCAI), the Tebtebba
Foundation, the Asociación Interétnica de Desarrollo de la Selva
Peruana (AIDESEP), the International Alliance of Indigenous and
Tribal Peoples of the Tropical Forests and the Asian Indigenous,
Hokkaidō Utari Association and Tribal Peoples Network. These
associations have mobilized human and material resources in a
coordinated way, despite numerous legal, political and economic
obstacles. Explaining the aims of CONAIE, the most important

organization of indigenous peoples in Ecuador, Luis Macas (2003: 195) remarked:

> CONAIE was formed in November 1986 to carry on the struggles of the indigenous peoples' movement in Ecuador, including the fight to recoup our lands and to rescue our language and culture. Above all, it was formed to search for unity among all indigenous nations through these common struggles, where before they had fought for their rights in isolation.

Alongside local indigenous networks and national organizations – like the American Indian Movement (AIM) in the United States, the Assembly of First Nations (AFN) in Canada and the National Congress of Australia's First Peoples – indigenous peoples also established working partnerships with non-indigenous national and international NGOs, such as Survival International, International Work Group for Indigenous Affairs (IWGIA), Minority Rights Group (MRG), Cultural Survival, Conselho Indigenista Missionário (CIMI), the Kalahari Peoples Fund (KPF), Centre for World Indigenous Studies (CWIS), Human Rights Watch, Centro de Investigación y Promoción del Campesinado (CIPCA), Amnesty International, Working Group of Indigenous Minorities in Southern Africa (WIMSA), Amazon Watch, European Network for Indigenous Australian Rights (ENIAR) and Friends of Peoples Close to Nature (FPCN). Through these NGOs, indigenous peoples' organizations can access additional support for educational and advocacy programmes, publications and training. Such organizations are also useful allies in mobilizing public opinion and pressuring governments and transnational companies in defence of indigenous rights. Unofficial channels for the making of human rights claims such as those offered by NGOs are attractive to indigenous groups because they can mount independent pressure on those who formulate human rights standards. But equally important is the fact that NGOs can produce press releases, media reports, studies, films and other materials to draw attention to the many human rights issues at stake and thereby influence governments sensitive to public opinion. However, despite their effective contribution to the protection and advancement of rights, NGOs may still be informed by 'Western, legal, and universalizing ideologies' (Landman 2006: 25).

Alongside the official route to recognition through the international system have been direct actions taken by indigenous peoples to assert their rights and sovereignty. Direct action groups are generally distrustful of liberalism, often seeing it as a means of legitimating colonialism. In 1994, indigenous peoples increased their visibility through the mobilizations that led to the Zapatista uprising and the founding of independent municipalities in defiance of Mexico. The Zapatistas currently control about a third of the province of Chiapas with a support base of a quarter of a million people, 22 per cent of the indigenous population of the territory (Klein 2015: xvii). Neoliberal economic policies represented by NAFTA triggered the mobilization of thousands of indigenous peoples who demanded an end to social exclusion, economic marginalization and discrimination and the implementation of basic rights to health, education, work, gender equality and land, while demanding a wider participation in the political process. The tone and themes of the Zapatistas' six Lacandon manifestos were clear and direct. For example, in the fourth declaration:

The arrogant wish to extinguish a rebellion which they mistakenly believe began in the dawn of 1994. But the rebellion which now has a dark face and an indigenous language was not born today. It spoke before with other languages and in other lands. This rebellion against injustice spoke in many mountains and many histories. It has already spoken in nahuatl, paipai, kiliwa, cucapa, cochimi, kumiai, yuma, seri, chontal, chinanteco, pame, chichimeca, otomi, mazahua, matlatzinca, ocuilteco, zapoteco, solteco, chatino, papabuco, mixteco, cucateco, triqui, amuzzgo, mazateco, chocho, ixcaateco, huave, tlapaneco, totonaca, tepehua, populuca, mixe, zoque, huasteco, lacandon, mayo, chol, tzeltal, tzotzil, tojolabal, mame, teco, ixil, aguacateco, motocintleco, chicomucelteco.
Today, this January 1 of 1996, the Zapatista Army of National Liberation signs this fourth declaration of the Lacandon jungle. We invite all the people of Mexico to subscribe to it. (Hayden 2002: 241–2)

Relying on the use of online media platforms to expand their visibility to global audiences, recent mobilizations on the streets of San Cristobal de Las Casas, Quito, Manila, Lima, Temuco, Manaus, Guatemala City, Nairobi, Sydney, Salt Lake City and Vancouver have been aimed at attracting national and international attention to indigenous claims. The Zapatista uprising, rather than being an isolated event, acted as a pivotal moment for indigenous peoples to globalize their longstanding struggle against colonial violence, territorial displacements, land grabbing, assimilation policies and violations of their human rights. In doing so, the Zapatistas have forged common cause with indigenous political prisoners such as Leonard Peltier in the United States, underpaid and exploited teachers in Mexico and Palestinians seeking freedom from Israeli occupation

(Soto 2015). They have also emphasized indigenous women's rights and have been led by many women. Zapatista women such as Major Ana María, Comandanta Ramona and Comandanta Esther have played military and political roles and have appeared in the media in the trademark ski masks (Klein 2015: xvi).

Both active resistance and formal political engagement led to official legal and bureaucratic changes that modified the colonial relationship between states and indigenous peoples. Table 5.1 provides a general overview of the activities within the UN system and other regional organisms by indigenous peoples, leading to the 2007 Declaration on the Rights of Indigenous Peoples.

United Nations Declaration on the Rights of Indigenous Peoples (2007)

Undoubtedly UNDRIP would not have happened if indigenous peoples had not been engaged in active resistance and became significant international actors. However, despite these achievements on the International Day of the World's Indigenous Peoples in 2014, the UN Special Rapporteur on the rights of indigenous peoples, Victoria Tauli-Corpuz (2014), cautioned:

> Today, the International Day of the World's Indigenous Peoples is a day to celebrate the gains and victories achieved by indigenous peoples in their bid to claim their rights and realize their life plans or development visions. However, for many indigenous peoples in many parts of the world, there is not much to celebrate. Countless violations of their civil, political, economic, environment, social and cultural rights continue on a daily basis. Justice still remains elusive for many of them.

Notwithstanding its nonbinding status and initial opposition of prominent settler colonial states, the Declaration provides a set of human rights standards for the protection and advancement of indigenous rights. It is also a framework from which international specialized agencies such as the UN's Development Program's Policy of Engagement with Indigenous Peoples, the World Bank Operational Policy and Bank Policy on Indigenous Peoples, and the Inter-American Development Bank's Operational Policy on Indigenous Peoples can review and develop indigenous policies that respect the broad rights 'to self-determination and free, prior and informed consent' (UNHRC 2008: 21).

UNDRIP also plays an important role in judicial resolutions on

Table 5.1   Significant moments in indigenous peoples' rights activism in the 20th and 21st centuries

1923	Haudenosaunee Chief Deskaheh travelled to the League of Nations in Geneva to defend their rights in Canada. He was not allowed to speak.
1925	Maori leader T. W. Ratana travels to the League of Nations in Geneva to protest the breaking of the Treaty of Waitangi that was signed between the Maori and New Zealand in 1840. He was not allowed to speak.
1957	The Indigenous and Tribal Populations Convention (ILO)
1969	International Convention on the Elimination of All Forms of Racial Discrimination (ICERD)
1974	The United Nations Economic and Social Council granted consultative status for the first time to a non governmental organization (NGO) of indigenous peoples
1985–1993	UN Working Group on Indigenous Populations (UN WGIP)
1989	International Labour Organization (ILO) Convention No. 169 on Indigenous and Tribal Peoples in Independent Countries
1994	The Zapatista uprising in Chiapas, Mexico
1994	United Nations Draft Declaration on the Rights of Indigenous Peoples (UN WGIP)
1997	OAS Draft American Declaration on the Rights of Indigenous Peoples
1996–2006	United Nations Working Group of the Commission on Human Rights (UN WGDD)
1992	International Year of the World's Indigenous People
1993–2003	First International Decade of the World's Indigenous People
2000	ACHPR Working Group on Indigenous Peoples/ Communities (WGIP)
2005–2014	Second International Decade of the World's Indigenous People
2000	The United Nations Permanent Forum on Indigenous Issues (UNPFII or PFII)
2001	Special Rapporteur on the rights of indigenous peoples
2007	United Nations Declaration on the Rights of Indigenous Peoples

indigenous issues. In fact, just a month after the Declaration was approved in the General Assembly, the Supreme Court of Belize issued the first judgment using UNDRIP, ruling in favour of a Mayan community that claimed property rights over their lands against government denials of such rights *(Aurelio Cal et al. v. Attorney General of Belize*), and the decision was also based on the ILO's Convention No. 169, to which Belize is not a signatory (Korman 2010: 167).

Undoubtedly, UNDRIP represents a significant political achievement. Rodolfo Stavenhagen (2007), the Special Rapporteur on the Rights of Indigenous Peoples in post at the time, summarized its main points:

> The Declaration reaffirms that indigenous peoples, both individually and collectively, enjoy all rights already recognized at the international level, and that the special circumstances of their existence as discriminated peoples and long dispossessed of their ancestral resources, demand particular attention by States and by the international community.
>
> Indigenous peoples' ancestral lands and territories constitute the bases of their collective existence, of their cultures and of their spirituality. The Declaration affirms this close relationship, in the framework of their right, as peoples, to self-determination in the framework of the States in which they live.

UNDRIP comprises 46 articles and covers a comprehensive range of issues that address elements of indigenous dispossession occasioned by colonialism. In emphasizing new specifically indigenous rights, it highlights the ways in which assimilation policies and violence limited the expression and exercise of indigenous peoples' human rights. Although much needs to be done to provide the legal and intellectual arguments to ensure that it is implemented, at a basic level UNDRIP simply holds states to their liberal principles of civil and human rights, including rights to cultural and, therefore, legal pluralism (Echo-Hawk 2013). The Declaration sets out a few guiding principles that hold all the rights together; these are as follows.

Self-determination

The cornerstone of the Declaration is the right to self-determination. As Morgan (2009: 128) explains, 'a conceptualization of self-determination as a territorialised right is of paramount importance to indigenous peoples, whose interests in a secure land base are economic, political, social and cultural'. In relation to these points:

> Indigenous peoples have the right to self-determination. By virtue of that right they freely determine their political status and freely pursue their economic, social and cultural development. (Article 3)

> Indigenous peoples, in exercising their right to self-determination, have the right to autonomy or self-government in matters relating to their

internal and local affairs, as well as ways and means for financing their autonomous functions. (Article 4)

The inclusion of self-determination in the Declaration provoked the initial opposition of many African states, the United States, Australia, New Zealand and Canada, as well as former colonial powers such as the United Kingdom. Their state representatives expressed concerns about the implications of this principle in relation to preserving the territorial integrity of sovereign states and the integrity of unified social, legal and political orders. Engle (2011: 146) points out that these concerns were appeased with the inclusion of Article 46 (1) which states:

> Nothing in this Declaration may be interpreted as implying for any State, people, group or person any right to engage in any activity or to perform any act contrary to the Charter of the United Nations or construed as authorizing or encouraging any action which would dismember or impair, totally or in part, the territorial integrity or political unity of sovereign and independent States.

Engle (2011: 147) further suggests that this concession came at a cost and to a certain extent modified previous indigenous demands for the possibility of external self-determination: 'Yet, something has been lost in the compromise. The declaration seals the deal: external forms of self-determination are off the table for indigenous peoples, and human rights will largely provide the model for economic and political justice for indigenous peoples.' Herein lies one of the fundamental ambiguities of UNDRIP. Indigenous peoples' rights to self-determination are affirmed, but only within the legal apparatuses of the states that have withdrawn these rights in the first place. As Champagne (2013: 11) argues:

> The implementation of UNDRIP with nation-states is one plan for addressing indigenous issues and will represent progress over past historical actions. However, the plan to address indigenous issues within nation-state institutions and governments does not address the full complexities of nation-state and indigenous nation relations. In many ways, UNDRIP treats indigenous peoples either as citizens of nation states or as ethnic minorities with certain collective political, cultural, and economic rights and historical claims.

Individual and collective rights

Bearing these points in mind, another important dimension of the Declaration is the articulation of individual and collective rights. As mentioned earlier, indigenous peoples enjoy all the rights guaranteed by UN declarations and conventions. However, UNDRIP guarantees indigenous peoples rights to self-determination, cultural identity and heritage, lands, territories and resources, and to FPIC in relation to industrial and other projects that affect them, in the fields of education, knowledge and the environment. The basis for these rights is the collective nature of indigenous peoples, and the enjoyment of their rights therefore presupposes a community as a legal entity. In this regard, UNDRIP enunciates the right to maintain and strengthen indigenous peoples' distinct political, legal, economic and cultural institutions (Article 5) and to maintain and develop their institutional structures and their distinctive customs, spirituality, traditions and juridical systems (in accordance with international human rights standards) (Article 34). This includes also the right to control and establish educational systems of their own choosing.

Territories and land

The preservation of their territories, land and resources is integral to the notion of indigenous identity, self-determination and collective rights. Article 26 specifies that:

1 Indigenous peoples have the right to the lands, territories and resources which they have traditionally owned, occupied or otherwise used or acquired.
2 Indigenous peoples have the right to own, use, develop and control the lands, territories and resources that they possess by reason of traditional ownership or other traditional occupation or use, as well as those which they have otherwise acquired.
3 States shall give legal recognition and protection to these lands, territories and resources. Such recognition shall be conducted with due respect to the customs, traditions and land tenure systems of the indigenous peoples concerned.

As discussed in Chapter 2, if there is one issue that epitomizes the antagonistic relationship between indigenous peoples and states, it is the ownership of indigenous territories. Regarding this, Gray (2009) provides an important distinction. While territories are understood as a 'fundamental part of the political organisation of indigenous peoples' (p. 22), land for states is often more an economic than cultural issue, and deals with 'access to resources and territorial control' (p. 24). As we have seen, external access to indigenous lands has weakened their social organizations, and displaced them and confined them to other locations, often away from their traditional territories. By depriving them of the uses of their lands, many groups descended into poverty, and this has given them little alternative other than to petition the very states whose actions had undermined their self-sufficiency in the first place. UNDRIP partially addresses this problem in Article 27, stating that 'states shall implement fair, independent and impartial processes recognizing indigenous laws, traditions and customs to recognize indigenous land claims'. We know, however, that such procedures today often fall far short of any standard of fairness. For example, under the notorious 'certainty' provisions, Canada's Comprehensive Land Claims process legitimates non-native encroachment on indigenous lands, demands that indigenous peoples forfeit their aboriginal rights and facilitates massive transfers of land to the Crown (Samson and Cassell 2013; Samson 2016), while in Australia the Native Title Act of 1993 has resulted in negligible restitution of land and has favoured mining and other commercial interests over indigenous title-holders (Short 2003, 2008). Although there have now been more than 200 Native Title determinations, the rights they confer were intended to accommodate competing non-Aboriginal property interests, giving Aboriginal communities no meaningful rights to control lands falling under their title. Under current land policies in Canada and Australia, the consent of indigenous peoples to the annexation of their lands is severely compromised.

Against these practices, the principle of FPIC included in the Declaration establishes a minimum standard for states when discussing economic development projects that affect indigenous territories and lands:

> Indigenous peoples shall not be forcibly removed from their lands or territories. No relocation shall take place without the free, prior and informed consent of the indigenous peoples concerned and after agreement on just and fair compensation and, where possible, with the option of return. (Article 10)

This is an important principle, which is intended to protect the right of indigenous peoples to live in their traditional territories and to be a meaningful part of any decision making process that could jeopardize this right. Wiessner (2011: 134) emphasizes the connections between culture and land that UNDRIP secures:

> Equally crucial to the effective protection of indigenous peoples' cultures is the safeguarding of their land. Being 'indigenous' means to live

within one's roots. Indigenous peoples, in a popular definition, have thus 'always been in the place where they are'. While this definition may not reflect empirical truth as, historically, a great many migrations of human communities have taken place, the collective consciousness of indigenous peoples, often expressed in creation stories or similar sacred tales of their origin, places them unequivocally and since time immemorial at the location of their physical existence. More importantly, their beliefs make remaining at that place a compelling dictate of faith.

This is a central point to remember. Without indigenous peoples doing indigenous things on their lands, the plurality of human knowledge and distinctive cultural identities will diminish. The retention of land is essential to protect the rights to maintain and modify indigenous land-based ways of life. This is why worldwide efforts are being made to enable people to take advantage of the newly articulated indigenous rights by supporting hunting and gathering practices, restoring animal and fish populations, 'rewilding' landscapes, removing dams, and recovering seeds, plants and indigenous foods (Samson 2013: 197–231).

In practice, the rights of indigenous peoples to the territories needed to maintain their cultures remain central to most of the challenges that they face today, especially in regard to the advance of extractive industries across the world, as we saw in Chapter 4. The ability to challenge, however, is heavily compromised. In addition to contested claims to restitution of territories, lands and resources, Stavenhagen (2008: 266) observes that exercising such rights involves costly and lengthy procedures of demarcation and litigation in national courts. Even if the legal processes were not so arduous, indigenous peoples' marginalization makes them easy prey to the corruption of leaders from resource extraction companies with big budgets (Whitmore 2012: 17; Veltmeyer and Petras 2014: 43). More problematic is that climate change is increasingly making the exercise of rights to lands and seas meaningless because the unpredictable weather patterns, deforestation, desertification, flooding and species extinctions are making traditional uses of these territories difficult or impossible (Wright 2014: 249–52).

Rights to culture

The right to cultural identity presents a rebuke to many of the foundational liberal narratives of states with indigenous populations. The Declaration guarantees indigenous peoples' right 'to practise and revitalize their cultural traditions and customs' (Article 11). From this springs the right to their distinct heritage, language and education, and the repatriation of human remains and intellectual property. Article 12 includes the protection of indigenous spiritual and religious traditions, while Article 13 protects languages, oral traditions, philosophies and literatures, and Article 24 does the same for indigenous medicines and health systems.

The aim of these Articles is to give rights to enjoy indigenous cultures and, in doing so, validate these as being vital to the corpus of human knowledge. Other articulations of international standards strengthen these aims of UNDRIP. For example, the UN report on the *State of the World's Indigenous Peoples* (UN DESA 2009: 64) stresses these connections:

> Indigenous traditional knowledge refers to the complex bodies and systems of knowledge, know-how, practices and representations maintained and developed by indigenous peoples around the world, drawing on a wealth of experience and interaction with the natural environment and transmitted orally from one generation to the next.

Although now incorporating some non-indigenous technologies and ideas, indigenous environmental knowledge continues to be preserved and transmitted and is a valuable source of understanding general human relationships to our planet. According to UNESCO's *Convention for the Safeguarding of the Intangible Cultural Heritage* (2003: Art. 2.1):

> intangible cultural heritage, transmitted from generation to generation, is constantly recreated by communities and groups in response to their environment, their interaction with nature and their history, and provides them with a sense of identity and continuity, thus promoting respect for cultural diversity and human creativity.

While the UN has sought to ensure the perpetuation of most aspects of indigenous cultures, controversy arose regarding the protection and possible recognition of indigenous laws, especially in Article 27. Arguably, laws are cultural products and the protection of these is of the same order as the protection of indigenous languages and medicines. However, the recognition of indigenous laws introduces parallel and possibly contradictory legal arrangements to those of the state. Believing the validity of their own legal systems to be unquestionable, the settler colonial states that voted against UNDRIP were particularly opposed to both indigenous laws and the more culturally appropriate, collective rights (despite the fact that in essence business corporations have collective rights).

Indigenous women's rights

In preserving and transmitting cultural heritage, the role of women has been particularly salient. For example, in the Lima Declaration (World Conference of Indigenous Women 2013: 2), the key contribution of women was emphasized:

> we affirm that Indigenous women have knowledge, wisdom, and practical experience, which has sustained human societies over generations. We, as mothers, life givers, culture bearers, and economic providers, nurture the linkages across generations and are the active sources of continuity and positive change.

In part because of the effects of the colonial displacing of indigenous women from the more elevated social statuses they often held compared to European women, UNDRIP specifically enunciates indigenous women's rights. They are contained in Article 22:

1 Particular attention shall be paid to the rights and special needs of indigenous elders, women, youth, children and persons with disabilities in the implementation of this Declaration.
2 States shall take measures, in conjunction with indigenous peoples, to ensure that indigenous women and children enjoy the full protection and guarantees against all forms of violence and discrimination.

Although this article is generic, it provides a platform to elaborate on indigenous women's rights and reflects an increased awareness of the need to introduce a gender perspective on rights. A number of expert meetings on the subject have taken place within the UNPFII and in different regions of the world. Three main themes stand out in these discussions: (1) indigenous women's rights have to be understood in the context of colonialism; (2) the importance of the recognition and protection of sexual and reproductive health rights; and (3) protection against any form of violence.

Indigenous women's representatives have articulated their rights as intertwined with their collective rights as indigenous peoples. Therefore, the demands of self-determination, territorial and land rights, and cultural identity are recognized in UNDRIP to form a basis for indigenous women's rights. This recognition builds on independent activism by indigenous women and feminist scholarship. For example, FIMI (2006: 7) coordinates indigenous women leaders representing diverse constituencies across the world: 'For Indigenous Peoples and Indigenous women, exercising our rights – both as Indigenous Peoples and as women – depends on securing legal recognition of our collective ancestral territories.' The representative here is arguing that indigenous women's rights and land rights are inseparable and echoes work done by scholars such as Andrea Smith (2005) that situate sexual violence as central to colonialism. Displacement, land confiscation and relocation often involved sexual violence, while at the same time transforming gender relations that created the conditions for internal violence against indigenous women to arise.

> For Indigenous women, the systematic violation of their collective rights as Indigenous People is the single greatest risk factor for gender-based violence – including violence perpetrated within their communities. (FIMI 2006: 7)

> For Indigenous women, gender-based violence is shaped not only by gender discrimination within Indigenous and non-Indigenous arenas, but by a context of ongoing colonization and militarism; racism and social exclusion; and poverty-inducing economic and 'development' policies. (FIMI 2006: 8)

Sexual and reproductive health rights have become prominent in a number of international meetings on indigenous women's rights. For example, the International Expert Group Meeting on Sexual and Reproductive Health (UNPFII 2014) provides a detailed description of the challenges that indigenous women have to face in relation to sexual and reproductive rights, not only in relation to the state but also within their communities. It focuses on discriminatory practices, the need to improve access to health care services and the implementation of intercultural programmes that integrate women's cultural identity as an essential part of health care. 'Violence against indigenous women and girls, discrimination against indigenous women, high rates of maternal mortality, poor access to health services, especially reproductive health services, still remain as major problems for indigenous women (Tauli-Corpuz 2014).

The articulation of indigenous women's rights is applicable to combatting the eugenic policies of sterilization against indigenous women which were implemented in the recent past in many countries, including the United States (Lawrence 2000), Mexico (Smith-Oka 2009: 2075) and Peru (Boesten 2007: 3):

Structural determinants, such as the ongoing effects of the colonization, occupation and militarization of indigenous peoples' territories, and the persistence of hegemonic views that continue to regard indigenous cultures as inferior, were also cited to explain the gaps between indigenous peoples and the non-indigenous population in the realization of sexual and reproductive health and rights. (UNPFII 2014, No. 15)

The discussion of indigenous women's rights, and in particular the violence that they experienced as women has also been a matter of concern in different countries. The interagency study *Breaking the Silence on Violence against Indigenous Girls, Adolescents and Young Women* (UNICEF et al. 2013) provides a thorough analysis of the challenges that indigenous women experience globally. Again, it starts by observing that indigenous women's rights are connected with their rights as indigenous peoples:

Violence against indigenous girls and women cannot be separated from the wider contexts of discrimination and exclusion to which indigenous peoples as a whole are often exposed in social, economic, cultural and political life. Challenges – such as land dispossession, conflict, insecurity, displacement, low rates of birth registration, limited access to culturally appropriate education and health services (including sexual and reproductive health), the lack of access to justice and other essential services, including social services – create conditions affecting their development, human security and the exercise of their human rights. (UNICEF et al. 2013: 3–4)

The study also highlights the violence experienced by indigenous women within indigenous communities:

Indigenous girls and women are also at risk of violence in communities where intra-communal and inter-communal conflicts have arisen, as well as in those communities that conform to deeply rooted patriarchal systems and practices that relegate women and girls to subordinate roles and positions in society. (2013: 4)

Other reports have documented the violence experienced by indigenous women in specific countries. Amnesty International's *Maze of Injustice: The Failure to Protect Indigenous Women from Violence in the USA* (2007: 9) provides a scathing assessment of the context of violence and impunity that engulfs indigenous women's experiences:

Overall, Amnesty International's findings indicate that many American Indian and Alaska Native victims of sexual violence find access to legal redress, adequate medical attention and reparations difficult, if not impossible. Impunity for perpetrators and indifference towards survivors contribute to a climate where sexual violence is seen as normal and inescapable rather than criminal, and where women do not seek justice because they know they will be met with inaction.

According to a review of research by the Indian Law Resource Center and interviews of survivors of gender-based violence in the US:

One in three Native women will be raped in their lifetime, and three in five will be physically assaulted. Native women are more than twice as likely to be stalked than other women and, even worse, Native women are being murdered at a rate ten times the national average. Due to under-reporting, the actual numbers are almost certainly higher. While data on violence against Native girls is sorely lacking, a recent national survey found violence against Native girls may be disproportionately high as well. (Indian Law Resource Center 2010)

One of the key demands in this regard by Native American leaders was to allow Tribal Courts to prosecute non-Native offenders for violence against Native American women committed in tribal lands. In 2013 the Obama administration reauthorized the Violence Against Women Act (VAWA) of 1994 and extended the jurisdiction of Tribal Courts to non-Native offenders.

A longstanding tragedy over the victimization and disappearances of large numbers of Aboriginal women has also occurred across Canada. In 2004, Amnesty International published *Stolen Sisters: Discrimination and Violence against Indigenous Women in Canada*, which examines the factors that have contributed to the high levels of violence experienced by indigenous girls and women. It stresses that these factors are not isolated but longstanding patterns. The 2013 Human Rights Watch report, *Those Who Take Us Away*, exposed the failure of the criminal justice system and the culpability of the police in British Columbia in not dealing with the numerous murders and disappearance of indigenous women:

For many indigenous women and girls interviewed for this report, abuses and other indignities visited on them by the police have come to define their relationship with law enforcement. At times the physical abuse was accompanied by verbal racist or sexist abuse. Concerns about police harassment led some women – including respected community leaders – to limit their time in public places where they might come into contact with officers. (HRW 2013b: 8)

The courts

If the UN has been the most important space for the advancement of indigenous rights, it has been the international and national judicial system where the concrete battles for their rights have been taking place. Indigenous peoples are no strangers to the use of the courts in settler societies. For example, in colonial Spanish America indigenous peoples often appealed to Spanish judicial institutions to denounce abuses and land usurpation by settlers and protest tax increases. Native Americans in the United States also used the judicial system in order to challenge federal policies and the lack of enforcement of policies protecting native peoples' rights. Similarly, in Canada numerous Aboriginal groups have had their complaints about the failure of the state to recognize underlying Aboriginal title taken all the way to the Supreme Court. Indigenous peoples continue to challenge states in national and international judicial forums around the world. Some national courts are gradually adopting human rights frameworks when dealing with indigenous claims. In particular, the jurisprudence of the Inter-American Court of Human Rights has been generally favourable in protecting the collective property rights of indigenous peoples (see Johansen 1998; Pasqualucci 2006, 2009; Contreras-Garduño and Rombouts 2010; CIDH 2010). Table 5.2 highlights selected national and regional rulings in favour of indigenous peoples.

The sheer volume of court cases and human rights reports dealing with indigenous issues is creating a substantial legal corpus on the promotion and protection of indigenous peoples' rights (see Gigoux and Samson 2016: 280–2). Similar patterns emerge from these rulings: (1) indigenous peoples' collective rights over their lands and resources are ignored and infringed by the state and third parties such as extractive industries and conservation projects; (2) indigenous peoples present petitions and libels against the states for not protecting their land rights; (3) the trials create a space for negotiating rights and discussing indigenous identities under legal and cultural frameworks; (4) the international instruments that protect indigenous collective rights provide a supranational legal framework for human rights commissions and national courts when dealing with these cases; (5) the states are mandated to recognize and protect indigenous collective land rights, provide redress for the communities and guarantee the implementation of FPIC for any project affecting indigenous lands. Since its inception, UNDRIP has been invoked as a source of legal authority in court cases that have instructed states to

Table 5.2 Selected court cases involving indigenous peoples' rights

Year	Country	Indigenous peoples	Case	Court
1992	Australia	Meriam People	*Mabo v. Queensland (No. 2)*	High Court of Australia
1997	Canada	Gitxsan and Wet'suwet'en Nations	*Delgamuukw v. British Columbia*	Supreme Court of Canada
1997	Japan	Ainu	*Kayano et al. v. Hokkaidō Expropriation Committee* (The Nibutani Dam Decision)	Sapporo District Court
2001	Nicaragua	Awas Tingni	*Mayagna (Sumo) Community Awas Tingni v. Nicaragua*	Inter-American Court of Human Rights
2002	Malaysia	Orang Asli	*Sagong Tasi v. Selangor State Government*	Federal Court, Malaysia
2002	United States	Western Shoshone	*Mary and Carrie Dann vs United States*	Inter-American Court of Human Rights
2005	Paraguay	Yakye Axa	*Yakye Axa v. Paraguay*	Inter-American Court of Human Rights
2006	Paraguay	Sawhoyamaxa indigenous community	*Sawhoyamaxa v. the State of Paraguay*	Inter-American Court of Human Rights

Year	Country	Group	Case	Court
2007	Belize	Maya	*Aurelio Cal et al. v. Attorney General of Belize*	Supreme Court of Belize
2010	Kenya	Endorois	*Centre for Minority Rights Development (Kenya) and Minority Rights Group International on behalf of Endorois Welfare Council v. Kenya*	African Commission on Human and Peoples' Rights
2012	Ecuador	Sarayaku	*Sarayaku v. Ecuador*	Inter-American Court of Human Rights
2012	Indonesia	Indonesia's national indigenous peoples' organization, AMAN	Review of Law No. 41 Year 1999 concerning Forestry against the 1945 Constitution of the State of the Republic of Indonesia	The Constitutional Court of the Republic of Indonesia
2013	Canada	Métis	*Daniels vs. Canada*	Federal Court of Canada
2013	Indonesia	The Indigenous People's Alliance of the Archipelago	Decision No. 35/PUU-X/2012 on the judicial review of Law No. 41 Year 1999 on Forestry	The Constitutional Court of Indonesia
2014	Guatemala	Maya	*Mayan Council of Sipacapa v. the State of Guatemala*	Appeal Court Guatemala City, Guatemala
2015	Belize	Maya	*Maya of Toledo v. State of Belize*	Caribbean Court of Justice, Belize City, Belize
2016	Suriname	Kaliña and Lokono	*Kaliña and Lokono Peoples v. Suriname*	Inter-American Court of Human Rights

alter their policies. Most recently, in 2016, the Inter-American Court of Human Rights found Suriname to be in violation of numerous human rights standards in 'its failure to recognize and guarantee the legal personality and territorial rights of the Kaliña and Lokono, as well as active violations of those and other rights in connection with bauxite mining, grants of individual titles to non-indigenous persons and both the existence of and restrictions imposed in two nature reserves' (Forest Peoples Programme 2016). According to the Forest Peoples Programme, this case demonstrates the power of UNDRIP to shape existing state laws.

However, effective implementation of these rulings depends on the political and institutional framework of the state. For example, in the *Sawhoyamaxa v. the State of Paraguay* case, the IACHR ruled in 2006 that the Paraguayan state had to return 14,000 hectares of traditional lands to the Enxet peoples, compensate them and support them with a development fund. It was only in 2014 that the Paraguayan government passed a law to expropriate ranchers who were, in effect, squatting on indigenous lands. In turn, the ranchers appealed to the Supreme Court in 2015, but their claims were rejected (Tierraviva 2015). Like Paraguay, the US government has also proved reluctant to honour international court rulings. In 2002, the United States was asked to have a judicial hearing on land title and review all law and policy relating to Native American property rights in the IACHR *Dann* case involving the Western Shoshone. The US, however, agreed only to pay compensation, not review property rights, contending that 'general encroachment' is sufficient to invalidate the 1863 treaty guaranteeing Western Shoshone land title. In 2005, the UN Committee on the Elimination of Racial Discrimination (CERD) ruled that this position amounted to racial discrimination (Akhtar 2007; Fishel 2008).

Finally, indigenous peoples in the United States, Canada, Colombia, Bolivia, Venezuela, Panama and Mexico have obtained the right to establish their own courts in order to deal with a number of offences and infringements of their customary laws (Tobin 2014). Although this right is restricted to specific offences, and courts are non-indigenous institutions, nonetheless it allows a limited exercise of self-determination.

The criminal justice system

No discussion of the rights of indigenous peoples should forget the relationships they have within national criminal justice systems.

According to Davies et al. (2009: 8), the criminal justice system (CJS): 'is about society's formal response to crime and is defined more specifically in terms of a series of decisions and actions taken by a number of agencies in response to a specific crime or crime in general'. Four subsystems of criminal justice can be distinguished within the CJS: (1) law enforcement: involving the police and prosecuting agencies; (2) courts; (3) penal system: involving probation, prisons and other agencies that punish and incarcerate and/or seek to monitor, control and reduce offending behaviour; (4) crime prevention.

The main purpose of the CJS is to deliver impartial and prompt justice whenever the law is broken. It presupposes the rule of law within a legitimate democratic system, the existence of independent judicial institutions and due process. However, the legitimacy of the CJS is problematic because it was used everywhere as a means of dispossessing and criminalizing indigenous peoples. For example, one of the fundamental principles protected by law is the right to private property. As we have seen, historically indigenous peoples were not recognized to have any specific rights to their lands unless granted by the state or colonial governments. In settler states, property rights were granted to settlers as they advanced into indigenous territories, making the mere presence of indigenous peoples on their lands a crime of trespass. When indigenous peoples reacted by defending their right to live in their traditional territories in settler states, they were at times repelled by vigilante groups often with the backing of the law. This was particularly the case when there were great riches at stake, as in California after the Gold Rush (Lindsay 2012). Furthermore, when indigenous peoples were relocated to reservations, stations, villages and settlements, the negative social impact on their ways of life led to conditions conducive to criminality such as high rates of poverty, unemployment, psychological depression, health problems, substance abuse, suicide and violence. Native peoples in many countries were frequently incarcerated and this remains the case today.

Second, it cannot be assumed that indigenous peoples and criminal justice personnel such as lawyers and judges share the same commitment to or understanding of basic concepts within the system. Often they do not speak the same language, and it is a rare case that is heard in an indigenous language in any state. A whole host of cultural and conceptual differences around the definition of crime, culpability and guilt are apparent (LaRocque 1997: 78–9). More basic is that many indigenous groups, especially hunters who are committed to what Brody (2001: 297) referred to as 'egalitarian individualism', find the adversarial procedures of the courtroom, and the necessary punishment, sentencing and humiliation of labelled criminals, bizarre and counterproductive (Samson 2003: 318–22).

A comparative analysis of the relationship of the CJS and indigenous peoples in settler colonial societies reveals similar patterns (Cunneen 2013): (1) the statistics show the overrepresentation of indigenous peoples at each stage of the CJS; (2) the access and legal representation of indigenous peoples to the CJS is undermined by issues such as language, geographical distance, cultural difference and poverty; (3) the CJS is informed by institutional racism and discriminatory practices; (4) there is a high level of distrust in law enforcement; (5) indigenous peoples are disproportionately represented as victims of crime compared to non-indigenous peoples; and (6) indigenous peoples have their own customary law and ideas about justice by which they have traditionally dealt with infringement to their community values.

These facts are constantly acknowledged in reports and studies on the relationship of the CJS and indigenous peoples in different countries. The first appointed Aboriginal person as a judge on the Ontario Court of Appeal, Mr. Justice Harry S. LaForme (2005: 15), confirmed discriminatory patterns in Canada's justice system: 'Indeed, over the past 20 years, various commissions of inquiry have confirmed the existence of systemic racism against Aboriginal people at all stages of Canada's criminal justice system.' In Australia, a report published in 2013 (Closing the Gap Clearinghouse 2013: 3) pointed to the overrepresentation of Aboriginals in the Australian CJS. Among the indicators, one out of four incarcerated is Aboriginal; the imprisonment rate is 15 times higher than for non-Aboriginals. It also highlights how the number of Aboriginal prisoners is increasing every year.

In the United States, Native Americans are overrepresented in the CJS. They account for about 1 per cent of the population and for 6 per cent of the prison population; native women account for 9 per cent of the prison population (Walker et al. 2011: 406). The rates of incarceration are also much higher for Native Americans than for whites, although lower than for African Americans. Nielsen (2009: 1) points at the colonial legacies that underlie these statistics:

> Native American involvement in the American criminal justice system is a complex story with its roots deep in colonialism. This issue cannot be understood without recognizing its interrelatedness with other issues facing Native Americans today. Political power and its lack, land and its loss, economic development and its success or lack of success, individual esteem or individual despair – these and other issues must be considered in exploring Native American criminal justice involvement.

6

Culture

It appalls us that the West can desire, extract and claim ownership of our ways of knowing, our imagery, the things we create and produce, and then simultaneously reject the people who created and developed those ideas and seek to deny them further opportunities to be creators of their own culture and own nations.

Smith (2012: 1)

Cultural reaffirmation is a revolutionary act

As Linda Tuhiwai Smith observes, a vast part of the colonial process involves the production of authoritative representations of indigenous peoples. This has generated impetus for the reclamation of knowledge production and representation as evidenced in recent and contemporary indigenous creative activity. From the large Andean and Mesoamerican civilizations to smaller societies of hunter-gatherers, pastoralists and farmers, indigenous peoples have developed different knowledge systems that have shaped complex and unique cultural forms in the visual arts, architecture, orature, literature, science and medicine. These are all part of distinctive cultural systems that reaffirm indigenous identity, community and self-representation in different parts of the world. The fact that indigenous peoples, along with their cultural practices and knowledge, have managed to survive despite the belittling and ignorance of their ideas and practices is remarkable.

In many parts of the world, cultural politics rose to prominence together with demands for the recognition of the rights of disenfranchised groups in the 1960s. Indigenous peoples in the United States formed the American Indian Movement (AIM) as a social forum for active political and cultural engagement (Smith and Warrior 1997; Cobb 2008). According to Nagel (1994: 113), community poverty, the persistence of racial discrimination and opposition to federal Indian policies acted as a catalyst for an 'American Indian ethnic rebirth'. Driven by calls for international sovereignty through the occupations of Alcatraz island in 1969, the BIA head office in 1972 and Wounded Knee in 1973, this new militancy helped shape a more vocal indigenous identity that survives to this day.

The parallel movement in Canada was the Canadian National Indian Brotherhood, which had a huge influence on the affirmation of indigenous culture through education. Their 1972 policy docu- ment 'invited Canadians to learn and share the history, customs, and cultures of Native people. It provided a philosophy, and a set of goals, principles, and directions that emphasized Native culture' (Agbo 2002: 283). In Australia, a similar process took place in the late 1960s, and the Black Power Movement there led to mobiliza- tions in defence of Aborigines' cultural rights. These movements inspired Aboriginal authors to assert Aboriginal rights in their works. As Heiss and Minter (2008: 5) point out: 'With the political agenda focused on land rights and cultural self-determination, Aboriginal literature began to play a leading role in the expression of Aboriginal cultural and political life . . . As new forms of agency were articulated in Aboriginal social and political life, new categories of authorship were explored and invented.'

Indigenous cultural reaffirmation also took place in Japan, where Ainu activism over the building of the Nibutani Dam on Ainu lands in 1997 'served as the turning point in Ainu movements; from that point on people strategically took on a new Ainu identity and changed Ainu policy from assimilation to ethnic independence' (Yamada 2001: 244). Part of this included the establishment of the Nibutani Ainu Cultural Museum in the Nibutani area of Biratori, and further reinforced a sense of ethnic cultural independence. Beyond this, festivals were revived as Ainu started to openly demonstrate their unique and distinct cultural identity. Similarly, the successful Saami political activism over the building of the Alta hydroelectric project and dam became an important affirmation of Saami cultural identity in Norway (Thuen 1995; Sand 2014).

The rise of indigenous cultural politics had two immediate effects. It brought indigenous rights to the forefront of national and, in some cases, international political life and it shaped the way that many non-indigenous scholars and researchers viewed their relationship with indigenous peoples. For example, in 1971 Latin American anthropologists gathering in Barbados for the symposium on 'Inter-ethnic conflict in South America', released a Declaration for the 'Liberation of the Indians'. The Declaration is a call for a militant anthropology that sides with indigenous peoples' quests for liberation:

> The anthropology now required in Latin America is not that which relates to Indians as objects of study, but rather that which perceives the colonial situation and commits itself to the struggle for liberation. In this context we see anthropology providing, on the one hand, the colonized peoples those data and interpretations both about themselves and their colonizers useful for their own fight for freedom and, on the other hand, a redefinition of the distorted image of Indian communities extant in the national society, thereby unmasking its colonial nature with its supportive ideology. (Declaration of Barbados 1971: 7)

In the 1990s indigenous movements became a central point of resistance to the forces of cultural homogenization. Referring to the parallel emergence of black diasporic identity, Hall (1990: 224) argues that cultural identity is a dynamic process of creation based 'not [on] the rediscovery but the production of identity. Not an identity grounded in the archaeology, but in the re-telling of the past.'

Since the 1960s, indigenous peoples have been retelling their own stories in public and private. Regarding the Yakama, Jacob (2013: 12) argues that 'cultural revitalization activists have two interconnected goals: (1) recovering traditional cultural practices, and (2) dismantling oppressive systems that harm our people, land, and culture'. In the words of artist Jimmie Durham (1993: 8), 'the struggle to maintain culture is in itself a revolutionary struggle':

> It is a universal truth that human beings do not exist outside of their culture, their society. A biologically human animal is not fully human without, for example, a language which is cultural/political phenomenon. To speak of an alienated society is to speak of people robbed of their culture, always so that some political system can exploit them. That is what makes culture so important to liberation, and that is why it can never be considered a separate piece of human activity. (1993: 12)

Because much of the endeavour is to recover and re-tell, indigenous cultural revitalization is not exclusively focused on male leadership, youth and novelty, but has become a site of political struggle where the roles of elders and women acquire a prominent position. Smith (2012: 115) points out: 'The cultural and linguistic revitalization movements have tapped into a set of cultural resources that have recentred the roles of indigenous women, of elders and of groups who have been marginalized through various colonial practices'. In contrast to the more individualistic emphasis on achievement in Western culture, indigenous cultural revitalization has been based on the collective and the community: 'Indigenous cultural revitalization efforts depend on intergenerational teaching and learning; it is a form of education that is rarely featured in Western educational systems. Tribal elders privilege oral histories, as opposed to textbooks, as part of the teachings they learned from previous generations of elders' (Jacob 2013: 83).

Vizenor (1994: 5) argues that, against dominant narratives of American Indians and American Indian cultures, indigenous cultural politics becomes a landmark for survival and resistance in which the simulated past represented by colonial ideas ('the absence of the real') is replaced by forms of survival that are inventive and at the same time draw upon indigenous peoples' own stories:

> The postindian warriors hover at last over the ruins of tribal repre-
> sentations and surmount the scriptures of manifest manners with new
> stories; these warriors counter the surveillance and literature of domi-
> nance with their own simulations of survivance. The postindian arises
> from the earlier inventions of the tribe only to contravene the absence
> of the real with theatrical performances; the theatre of tribal conscious-
> ness is the recreation of the real, not the absence of the real in the
> simulations of dominance.

In a different indigenous cultural context, the Mapuche poet David Aniñir Guilitraro conveys Vizenor's notion of survivance (see Wadi 2011):

> It is a half-open view to a world of identity reconstruction in urban
> Mapuche. The political and social context that has occurred in Latin
> American, indigenous people go hand in hand with artistic expression.
> Mapurbe [Mapuche culture in urban areas] poetics is an aesthetic
> concept in tune with the artistic movement in Chile. The revival of a
> culture that modifies to survive, adapting new forms of expression that
> are proposing a cultural and political reflection. A vanguard expres-
> sion of art that has questioned its origin and now identifies itself as
> Mapuche. This state of culture should not propose a contemporary
> form of identification before a culture of domination. Therefore, it is a
> culture that is in constant motion. That's Mapurbe – a poetic concept
> of identity and part of the people's contemporary heritage.

Museums

During the heyday of the Great Land Rush and the advent of more widespread world travel and global scientific exploration, museums found ready supplies of indigenous artefacts. These were presented as expressions of exotic, yet immobile and evolutionarily prior, indigenous cultures. Museums have housed a vast amount of indigenous sacred objects, crafts, archaeological materials, fine art and scientific products. These were obtained (and often stolen) from indigenous peoples by networks of European dealers, ethnographic collectors, curators, explorers and academics (Shelton 2000: 160). Human remains and other products of grave robbing were also brought back to Europe and North America, and contributed to many museum collections. Bouquet (2012) suggests that the purpose of the curated display of indigenous cultures was to 'make difference visible and intelligible' to an audience by adopting a social Darwinist narrative and transmitting colonial worldviews. In Britain, the Pitt Rivers Museum in Oxford and the British and Horniman Museums in London are sites for the display of indigenous and other non-European cultural products. There are many equivalents elsewhere, including the Musée du quai Branly in Paris, the Museum of Civilizations in Ottawa, and the Smithsonian in Washington, DC.

However, more recently, the evolutionary frameworks of interpretation have been silently dropped, and museums have paid more respect to donor communities. In the United States, numerous museums have emerged – such as the Heard Museum in Phoenix, Arizona – that specialize in particular regional Native American groups, or that combine such a focus with exhibitions by indigenous artists more generally. The process of revisiting the representation of indigenous peoples has increasingly been concerned with the design, curatorship, implementation and administration of exhibitions, cultural centres and museums. As Lonetree (2012: 1) argues, 'the efforts today by tribal communities to be involved in developing exhibitions point to the recognition that controlling the representation of their cultures is linked to the larger movements of self-determination and cultural sovereignty'. Prominent venues such as the National Museum of the American Indian in New York and Washington, DC and the Melbourne Museum in Australia illustrate sustained collaborations between the museums and indigenous peoples. These have established new epistemologies in the displays of colonial histories and indigenous peoples' cultures. Indigenous cultural displays are perceived as powerful strategic tools for educating visitors, and providing both commentary on past presentations of indigenous peoples and new forms of self-presentation.

The Mashantucket Pequot peoples have established what is called on their website 'the largest Native American Museum' at their corporate Foxwoods casino in Connecticut. Some of their exhibitions feature displays on the erroneous observations or unethical behaviour of anthropologists and other visitors. A prime example of this elsewhere is the commentary on anthropologist Frank Cushing in the much smaller and noncorporate, but no less significant, museum in Zuñi, New Mexico. Although Cushing helped protect the Pueblo from settlers and the American government, he was made privy to secret information that he published against the wishes of his hosts. On a visit in 2010, Colin Samson observed a plaque under the heading 'Anthropologists' in the Zuñi Pueblo museum that reads: 'These attempts to document and "understand" the Zuñi, however well meaning in their purpose, ultimately represented intrusions into the private world and life of the community.'

However, indigenous cultural centres can also have important ambivalences and shortcomings. For example, Nakamura (2007: 334) observes that Ainu museums in Hokkaidō tend to display traditional Ainu culture as it was lived in the past, while ignoring contemporary political struggles: 'The lack of contemporary Ainu culture from the permanent exhibition is a major problem in the Japanese museum system since it often forms an inappropriate imagination among the Japanese public that the Ainu no longer exists in the contemporary Japanese society.'

Strikingly, the cultural centres in Shiraoi and Nibutani, although representing the rich material and spiritual Ainu cultural traditions, do not display the Ainu's contemporary political struggles. By contrast, the displays of the Hokkaidō Ainu Center in Sapporo and the Ainu Culture Center in Tokyo reveal the history of Ainu resistance while providing educational space for understanding Ainu culture and politics in a contemporary frame. The Ainu example illustrates a tension underlying indigenous cultural centres around the world, as colonial frameworks that conveniently placed them in the past constantly diminish indigenous identity and avoid the political implications for the present.

Another important concern of indigenous communities is recovering cultural heritage contained in museums around the world. The loss of indigenous cultural heritage has, over the last few decades, been tackled by indigenous peoples involved in complex processes of reparation claims through national and international laws (Vrdoljak

2008). The most salient example of this is the repatriation of human remains from European and North American museums. In 2013 the Museum of Medical History at the Charité Hospital in Berlin returned 33 skulls and skeletons to Australian Aboriginal peoples and to members of tribes from the islands of the Torres Straits (Carvajal 2013), yet this represents just a tiny fraction of the Aboriginal remains and artefacts stolen during the colonizing process. Similarly, under the Native American Graves and Repatriation Act of 1990, thousands of human remains, funerary objects and objects of cultural patrimony have been returned to Native Americans. Yet, as of 2010, only about 27 per cent of the confiscated Native American objects had been returned (Nash and Colwell-Chanthaphonh 2010: 99).

Elsewhere, the Rapa Nui peoples of Easter Island are requesting the restitution of the wooden tablet engraved with the Rongo Rongo inscription and the Hoa Hakananai'a Moai held in the British Museum after being taken to England by sailors on HMS *Topaze* in 1868. Augmenting the problems of repatriating indigenous possessions is the fact that chemicals used over decades while objects were on display or in storage have contaminated many objects. Additionally, the legal processes involved are often expensive, bureaucratic, time-consuming and involve long-distance international travel.

More positively, a number of initiatives have emerged that go beyond museums and create new spaces for the articulation of cultural identities. Champagne (1999: 9) highlights how tribal identities have been preserved in US urban spaces such as community centres, university American Indian Studies departments and powwows. A number of North American university programmes and international NGOs contribute to these cultural projects. For example, the US-based Vanishing Cultures Project (VCP) has a mission to document, support, fundraise for and protect indigenous cultures under threat from land grabbing, extractive industry and assimilation policies. VCP engages with indigenous communities that face an immediate danger of cultural change, like the Loba of Upper Mustang in Nepal, the Nomadic Herders from Mongolia and the Xikrin-Kayapó of the Brazilian Amazon. Cultural representation can therefore be a political act of defiance, affirming self-determination.

Education and endangered languages

A central theme of cultural revitalization is the promotion of indigenous languages. This comes in response to a wider global process that is leading to the rapid extinction of many languages. If linguistic anthropologists such as Daniel Nettle (1999: 113) are correct in their projections that at least 100,000 speakers are needed for a language to survive 'the cultural-economic juggernauts', almost 84 per cent of the world's languages will soon die out.

Because language is more than a mode of communication, but also conveys fundamental cosmological assumptions about the world, its loss means the parallel dissolution of ways of thinking. For example, Brody (2001) shows that the Inuit language conveys modesty about oneself and one's achievements, including strictures against boasting and putting oneself above others. The vocabularies of Inuktitut are therefore important to a more global human sense of humility and modesty as well as the stability of Inuit society. Similarly, more nuanced distinctions are made in native languages about the natural world and the person. When statements of fact are made, the languages often contain more precision about how the fact was arrived at – by perception, vicariously, by evidence of a specific nature. They may also encode communication about the perceptual status of the speaker, and their relation to another person (Adams 1995: 140; Nettle and Romaine 2000: 60). These differences mean that indigenous languages provide additional information about how knowledge is acquired and what knowledge consists of, thus breaking out of the commonly held Western notion that there is a singular scientific or empirical truth.

In view of many similar considerations, some cultural revitalization processes embrace the fundamental right to speak and learn native languages, and these have been central to indigenous cultural and political struggles, including collaborations between indigenous communities, schools and universities (McCarty et al. 1997). In this regard, many indigenous communities are making efforts to rescue and strengthen their languages. As Hobson et al. (2010: xxvi) argue:

> Language revitalisation is underpinned more fundamentally by notions of cultural sovereignty – Indigenous people asserting their ownership and pride in their heritage – past, present and future. To move from being an act of colonial resistance, to genuine acceptance of the value of Indigenous languages and cultures in Australian society more broadly, the legitimacy of language work can no longer be in question.

Therefore cultural revitalization includes strengthening cultural identity not only in terms of content, but also in relation to community involvement in the design, implementation and assessment of educational policies affecting indigenous communities. A cornerstone of these demands is the inclusion of indigenous teachers and indigenous languages in the educational process. Aikman (1997: 81) points out that this process implies an active participation as citizens in support of their rights, something that is enshrined in Article 14 of UNDRIP as rights to establish and control indigenous educational systems, and for indigenous children to be taught about their own culture and in their own language. A direct consequence of these convictions has been the demand for the implementation of intercultural education in schools with indigenous children.

This process has been particularly popular in Latin America. In Brazil, for example, a number of initiatives have been implemented in order to fortify intercultural education for indigenous peoples (Hauanna Cassula and Mendonça Bernardino 2012). Other formal efforts to incorporate indigenous and local knowledge in classroom settings have been made in colleges and universities across the world. An accord to bring indigenous knowledge into Canadian university classrooms was signed in Montreal in 2010 (Church 2010). Whatever their character, indigenous educational projects undoubtedly enlarge and diversify the predominantly European base of educational systems, and this extends beyond pure academic content into realms of cosmology. If education was a means of colonial control, now it may become a means of self-determination and assist with the enlightenment of non-indigenous populations.

Performance arts, film and media

In 1987, at the Museum of Man in San Diego, the artist James Luna presented his performance *The Artifact Piece*. Luna, a Pooyukitchum (Luiseño) and Mexican American lay flat on his back for hours inside a sand-box vitrine covered only by a plain cloth. Surrounded by American Indian artefacts, he also displayed a number of cultural icons, memorabilia and personal effects that defined his life on the reservation. As Luna (2004) explains, his performance was a challenge to colonial epistemologies:

> that questioned American Indian presentation in museums-presentation that further stereotype, denied contemporary society and one that did not enable a Indian viewpoint. The exhibit through 'contemporary artifacts' of a Luiseño man, showed the similarities and differences in the cultures we live, and putting myself on view brought new meaning to 'artifact'.

Luna represents indigenous cultures in a contemporary frame where the visitor and the Native American share a complex but common time and space. In his later performance, *Take a Picture with a Real Indian*, which took place in several countries in the 1990s and 2000s, Luna continues to parody stereotypes by interacting with the audience wearing traditional clothes and surrounded by three gigantic photographs of himself dressed in attire that evokes images of the traditional and the contemporary. He invites spectators to come forward and be photographed with him. In doing so, he provokes the audience to confront their own perceptions of indigenous identity. The performance poses questions about what Indians are to the audience, and also to the performer. In discussing his work as a whole, Luna (1991: 46–7) remarked:

> In the United States, we Indians have been forced, by various means, to live up to the ideals of what 'being an Indian' is to the general public; in art, it means the work 'looked Indian', and that look was controlled by the market. If the market said that it (my work) did not look 'Indian', then it did not sell. If it did not sell, then I wasn't Indian.
>
> It is my feeling that artwork in the medias of performance and installation offers an opportunity like no other for Indian people to express themselves in traditional art forms of ceremony, dance, oral traditions and contemporary thought without compromise. Within these (nontraditional) spaces, one can use a variety of media, such as found/made objects, sounds, video and slides so that there is no limit to how and what is expressed.

James Luna is not unique in using performance and installation as a way of addressing indigenous issues. Others, such as Shelley Niro, a Six Nations artist who, like Luna, has exhibited at the Venice Biennale and remains living in her own community, also uses her body in her art. In '500 Year Itch', for example, she re-enacts the famous scene of Marilyn Monroe with her dress blown up to comment on the 500 years of colonization. Marcus Amerman, a Choctaw, has created a number of visual representations of identity, such as beadwork, fashion, photography, glass and painting. His collection of photographs set against turn of the twentieth century photographs taken by Edward Curtis plays with established views on American Indian cultures. Reflecting on his work Amerman argues: 'To me, a stereotype is like a prison cell. It's a place society puts you in to keep you contained. Well, I'm not waiting for anyone to parole me, I've got a tunnel going, I've got files being smuggled to me in cakes, and I have friends who'll ram a truck through the prison wall' (The Magazine 2008).

In Australia a new generation of Aboriginal artists has embraced questions of identity, racism and the issues about Australia's history exposed by the *Stolen Generation Report*. Jimmy Chi's musical, *Bran Nue Dae* (1991), is a romantic story set against the social issues confronting Aboriginal children in boarding schools and the racial tensions in the wider society. Written and mostly acted by Aboriginal people it reveals an alternative to the dominant state narrative of Australia's past. In a similar vein, the Yirra Yaakin Theatre Company based in Perth has opened up the possibility for young Aboriginal actors to share their stories with Aboriginal and non-Aboriginal audiences. In Canada, the play *Chocolate Woman Dreams the Milky Way* (2011), by playwright and actor Monique Mojica, combines indigenous language, healing, beliefs and indigenous identity in a powerful performance. Similarly, artist Thomson Highway blends Cree and several other languages in musicals, plays and other works, including children's books which retell and reinvent Cree tales in contemporary contexts.

As Gilbert and Tompkins argue (1996: 205), 'the post-colonial stage offers opportunities to recuperate the colonised subject's body'. Although 'postcolonial' is an inappropriate description, it is possible to agree with the authors that the theatre or stage can help make visible to indigenous and non-indigenous audiences the struggles for identity and rights. Here, Gilbert's (1994: 106) distinctions about the functions of the body in performance are insightful: 'As a physical body it is a sign of otherness that resists appropriation through its presence on the stage. As a social body it becomes a site of contestation showing the historical inscriptions of indigenous and colonizer cultures and their competing ideologies.'

Indigenous film and media

Arguably, one of the most salient features of contemporary processes of indigenous revitalization is the convergence of the politics of culture and media technology. This has led to the creation and production of indigenous documentary and feature films made by both non-indigenous and indigenous filmmakers and producers. Although such films are produced in different locations, it is possible to discern common themes: the centrality of oral history and collective memory; the active participation of the indigenous communities involved; the relevance of everyday lives; social issues that affect the communities, like substance abuse, violence, poverty, migration, discrimination and environmental degradation; and the social mobilization for

human rights. Ginsburg (2008: 139) highlights how these productions are clearly connected to indigenous peoples' struggles for rights:

> The cultural activists creating these new kinds of cultural forms have
> turned to them as a means of revivifying relationships to their lands,
> local languages, traditions and histories and articulating community
> concerns. They also see the media as a means of furthering social and
> political transformations by inserting their own stories into national
> narratives as part of ongoing struggles for Aboriginal recognition and
> self-determination.

Ginsburg (2008: 140) also discusses how indigenous productions
represent efforts to counter monopolies of power on the production
and distribution of knowledge by providing alternative indigenous
interpretations of history and identity:

> Indigenous digital media have raised important questions about the
> politics and circulation of knowledge at a number of levels; within com-
> munities this may be about who has access to and understanding of
> media technologies, and who has the right to know, tell, and circulate
> certain stories and images. Within nation-states, the media are linked
> to larger battles over cultural citizenship, racism, sovereignty, and
> land rights, as well as struggles over funding, air space and satellites,
> networks of broadcasting and distribution, and digital broadband, that
> may or not be available to indigenous work.

At a fundamental level, indigenous films and videos have a double
aim. On the one hand, they represent an opportunity to educate
non-indigenous audiences on indigenous ways of life, identities and
struggles. But, such media also attempt to educate and inspire indigenous communities, and in particular youth, on their ways of life,
histories and collective identities, countering the images produced in
the dominant media outlets. We present below a small sampling of
the recent offerings of indigenous media and film.

A prominent example of the efforts of indigenous peoples to create
'visual sovereignty' is the work of numerous Inuit who have adapted
photographic and cinematic technologies to represent themselves and
creatively tell stories that have wider significance (Norman 2014).
The Inuit were the subjects of the first documentary drama in Robert
Flaherty's silent movie *Nanook of the North* in 1922. While the popu-
larity of Flaherty's film ensured that external images of the 'carefree
Eskimo' would survive long after its release, Inuit have produced
different narratives, such as those by Isuma Igloolik Productions,

an independent and community-based company that promotes the making of films in Inuktitut, as well as an online network as a platform for these.

Founded in 1990 by Zacharias Kunuk and Norman Cohn, *Isuma* became internationally known through Kunuk's 2001 film *Atanarjuat: The Fast Runner*. The film initially suffered setbacks because Canadian funders recognized it *only* as an Aboriginal film (Ginsburg 2003), but showing its broad appeal it went on to win the Caméra d'Or award at the Cannes Film Festival. It is based on an Inuit legend that reflects the importance of community values like solidarity, cooperation and humility, while imparting a complex (and, arguably, anticolonial) moral tale about the fatal consequences of individualism and conflict. After the critical and box office success of *Atanarjuat*, the 2008 launch of Isuma TV and its web platform not only consolidated Inuit audiovisual enterprises, but created a base for indigenous productions from all over the world, dealing with issues like land claims, environmental degradation, youth alienation and community involvement.

Similarly, in Australia the Central Australian Aboriginal Media Association (CAAMA) has provided a platform for Aboriginal musical, cultural and audiovisual productions since its early beginnings in 1980. More recently, in 2013 the creation of Obsidiana TV has also provided an online platform for indigenous productions in Latin America.

In Australia, there is a long tradition of Aboriginal audiovisual productions (McNiven 2015). One of the most internationally acclaimed recent feature films is *Samson and Delilah* (2009) by Warwick Thornton. The film depicts the harsh life of an Aboriginal community near Alice Springs through the romantic story of a young Aboriginal couple. The film highlights Aboriginal poverty, marginality, substance abuse, violence and homelessness in the Northern Territory. The love story is set against the backdrop of a racially segregated Australia and the struggles of Aboriginal youth to develop their lives and identities in the context of demoralizing living conditions. A subtle irony, sense of humour and beauty provide a hopeful cornerstone to a bleak and challenging environment. Nonetheless, the film provides a useful insight into contemporary Aboriginal lives in Australia. Dramas like *Atanarjuat* and *Samson and Delilah* are expensive and demanding to make, but nevertheless, 'indigenous dramatic features have gained a lot of ground in the last decade, going from a scattered handful to a dozen or so a year' (Pearson and Knabe 2015: 14).

Indigenous documentary films are far more numerous than feature films and have also multiplied in recent decades. A few examples illustrate their diversity. *Miss Navajo* by Billy Luther (2007) follows the journey of a young Diné woman as she participates in a Navajo beauty pageant. The film highlights the issue of tribal identity and the threats of cultural assimilation as it is negotiated within the form of a mainstream beauty pageant contest. McCarty (2002: 189) explains that while *Miss Navajo* is not understood as a traditional event, it nevertheless fulfils a quest for Diné identity among the youth because it 'represents a new kind of language and culture'. The contest moves away from the objectification of women's bodies through male heterosexual conceptions of physical appearance to a contest about cultural identity and indigenous pride. Navajo contestants must go through a demanding process where they have to prove their knowledge of the Diné language and show their abilities in performing tasks in the community like making crafts, teaching, cooking and spiritual duties. The film presents a journey of reconnection between the young Navajo women and their cultural heritage. House (2005: 33) points out 'the use of alteric discourse and narratives to develop and champion the image of distinctive and authentic Navajo-ness, and the Navajo-ization of Navajo institutions so that they are sites for both the creation and practice of Navajo-ness (Navajo culture and Navajo language).'

Others have more explicitly made documentaries to draw attention to human rights violations. In Canada, Alanis Obomsawim's series of films about the 'Oka Crisis' in 1990 served as a commentary on the Canadian military intervention to stop indigenous protesters from occupying sacred Mohawk lands sold by the non-indigenous Town Council for a golf course (Pearson and Knabe 2015: 7–8). Obomsawim's films contest the Canadian state narrative of the 'crisis' as one principally about law and order and not indigenous rights. Some non-indigenous filmmakers have worked in concert with indigenous artists and communities to add to these counter-narratives. One example is German filmmaker Sarah Sandring, whose collaborations with the Innu community of Natuashish led to *Nutshimit* (2009), which documents the contemporary land-based transmission of Innu knowledge between grandmothers and their grandchildren, and *Nutak* (2013), which explores Innu elders' memories of the forgotten history of attempted relocation of Innu far from their homelands in 1948.

In Argentina, *Los Coihues: Escondidos al Oeste de Pichi Leufu* (2012) is a documentary by Natalia Cano that portrays the impact of coloni-

6.1 Poster for 2012 film 'Nutshimit', a collaboration between the Mushuau Innu community of Natuashish, Labrador, Canada and filmmaker Sarah Sandring. The film explores the cultural continuity of the Innu and the inter-generational transmission of land-based knowledge.

Source: Sarah Sandring

zation over a Mapuche community. Through a number of interviews, Cano rescues the collective memory of forced displacement by the national army from Mapuche territories. Elders' testimonies provide the structure and the content to this production. The images of the landscape and the economic poverty of the community are illustrated by the accounts of dispossession, discrimination and marginalization. These all powerfully defy sanitized versions of official Argentine national history that highlight valiant European settlers.

Other recent successes include *Sachata Kishpichik Mani* (2003) by the Kichwa director Eriberto Gualinga, which won the 2004 Anaconda Prize for Indigenous Video. It highlights how extractive industries threaten indigenous communities around the world. The documentary shows the resistance to a project sponsored by the state and carried out by a transnational company that seeks to extract oil from indigenous territories. It underlines the unequal and unjust struggle that many indigenous communities confront as transnational companies and national governments, all too keen to attract foreign investment, target their lands. In particular, the role of women is highlighted as they take leadership positions in defending the community. The interaction between the environment, indigenous rights, resistance and global interests provides this film with a truly global and contemporary outlook.

In a different register, *Dulce Convivencia* (Sweet Gathering) by Filoteo Martínez (2004) describes the process of the production of *panela* (brown sugar) in San Miguel Quetzaltepec, a small Mixe village located in Oaxaca in southwest Mexico. The rich ecosystem of the mountainous surroundings provides the setting for the daily interaction of the indigenous community as they share different tasks associated with the small-scale production of *panela*. The subtle use of the camera allows for silence and time to be central to the story in what is an intimate documentary. *Dulce Convivencia* reveals a simple yet complex community life, where solidarity, work and friendship play significant roles in defining social bonds. The documentary brings to light the life of an indigenous community that is similar to many, but it also acts as a memory of collective life and traditions for both indigenous and non-indigenous audiences.

In Africa, the struggles for indigenous peoples' rights to preserve their cultural identity, territories and resources has led to an increasing number of collaborative films and documentaries on these issues. The participatory video *Maasai Voices on Climate Change* (2011) is the outcome of US and Danish university collaborations with a number of Maasai people who were trained in using video cameras to document their everyday lives. The short video was shot and edited by Maasai participants and uncovers a number of changes and challenges, such as access to the land, the impact of the tourist industry on water sources for their cattle, land demarcation and drought. The interviews are intimate and revealing, while at the same time filming of the landscape and living conditions provides a useful contemporary framework to their accounts. One of the authors, Sasine ole Neboo, explains the importance of the project: 'The movie we are making is very important for us and the community. It gives a comparison between the past and the present. Long ago, you could see that the Talek River was really a river. Now, it's not a river anymore' (Roque de Pinho 2013: 84).

In South Africa, independent filmmaker Weaam Williams produced and directed three short documentaries on the Khoe and San peoples: *Reclaiming the Mother Tongue* (2014), *Returning the Remains* (2014) and *Stories from the Caves* (2014). Although Williams is not a Khoe or a San, she worked closely with the people of the communities to uncover the colonial legacies through their own voices, memories and experiences. Issues of cultural heritage, social change, colonial genocide, indigenous knowledge and language extinction are all highlighted as visual reminders of the social and cultural threats to which the Khoe and San are exposed. Anthropologist Hugh Brody also worked closely with San in his 2012 *Tracks Against the Sand*. This film traces the quests of a group of Khomani San, thought to have disappeared as 'coloureds' under apartheid, in winning a land claim in South Africa.

The expansion of these audiovisual productions has been made possible through a conjuncture of factors: the increasing availability and low cost of audiovisual technologies, the rise and expansion of the Internet, the funding provided by governments and NGOs for the development of workshops in the use of these technologies, and the proliferation of indigenous film and video festivals where indigenous productions could be screened and distributed to wider audiences. Gleghorn (2013) explains how the development of indigenous films in Mexico started in the 1980s and how one of the most salient features here was to transfer audiovisual technologies to the communities to establish grassroots video artists and filmmakers.

For example, in 1985 the first Latin American Festival of Indigenous Films and Videos was organized in Mexico City and the Latin American Organization of Indigenous Films and Communications (CLACPI) was formed. The aims of CLACPI (2013) are to contribute to the production and commercial distribution of indigenous films and videos, and promote workshops and training for indigenous communities so they can create, produce and direct their own audiovisual work. The festival, which takes place every two years, provides an important site for audiences to view indigenous productions from different parts of Latin America. The fact that the twelfth version of the festival took place in Mapuche territory (Wallmapu) in Chile and Argentina in 2015 is a clear statement of how a film festival can be central to resistance and indigenous rights across national borders. Additionally, Castells i Talens (2003) argues that these productions can be understood as sites of cultural resistance because they break dominant stereotypes and use indigenous languages and the indigenous fictional presentations have subversive overtones.

The issues raised in the indigenous-produced or collaborative films, although responding to different contexts, share some common traits. The emphasis on the community and collective identity in

many of them is a startling contrast to the individualism of the surrounding non-indigenous societies. As Leuthold (1999: 197) argues
in relation to Native American media: 'Native Americans base their
model of community on assumptions of togetherness, interdependence, and mutual accountability. By contrast, American cultural
traditions, with their emphasis on self-reliance, may leave individuals
isolated.'

The importance of older people in keeping and transmitting traditions is also a central feature of the films, as it is through them that
the collective identity is communicated. Thus, oral history becomes
an important research methodology that filmmakers use in order to
describe the different dimensions of indigenous communities. The
use of interviews brings to the forefront the often excluded voices
and histories of indigenous communities. As Thompson (2000: 3)
points out, 'it [oral history] can give back to the people who made
and experience history, through their own words, a central place'.
Another important dimension present in these films is the centrality
of daily interaction in the communities. This is reflected in the work
routines or in the social conflicts that result from being marginalized
in reservations, settlements and villages; often in the background, we
find threats posed by national governments and corporations against
indigenous territories and resources. Rather than being productions
that locate indigenous communities in an ahistorical and timeless
place, the ongoing colonial conditions are vividly exposed. In many
productions, the role of humour, irony and silence in the daily
interaction of community members provides a vivid contrast to the
sombre shadows hanging over people's lives.

Information and communication technologies

While audiovisual productions such as films are important means
of indigenous cultural production, it is clear that the Internet makes
these productions available to a larger audience. The expansion of
digital media is one of the most central features of globalization and
may play a significant role in cultural revitalization. The development of information and communication technologies (ICTs) has
enormously expedited global communications, and is an increasingly
important tool of social and cultural inclusion. Failure to adopt and
use ICTs often leaves individuals and communities unheard and
silent. Thus ICTs have become a strategic site for all social movements, including those of indigenous peoples. There is a growing lit-

erature that analyses the links between ICTs and social movements. Milan (2013: 1) points out the emancipatory capacity in the use of ICTs: 'In recent decades activist groups have increasingly challenged media corporations and state-owned broadcasters on their own terrain. They have created alternatives to existing communication infrastructure by setting up community radio and television stations, and alternative websites for self-produced information.' ICTs therefore represent an opportunity but also a threat to indigenous peoples. According to the UNESCO (2011: 3) report *ICTs and Indigenous People*: 'In many ways ICTs may be viewed as a two-edged sword that has the potential to accelerate the erosion of indigenous culture and knowledge. On the other hand, the new digital technologies offer the potential to empower and support the creation of new culturally responsive learning resources and environments for indigenous children.'

Indeed ICTs can have a detrimental impact on indigenous communities, in particular among the youth, as their societies and cultures are often absent from mainstream media and, when they are represented, the information on them may be stereotypical and racist. However, ICTs have provided an opportunity for indigenous self-representation and creativity. On its website, Isuma TV (2009) explains the aim of its 'action-oriented platform': 'Our tools enable Indigenous people to express reality in their own voices: views of the past, anxieties about the present and hopes for a more decent and honorable future. Our goal is to recognize and respect diverse ways of experiencing our world, and honor those differences as a human strength.'

The increased use of ICTs by indigenous peoples is a reflection of their will to resist colonial practices and advance their rights. Indigenous groups have worked in partnership with NGOs, international agencies and, in some cases, with state-funded institutions to actively develop training programmes for their communities. Echoing the importance of ICTs for indigenous communities, in 2012 the UN Development Program (UNDP) launched a special programme to train indigenous people in the use of information technology as a way of strengthening their political participation. Guaranteeing access to ICTs for women and youth is a priority of this and similar operations. Along these lines, curricula in schools attended by indigenous children have gradually incorporated ICT training as a way of reinforcing indigenous cultural identity.

Many indigenous communities and political bodies own and run their own websites, and these make it possible to learn about their history, traditions, organizations and languages as well as the struggles and conflicts they face. The websites act as a portal to the outside world, but also towards indigenous youth, who can see their cultures and societies being displayed and characterized differently. The development of indigenous websites and online platforms also highlights a more democratic process by which grassroots organizations, often excluded from mainstream media, develop their own contents. In many ways, these websites are important guides for any student researching indigenous issues.

For example, Mapuche organizations are using the Internet in order to highlight their claims and their conflict with the state. Many websites hosted abroad or in Chile advocate for Mapuches' rights and provide a platform for news related to their struggles. Adopting sometimes militant and direct language, these websites have become effective means by which to counter mainstream media, which often reflect the interests of the state or timber industries while excluding Mapuche voices. Websites like mapuexpress.org, mapuche-nation. org and the online newspaper azkintuwe.org are just a few examples of such online platforms. Similarly, many indigenous organizations around the world have websites that reflect their work and struggles. The Cordillera Peoples Alliance (CPA) in the Philippines, the Union of British Columbia Chiefs in Canada, the Navajo in the United States, CONAIE in Ecuador, the Pater Surui in Brazil, as well as pan-indigenous movements such as Idle No More, are but a few examples of the global nature of politicizing information about indigenous peoples.

Conclusion

We end with notes of caution and optimism regarding the continued articulation of indigenous peoples' struggles for cultural survival, freedom and autonomy. Our narrative began by emphasizing the inextricable link between indigenous peoples and their lands, a relationship that has been disrupted and often destroyed by colonial forces that justified themselves by appeals to Western modernity and liberalism. Given the corporate and military power of colonialism, many indigenous peoples are in no position to be creative, culturally engaged and resilient. In the midst of battles against the seizure of their lands, ubiquitous health problems and economic marginalization, there is often little energy and few resources for inventive resistance. Furthermore, in many cases indigenous communities are in a vulnerable position as they have experienced great demographic declines from which they are only now recovering. Many have also lost the attributes that made them strong: their languages, social organization, spirituality and lands. Another challenge to cultural reaffirmation and revitalization is the threat of cooptation. Governmental and international funding programmes that sponsor indigenous cultural initiatives may sever the links between culture and politics by ignoring indigenous projects that challenge dominant state development and assimilationist paradigms.

Yet, it is also true that the long and continuing colonial process generates resistance and opposition, as illustrated by the creative projects covered in this chapter, the activism for human rights discussed in Chapter 5 and the resistance to neoliberalism, extractive industry and state domination mentioned in previous chapters. While the future is very much in the balance, indigenous cultural projects can, along with newly acquired international human rights, help maintain distinctiveness and resistance in a world that many see moving towards cultural and political homogenization. We know that the modernist promises of a singular world of ever-increasing material consumption and increased standards of living do not deliver improvements in well-being and happiness, especially when these come at the cost of cultural meaning and purpose (Pretty 2013). The pressing problems posed by the destruction of the environment, the commercialization of nature, land and cultural dispossession, the violation of human rights and political domination will require more than Western scientific, commercial and political solutions. We are going to have to draw upon the plurality of human knowledge and embrace the multiplicity of cosmologies, and this crucially includes all that indigenous peoples have to offer. Efforts being made to reclaim, reconfigure and respect indigenous distinctiveness will be necessary for the sake of everyone.

References

Abdalla, M. (2012) 'The Alaskans Sitting on Billions of Barrels of Oil', BBC News, 29 November. Available at: http://www.bbc.co.uk/news/magazine-20310752 (Accessed 15 January 2015).

Aboriginal Affairs and Northern Development Canada (2003) *Resolving Aboriginal Claims: A Practical Guide to Canadian Experiences*. Available at: http://www.aandc-aandc.gc.ca/eng/1100100014174/1100100014179#intro (Accessed 15 January 2015).

ABS (Australian Bureau of Statistics) (2011) *Estimates of Aboriginal and Torres Strait Islander Australians*. Available at: http://www.abs.gov.au/ausstats/abs@.nsf/mf/3238.0.55.001 (Accessed 15 January 2015).

Abu-Saad, I. (2008) 'Spatial Transformation and Indigenous Resistance: The Urbanization of the Palestinian Bedouin in Southern Israel', *American Behavioral Scientist* 51 (12): 1713–1754.

Adams, D. W. (1995) *Education for Extinction: American Indians and the Boarding School Experience, 1875–1928*. Lawrence: University Press of Kansas.

Adelson, N. (2008) 'Discourses of Stress, Social Inequities, and the Everyday Worlds of First Nations Women in a Remote Northern Canadian Community', *Ethos* 36 (3): 316–333.

Adelson, N. (2009) 'Toward a Recuperation of Souls and Bodies: Community Healing and the Complex Interplay of Faith and History', in L. J. Kirmayer and G. G. Valaskakis (eds.), *Healing Traditions: The Mental Health of Aboriginal Peoples in Canada*. Vancouver: University of British Columbia Press.

ACHPR (African Commission on Human and Peoples' Rights) (2007) *Advisory Opinion of the African Commission on Human and Peoples' Rights on the United Nations Declaration on the Rights of Indigenous Peoples*. Banjul: African Union.

ACHPR/IWGIA (African Commission on Human and Peoples' Rights/ International Work Group for Indigenous Affairs) (2005) *Report of the*

African Commission's Working Group of Experts on Indigenous Populations/ Communities. Copenhagen: IWGIA.

ACHPR/IWGIA (African Commission on Human and Peoples' Rights/ International Work Group for Indigenous Affairs) (2006) *Indigenous Peoples in Africa: The Forgotten Peoples? The African Commission's work on indigenous peoples in Africa.* Copenhagen: IWGIA.

African Union (1986) *African (Banjul) Charter on Human and Peoples' Rights.* Available at: http://www.achpr.org/files/instruments/achpr/banjul_charter. pdf (Accessed 15 January 2015).

Agbo, S. (2002) 'Decentralization of First Nations education in Canada: Perspectives on ideals and realities of Indian control of Indian education', *Interchange* 33 (3): 281–302.

Aikman, S. (1997) 'Interculturality and Intercultural Education: A Challenge for Democracy', *International Review of Education* 43 (5–6): 463–479.

Akhtar, Z. (2007) 'Human Rights and American Indian Land Claims', *International Journal of Human Rights* 11 (4): 529–534.

Albert, B. (2005) 'Territoriality, Ethnopolitics, and Development: The Indian Movement in the Brazilian Amazon', in A. Surrallés and P. García Hierro (eds.), *The Land Within: Indigenous Territory and the Perception of the Environment.* Copenhagen: IWGIA.

Albó, X. (2008) *Movimientos y Poder Indígena en Bolivia, Ecuador y Perú.* La Paz: PNUD & CIPCA.

Alfred, T. (1999) *First Nations Perspective on Indigenous Identity.* Ottawa: Assembly of First Nations.

Alfred, T. (2005) *Wasase: Indigenous Pathways of Action and Freedom.* Peterborough: Broadview Press.

Alfred, T. (2006) '"Sovereignty" – An Inappropriate Concept', in R. Maaka and C. Andersen (eds.), *The Indigenous Experience: Global Perspectives.* Toronto: Canadian Scholars' Press.

Alfred, T. (2009) *Peace, Power, Righteousness: An Indigenous Manifesto,* 2nd ed. Oxford: Oxford University Press.

Alfred, T. and Corntassel, J. (2005) 'Being Indigenous', *Government and Opposition* 40 (4): 597–614.

Aminzade, R. (2013) 'The Dialectic of Nation Building in Postcolonial Tanzania', *Sociological Quarterly* 54 (3): 335–366.

Amnesty International (2004) *Stolen Sisters: Discrimination and Violence against Indigenous Women in Canada.* Available at: http://www.amnesty. ca/sites/amnesty/files/amr200032004enstolensisters.pdf (Accessed 15 January 2015).

Amnesty International (2007) *Maze of Injustice. The Failure to Protect Indigenous Women from Sexual Violence in the USA.* Available at: http://www. amnestyusa.org/pdfs/MazeOfInjustice.pdf (Accessed 15 January 2015).

Amnesty International (2013) *Pushed to the Edge: Indigenous Rights Denied in Bangladesh's Chittagong Hill Tracts.* Available at: http://www.amnesty. org.uk/sites/default/files/pushed_to_edge.pdf (Accessed 15 January 2015).

Anaya, J. (2004) *Indigenous Peoples in International Law*. Oxford: Oxford University Press.

Andersen, C. (2015) 'Urban Landscapes of North America', in R. Warrior (ed.), *The World of Indigenous North America*. New York: Routledge.

Anderson, A. B. (ed.) (2013) *Home in the City: Urban Aboriginal Housing and Living Conditions*. Toronto: University of Toronto Press.

Anderson, B. (1983) *Imagined Communities: Reflections on the Origin and Spread of Nationalism*. London: Verso.

Anderson, D. (2000) *Identity and Ecology in Arctic Siberia: The Number One Reindeer Brigade*. Oxford: Oxford University Press.

Appelbaum, N. P., Macpherson, A. S. and Rosemblatt, A. (eds.) (2003) *Race & Nation in Modern Latin America*. Chapel Hill: University of North Carolina Press.

Arce, J. (1960) *José Arce Roca, 1843–1914. Su vida. Su obra*. Buenos Aires: Ministerio de Educación y Justicia.

Axelsson, P. and Sköld, P. (2011) 'Introduction', in P. Axelsson and P. Sköld (eds.), *Indigenous Peoples and Demography: The Complex Relation between Identity and Statistics*. New York: Berghahn Books.

Axtell, J. (2001) *Natives and Newcomers: The Cultural Origins of North America*. New York: Oxford University Press.

Bacci, M. L. (2003) 'Return to Hispaniola: Reassessing a Demographic Catastrophe', *Hispanic American Historical Review* 83 (1): 3–51.

Baker, E. W. (1989) '"A Scratch with a Bear's Paw": Anglo-Indian Land Deeds in Early Maine', *Ethnohistory* 36 (3): 235–256.

Baker, L. (1998) *From Savage to Negro: Anthropology and the Construction of Race, 1896–1954*. Berkeley: University of California Press.

Bannon, J. F. (1974) *The Spanish Borderlands Frontier, 1513–1821*. Albuquerque: University of New Mexico Press.

Barié, C. G. (2003) *Pueblos Indígenas y Derechos Constitucionales en América Latina: Un Panorama*, 2nd ed. Quito: Abya Yala.

Barker, A. (2015) '"A Direct Act of Resurgence, a Direct Act of Sovereignty": Reflections on Idle No More, Indigenous Activism, and Canadian Settler Colonialism', *Globalizations* 12 (1): 43–65.

Barnett, T. (2010) 'Guatemala Orders Marlin Mine to Close', *Cultural Survival*. Available at: https://www.culturalsurvival.org/news/guatemala-orders-marlin-mine-close (Accessed 15 January 2015).

Barume, A. K. (2010) *Land Rights of Indigenous Peoples in Africa*. Copenhagen: IWGIA.

Basso, K. (1996) *Wisdom Sits in High Places: Landscape and Language among the Western Apache*. Albuquerque: University of New Mexico Press.

Batalla, G. B. (1996) *México Profundo: Reclaiming a Civilization*, trans. Philip A. Dennis. Austin: University of Texas Press.

Beardsell, P. (2000) *Europe and Latin America: Returning the Gaze*. Manchester: Manchester University Press.

Becker, M. (2011) 'Correa, Indigenous Movements, and the Writing of a New Constitution in Ecuador', *Latin American Perspectives* 38 (1): 47–62.

Bengoa, J. (1996) *Historia del Pueblo Mapuche. Siglos XIX y XX*. Santiago: Ediciones Sur.

Bengoa, J. (2004) *La Memoria Olvidada: Historia de los Pueblos Indígenas de Chile*. Santiago: Publicaciones del Bicentenario, Presidencia de la República.

Berkhofer, R. (1978) *The White Man's Indian: Images of the American Indian from Columbus to the Present*. New York: Vintage.

Bhambra, G. (2007) *Rethinking Modernity: Postcolonialism and the Sociological Imagination*. Basingstoke: Palgrave Macmillan.

Bhambra, G. (2014) *Connected Sociologies*. London: Bloomsbury.

Bhukya, B. (2008) 'The Mapping of Adivasi Social: Colonial Anthropology and Adivasis', *Economic and Political Weekly* XLIII (39): 103–109.

Bieder, R. E. (1986) *Science Encounters the Indian, 1820–1880: The Early Years of American Ethnology*. Norman: University of Oklahoma Press.

Biesele, M. and Hitchcock, R. (2011) *The Ju/'hoansi San of Nyae Nyae and Namibian Independence*. Oxford: Berghahn.

Billson, J. M. (1990) 'Opportunity of Tragedy: The Impact of Canadian Resettlement Policy on Inuit Families', *American Review of Canadian Studies* 20 (2): 187–218.

Binns, T. (2014) 'Dualistic and Unilinear Concepts of Development', in V. Desai and R. Potter (eds.), *The Companion to Development Studies*, 3rd ed. London: Routledge.

Biolsi, T. and Zimmerman, L. (1997) 'Introduction: What's Changed: What Hasn't', in T. Biolsi and L. Zimmerman (eds.), *Indians and Anthropologists: Vine Deloria Jr. and the Critique of Anthropology*. Tucson: University of Arizona Press.

Blackburn, C. (2000) *Harvest of Souls: The Jesuit Missions and Colonialism in North America, 1632–1650*. Montreal: McGill-Queen's University Press.

Blackhawk, N. (2006) *Violence Over the Land: Indians and Empires in the Early American West*. Cambridge, MA: Harvard University Press.

Blanchard, P., Bancel, N., Boëtsch, G., Deroo, É., Lemaire, S. and Forsdick, C. (eds.) (2007) *Human Zoos: Science and Spectacle in the Age of Colonial Empires*. Liverpool: Liverpool University Press.

Blanton, R., Mason, D. and Athow, B. (2001) 'Colonial Style and Post-Colonial Ethnic Conflict in Africa', *Journal of Peace Research* 38 (4): 473–491.

Bloch, A. (2004) *Red Ties and Residential Schools: Indigenous Siberians in a post Soviet State*. Philadelphia: University of Pennsylvania Press.

Boccara, G. (2002) 'Colonización, resistencia y etnogénesis en las fronteras Americanas', in G. Boccara (ed.), *Colonización, Resistencia y Mestizaje en las Américas, Siglos XVI–XX*. Quito: Abya-Yala.

Boesten, J. (2007) 'Free Choice or Poverty Alleviation? Population Politics in Peru under Alberto Fujimori', *European Review of Latin American and Caribbean Studies* 82: 3–20.

Boischio, A. A. P. and Henshel, D. (2000) 'Fish Consumption, Fish Lore, and Mercury Pollution – Risk Communication for the Madeira River People', *Environmental Research* 84 (2): 108–126.

Borgerson, S. (2008) 'Arctic Meltdown: The Economic and Security Implications of Global Warming', *Foreign Affairs* 87 (2): 63–77.

Borras, S. and Franco, J. (2012) 'Global Land Grabbing and Trajectories of Agrarian Change: A Preliminary Analysis', *Journal of Agrarian Change* 12 (1): 34–59.

Borrows, J. (1997) 'Wampum at Niagara: The Royal Proclamation, Canadian Legal History, and Self-Government', in M. Asch (ed.), *Aboriginal and Treaty Rights in Canada: Essays on Law, Equity, and Respect for Difference*. Vancouver: University of British Columbia Press.

Bouquet, M. (2012) *Museums: A Visual Anthropology*. London: Berg.

Bowden, H. W. (1981) *American Indians and Christian Missions: Studies in Cultural Conflict*. Chicago, IL: University of Chicago Press.

Brantlinger, P. (2003) *Dark Vanishings: Discourse on the Extinction of Primitive Races, 1800–1930*. Ithaca, NY: Cornell University Press.

Brody, H. (1981) *Maps and Dreams*. New York: Pantheon.

Brody, H. (1991/1975) *The People's Land: Inuit, Whites and the Eastern Arctic*. Vancouver: Douglas and McIntyre.

Brody, H. (2001) *The Other Side of Eden: Hunter-Gatherers, Farmers and the Modern World*. London: Faber & Faber.

Brown, T. L. (2013) *Pueblo Indians and Spanish Colonial Authority in Eighteenth-Century New Mexico*. Tucson: University of Arizona Press.

Brugge, D., Benally, T. and Yazzie-Lewis, E. (eds.) (2006) *The Navajo People and Uranium Mining*. Albuquerque: University of New Mexico Press.

Brysk, A. (2015) 'From Civil Society to Collective Action: The Politics of Religion in Ecuador', in E. L. Cleary and T. J. Steigenca (eds.), *Resurgent Voices in Latin America: Indigenous Peoples, Political Mobilization and Religious Change*. New Brunswick, NJ: Rutgers University Press.

B'Tselem. (2015) 'Facing Expulsion: For the Second Time This Winter, the Civil Administration has Demolished All the Structures in Khirbet 'Ein Karzaliyah, Leaving the Residents Exposed to the Elements', 4 March. Available at: http://www.btselem.org/planning_and_building/20150304_ein_karzaliyah_demolished_again (Accessed 15 January 2015).

Buchan, B. and Heath, M. (2006) 'Savagery and Civilization: From Terra Nullius to the "Tide of History"', *Ethnicities* 6 (1): 5–26.

Burgess, K. (2000) 'The Pequots' Conversion to Christianity', in R. Niezen (ed.), *Spirit Wars: Native North American Religions in the Age of Nation Building*. Berkeley: University of California Press.

Burkholder, M. A. and Johnson, L. L. (2010) *Colonial Latin America*. New York: Oxford University Press.

Bussidor, I. and Bilgen-Reinart, U. (1997) *Night Spirits: The Story of the Relocation of the Sayisi Dene*. Winnipeg: University of Manitoba Press.

Buti, A. (2005) 'Neville Proof Fence', *Pacific Studies* 28 (1): 1–22.

Cambou, D. (2015) 'Addressing the Rights of Indigenous Peoples in the Development of Ethiopia: A Difficult Compromise or a Compelling Necessity?', in E. Brems, C. Van der Beken and S. Abay Yimer (eds.), *Human Rights and Development: Legal Perspectives from and for Ethiopia*. Leiden: Brill.

Campbell, J. R. (2004) 'Ethnic Minorities and Development: A Prospective Look at the Situation of African Pastoralists and Hunter-Gatherers', *Ethnicities* 4 (1): 5–26.

Canada's National Household Survey (NHS). Available at: http://www12.statcan.gc.ca/nhs-enm/2011/as-sa/99-011-x/99-011-x2011001-eng.cfm (Accessed 15 January 2015).

Canessa, A. (2007) 'Who is Indigenous? Self-Identification, Indigeneity, and Claims to Justice in Contemporary Bolivia', *Urban Anthropology and Studies of Cultural Systems and World Economic Development* 36 (3): 195–237.

Carvajal, D. (2013) 'Museums Confront the Skeletons in Their Closets', *New York Times*, 24 May. Available at: http://www.nytimes.com/2013/05/25/arts/design/museums-move-to-return-human-remains-to-indigenous-peoples.html?_r=0 (Accessed 15 January 2015).

Castells i Talens, A. (2003) 'Cine Indígena y Resistencia Cultural', *Chasqui, Revista Latinoamericana de Comunicación* 84: 50–57. Available at: http://www.redalyc.org/pdf/160/16008407.pdf (Accessed 15 January 2015).

Castells, M. (2004) *The Power of Identity*. Malden, MA: Blackwell.

Caulfield, S. (2003) 'Interracial Courtship in the Rio de Janeiro Courts, 1918–1940', in N. P. Appelbaum, A. S. Macpherson and K. A. Rosemblatt (eds.), *Race and Nation in Modern Latin America*. Chapel Hill: University of North Carolina Press.

CBC (Canadian Broadcasting Corporation) (2014) 'Catholic Church Withholding Millions from Victims, Alleges Government', 18 February. Available at: http://www.cbc.ca/news/aboriginal/catholic-church-withholding-millions-from-victims-alleges-government-1.2542363?cmp=rss (Accessed 15 January 2015).

CEH (Commission for Historical Clarification) (1999) *Guatemala: Memory of Silence*. Available at: http://www.aaas.org/sites/default/files/migrate/uploads/mos_en.pdf (Accessed 15 January 2015).

CFR (Code of Federal Regulations) (1978) *Procedures for Establishing that an American Indian Group Exists as an Indian Tribe*. Available at: https://www.law.cornell.edu/cfr/text/25/part-83 (Accessed 15 January 2015).

Chabot, L. (2007) *The Concept of Citizenship in Western Liberal Democracies and in First Nations: A Research Paper*. Ottawa: Department of Indian Affairs and Northern Development.

Chagnon, N. (1992) *Yanomamö: The Last Days of Eden*, 4th ed. Orlando, FL: Harcourt Brace College Publishers.

Chakma, B. (2010) 'The Post-Colonial State and Minorities: Ethnocide in the Chittagong Hill Tracts, Bangladesh', *Commonwealth & Comparative Politics* 48 (3): 281–300.

Champagne, D. (ed.) (1999) *Contemporary Native American Cultural Issues*. Walnut Creek, CA: AltaMira Press.

Champagne, D. (2013) 'UNDRIP (United Nations Declaration on the Rights of Indigenous Peoples): Human, Civil, and Indigenous Rights', *Wicazo Sa Review* 28 (1): 9–22.

Chatty, D. and Colchester, M. (2002) *Conservation and Mobile Indigenous Peoples*. Oxford: Berghahn.

Cheung, S. C. H. (2003) 'Ainu Culture in Transition', *Futures* 35: 951–959.

Child, B. J. (1998) *Boarding School Seasons: American Indian Families 1900–1940*. Lincoln: University of Nebraska Press.

Church, E. (2010) 'Educators Pledge Support for Aboriginal Learning', *Toronto Globe and Mail*, 1 June. Available at: http://www.theglobeandmail.com/news/national/educators-pledge-support-for-aboriginal-learning/article1211548/ (Accessed 15 January 2015).

CIDH (Comisión Inter-Americana de Derechos Humanos) (2010) *Derechos de los Pueblos Indígenas y Tribales sobre sus tierras ancestrales y recursos naturales: Normas y jurisprudencia del Sistema Interamericano de Derechos Humanos*. Available at: http://cidh.org/countryrep/TierrasIndigenas2009/Tierras-Ancestrales.ESP.pdf (Accessed 15 January 2015).

CIMI (Conselho Indigenista Missionário) (2014) *Violence Against Indigenous Peoples in Brazil: 2014 Data*. Available at: http://www.cimi.org.br/pub/Relatorio%20Violencia%202014/_Relat.pdf (Accessed 15 January 2015).

CIMI (Conselho Indigenista Missionário) (2015) 'Povos indígenas de Roraima realizam marcha e denunciam invasões a territórios homologados'. Available at: http://cimi.org.br/site/pt-br/?system=news&action=read&id=8259 (Accessed 15 September 2015).

Cladoosby, B. (2015) *State of Indian Nations*, 22 January. Available at: http://www.ncai.org/resources/testimony/2015-state-of-indian-nations (Accessed 15 March 2015).

CLACPI (Coordinadora Latinoamericana de Cine y Comunicación de los Pueblos Indígenas) (2013) Available at: http://www.clacpi.org (Accessed 15 January 2015).

Clemmer, R. (2009) 'Land Rights, Claims, and Western Shoshones: The Ideology of Loss and the Bureaucracy of Enforcement', *Political and Legal Anthropology Review* 32 (2): 279–311.

Closing the Gap Clearinghouse (2013) *Diverting Indigenous Offenders from the Criminal Justice System*. Resource sheet no. 24. Available at: http://www.aihw.gov.au/WorkArea/DownloadAsset.aspx?id=60129545614 (Accessed 15 January 2015).

COAC (Center for Orang Asli Concerns) (2015) Available at: http://www. coac.org.my/main.php?section=about&page=about_index (Accessed 15 January 2015).

Cobb, D. M. (2008) *Native Activism in Cold War America: The Struggle for Sovereignty*. Lawrence: University Press of Kansas.

Cobo, J. R. M. (1986) *Study of the Problem of Discrimination against Indigenous Populations*. United Nations, Economic and Social Council (UN ECOSOC), 11 March. E/CN.4/Sub.2/1986/7/ and Add.1-4.

Colchester, M. (1997) *Guyana: Fragile Frontier*. London: Latin America Bureau.

Colchester, M., La Rose, J. and James, K. (2002) *Mining and Amerindians in Guyana: Final Report of the Apa/Nsi Project on Exploring Indigenous Perspective on Consultation and Engagement Within the Mining Sector in Latin America*. Ottawa: North–South Institute.

Colson, E. (1971) *The Social Consequences of Resettlement: The Impact of the Kariba Resettlement on the Gwembe Tonga*. Manchester: Manchester University Press.

Cone, M. (2005) *Silent Snow: The Slow Poisoning of the Arctic*. New York: Grove Press.

Conklin, A. (2013) *In the Museum of Man: Race, Anthropology, and Empire in France, 1850–1950*. Ithaca, NY: Cornell University Press.

Connell, R. (2007) *Southern Theory*. Cambridge: Polity.

Contreras-Garduño, D. and Rombouts, S. (2010) 'Collective Reparations for Indigenous Communities Before the Inter-American Court of Human Rights', *Merkourios* 27 (72): 4–17.

Convención de Pátzcuaro (1940) Available at: http://www.iadb.org/ Research/legislacionindigena/pdocs/CONVENCIONPATZCUARO.pdf (Accessed 15 January 2015).

Cook, S. (1976) *The Conflict between the California Indian and White Civilization*. Berkeley: University of California Press.

Cooley, C. H. (1902) *Human Nature and the Social Order*. New York: Charles Scribner's Sons.

Coulthard, G. (2007) 'Subjects of Empire: Indigenous Peoples and the "Politics of Recognition" in Canada', *Contemporary Political Theory* 6 (4): 437–460.

Coulthard, G. S. (2014) *Red Skin White Masks: Rejecting the Colonial Politics of Recognition*. Minneapolis: University of Minnesota Press.

Courtoreille, L. (1997) 'The Legal Origins and Development of Aboriginal and Treaty Rights', in A. P. Morrison (ed.), *Justice for Natives: Searching for Common Ground*. Montreal: McGill-Queen's University Press.

Cronon, W. (1983) *Changes in the Land: Indians, Colonists and the Ecology of New England*. New York: Hill and Wang.

Cruikshank, J. (1998) *The Social Life of Stories: Narrative and Knowledge in the Yukon Territory*. Lincoln: University of Nebraska Press.

Crum, S. (2011) 'The Ruby Valley Indian Reservation of Northeastern

Nevada "Six Miles Square"', in S. Miller and J. Riding In (eds.), *Native Historians Write Back*. Lubbock: Texas Tech University Press.

Culbert, T. P. (1974) *The Lost Civilization: The Story of the Classic Maya*. New York: Harper and Row.

Cunneen, C. (2013) 'Colonial Processes, Indigenous Peoples, and Criminal Justice Systems', in S. Bucerius and M. Tonry (eds.), *The Oxford Handbook of Ethnicity, Crime, and Immigration*. New York: Oxford University Press.

Curtis, C. (2016). 'Remote Quebec Community of Kuujjuaq Reeling after Three Teen Suicides', *Montreal Gazette*, 17 February. Available at: http://montrealgazette.com/news/suicide-in-kuujjuaq (Accessed 21 April 2016).

Das, M. B., Hall, G. H., Kapoor, S. and Nikitin, D. (2012) 'India: The Scheduled Tribes', in G. H. Hall and H. A. Patrinos (eds.), *Indigenous Peoples, Poverty, and Development*. Cambridge: Cambridge University Press.

Daschuk, J. (2013) *Clearing the Plains: Disease, Politics of Starvation and the Loss of Aboriginal Life*. Regina, SK: University of Regina Press.

Davenport, C. and C. Robertson. (2016). 'Resettling the First American "Climate Refugees"', *New York Times*, 3 May. Available at: http://www.nytimes.com/2016/05/03/us/resettling-the-first-american-climate-refugees.html?emc=edit_th_20160503&nl=todaysheadlines&nlid=21277101&_r=0 (Accessed 4 May 2016).

Davies, M., Croall, H. and Tyrer, J. (2009) *Criminal Justice*, 4th ed. London: Longman.

Davis, M. (2002) *Dead Cities and Other Tales*. New York: New Press.

Debo, A. (1940) *And Still the Waters Run: The Betrayal of the Five Civilized Tribes*, Princeton, NJ: Princeton University Press.

Debo, A. (1970) *A History of the Indians of the United States*. Norman: University of Oklahoma Press.

Declaration of Barbados (1971) Available at: http://www.iwgia.org/iwgia_files_publications_files/0110_01Barbados.pdf (Accessed 15 January 2015).

Del Castillo, R. G. (1990) *The Treaty of Guadalupe Hidalgo*. Norman: University of Oklahoma Press.

Deloria, V. (1985) *Behind the Trail of Broken Treaties: An Indian declaration of independence*. Austin: University of Texas Press.

Deloria, V. (1999) *For This Land: Writings on Religion in America*. New York: Routledge.

Dersso, S. (ed.) (2010) *Perspectives on the Rights of Minorities and Indigenous Peoples in Africa*. Pretoria: Pretoria University Law Press.

De Souza, M. (2011) 'Oilsands Emissions Data Left Out of UN Report', *Vancouver Sun*, 30 May. Available at: http://www.pressreader.com/canada/the-vancouver-sun/20110530/284266706787683/TextView (Accessed 15 January 2015).

Devine Gúzman, T. (2013) *Native and National in Brazil: Indigeneity after Independence*. Chapel Hill: University of North Carolina Press.

Diabo, R. (2013) 'Harper Launches Major First Nations Termination Plan as Negotiating Tables Legitimize Canada's Colonialism', *The Bullet*, 10 January. Available at: http://www.socialistproject.ca/bullet/756.php (Accessed 15 January 2015).

Díaz Polanco, H. (1995) *Autonomía regional: La autodeterminación de los pueblos indios*. Mexico City: Siglo XXI.

Dieckmann, U. (2007) *Hai//om in the Etosha Region: A History of Colonial Settlement, Ethnicity and Nature Conservation*. Basel: Basler Afrika Bibliographien.

Dooley, K. and Griffiths, T. (eds.) (2014) *Indigenous Peoples' Rights, Forests and Climate Policies in Guyana: A Special Report*. Amerindian Peoples Association and Forest Peoples Programme. Available at: http://landportal.info/library/2015/09/indigenous-peoples'-rights-forests-and-climate-policies-guyana-special-report (Accessed 15 January 2015).

Dougherty, M. (2011) 'The Global Gold Mining Industry, Junior Firms, and Civil Society Resistance in Guatemala', *Bulletin of Latin American Research* 30 (4): 403–418.

Dowie, M. (2009) *Conservation Refugees: The Hundred-Year Conflict between Global Conservation and Indigenous Peoples*. Cambridge, MA: MIT Press.

Drahos, P. (2014) *Intellectual Property, Indigenous Peoples and their Knowledge*. Cambridge: Cambridge University Press.

Dunbar-Ortiz, R. (2014) *An Indigenous Peoples' History of the United States*. Boston, MA: Beacon Press.

Durham, J. (1993) *A Certain Lack of Coherence*. London: Kala Press.

Durland, S. (1991) 'Call Me in '93: An Interview with James Luna', *High Performance* XIV (4): 34–39.

Dussel, E. (1995) *The Invention of the Americas: Eclipse of 'the Other' and the Myth of Modernity*. New York: Continuum.

Earle, R. (2007) *The Return of the Native: Indians and Myth-Making in Spanish America, 1810–1930*. Durham, NC: Duke University Press.

Echo-Hawk, W. (2013) *In the Light of Justice: The Rise of Human Rights in Native America & the UN Declaration of the Rights of Indigenous Peoples*. Golden, CO: Fulcrum Publishing.

ECLAC (Economic Commission for Latin America and the Caribbean) (2014) *Summary: Guaranteeing Indigenous People's Rights in Latin America: Progress in the Past Decade and Remaining Challenges*. Santiago: United Nations.

Elkins, C. (2006) *Imperial Reckoning: The Untold Story of Britain's Gulag in Kenya*. New York: Henry Holt and Co.

Endicott, K. (ed.) (2016) *Malaysia's Original People: Past, Present and Future of the Orang Asli*. Singapore: National University of Singapore Press.

Engle, K. (2011) 'On Fragile Architecture: The UN Declaration on the Rights of Indigenous Peoples in the Context of Human Rights', *European Journal of International Law* 22 (1): 141–163.

Erueti, A. (2011) 'The International Labour Organization and the Internationalisation on the Concept of Indigenous Peoples', in S. Allen and A. Xanthaki (eds.), *Reflections on the UN Declaration on the Rights of Indigenous Peoples*. Oxford: Hart Publishing.

Escárcega, S. and Varese, S. (eds.) (2004) *La Ruta Mixteca: El Impacto Etnopolítico de la Migración Trasnacional en los Pueblos Indígenas de México*, Mexico City: Universidad Nacional Autónoma de México.

Escárzaga Nicté, F. (2004) 'La Emergencia Indígena contra el Neoliberalismo', *Política y Cultura* 22: 101–121.

Estatuto do Índio, República Federalista do Brasil (1973) Available at: http://www.planalto.gov.br/ccivil_03/Leis/L6001.htm (Accessed 15 January 2015).

EYROC (Executive Yuan, Republic of China) (2014) *The Republic of China Yearbook 2014*. Available at: http://www.ey.gov.tw/en/cp.aspx?n= BE8DFC05912B9563 (Accessed 15 January 2015).

Eze, E. C. (ed.) (1997) *Race and the Enlightenment: A Reader*. Oxford: Blackwell.

Fabian, J. (2002/1983) *Time and the Other: How Anthropology Makes Its Object*. New York: Columbia University Press.

Fanon, F. (1963) *The Wretched of the Earth*, trans. C. Farrington. New York: Grove Press.

Farley, M., Lynne, J. and Cotton, A. J. (2005) 'Prostitution in Vancouver: Violence and the Colonization of First Nations Women', *Transcultural Psychiatry* 42 (2): 242–271.

FIMI (International Indigenous Women's Forum) (2006) *Mairin Iwanka Raya: Indigenous Women Stand against Violence*. Available at: http://www.un.org/esa/socdev/unpfii/documents/vaiwreport06.pdf (Accessed 15 January 2015).

Fishel, J. A. (2006/2007) 'United States Called to Task on Indigenous Rights: The Western Shoshone Struggle and Success at the International Level', *American Indian Law Review* 31 (2): 619–650.

Fixico, D. (1986) *Termination and Relocation: Federal Indian Policy, 1945– 1986*. Albuquerque: University of New Mexico Press.

Fixico, D. (1998) *The Invasion of Indian Country in the Twentieth Century: American Capitalism and Tribal Natural Resources*. Boulder: University Press of Colorado.

Fixico, D. (2000) *The Urban Indian Experience in America*. Albuquerque: University of New Mexico Press.

Foggin, J. M. (2008) 'Depopulating the Tibetan Grasslands: National Policies and Perspectives for the Future of Tibetan Herders in Qinghai Province, China', *Mountain Research and Development* 28 (1): 26–31.

Forest Peoples Programme (2014) *World Bank Moves to Undermine the Rights of Indigenous Peoples*, Press Release, 29 July. Available at: http://www. forestpeoples.org/topics/safeguard-accountability-issues/news/2014/07/

press-release-world-bank-moves-undermine-rights (Accessed 15 January 2015).

Forest Peoples Programme (2016) 'Indigenous Peoples in Suriname Win Important Case in the Inter-American Court of Human Rights', 23 February. Available at: http://www.forestpeoples.org/topics/inter-ameri can-human-rights-system/news/2016/02/indigenous-peoples-suriname-win-important-case (Accessed 1 March 2016).

Forte, J. and Melville, I. (1989) *Amerindian Testimonies*. Boise, ID: Boise State University Press.

Forte, M. (2013) '"Who is an Indian?": The Cultural Politics of a Bad Question', in M. Forte (ed.), *Who is an Indian?: Race, Place and Politics of Indigeneity in the Americas*. Toronto: Toronto University Press.

Fournier, S. and Crey, E. (2006) '"Killing the Indian in the Child": Four Centuries of Church-Run Schools', in R. Maaka and C. Andersen (eds.), *The Indigenous Experience: Global Perspectives*. Toronto: Canadian Scholars' Press.

Freud, S. (1927) *The Ego and the Id*. London: Hogarth.

Fumoleau, R. (1974) *As Long As This Land Shall Last: A History of Treaty 8 and Treaty 11, 1870–1939*. Toronto: McClelland and Stewart.

Funk-Unrau, N. and Snyder, A. (2007) 'Indian Residential School Survivors and State-Designed ADR: A Strategy for Co-optation?', *Conflict Resolution Quarterly* 24 (3): 285–304.

Furi, M. and Wherrett, J. (2003) *Indian Status and Band Membership Issues*. Ottawa: Political and Social Affairs Division Parliamentary Information and Research Service. Available at: http://www.parl.gc.ca/content/lop/ researchpublications/bp410-e.pdf (Accessed 15 January 2015).

Gall, S. (2002) *The Bushmen of Southern Africa: Slaughter of the Innocent*. London: Pimlico.

García-Alix, L. (2003) *Handbook on the Permanent Forum on Indigenous Issues*. Copenhagen: IWGIA.

Gardiner-Garden, J. (2003) 'Defining Aboriginality in Australia', Current Issues Brief no. 10 2002–03. Available at: http://www.aph.gov.au/binaries/ library/pubs/cib/2002-03/03cib10.pdf (Accessed 15 January 2015).

Garfield, S. (2001) *Indigenous Struggle at the Heart of Brazil: State Policy, Frontier Expansion, and the Xavante Indians, 1937–1988*. Durham, NC: Duke University Press.

Garroutte, E. M. (2003) *Real Indians: Identity and the Survival of Native America*. Berkeley: University of California Press.

Gigoux, C. (2010) 'Colonizing Images: The Politics of Representation in the Archipelago of Tierra del Fuego', unpublished doctoral thesis, University of Essex.

Gigoux, C. and Samson, C. (2016) 'Globalization and Indigenous Peoples: New Old Patterns', in B. S. Turner and R. J. Holton (eds.), *The Routledge International Handbook of Globalization Studies*, 2nd ed. Abingdon: Routledge.

Gilbert, H. (1994) 'De-scribing Orality: Performance and the Recuperation of Indigenous Voices', in C. Tiffin and A. Lawson (eds.), *De-scribing Empire: Colonialism and Textuality*. London: Routledge.

Gilbert, H. and Tompkins, J. (1996) *Post-colonial Drama: Theory, Practice, Politics*. London: Routledge.

Gilbert, J. (2006) *Indigenous Peoples' Land Rights under International Law: From Victims to Actors*. Ardsley, NY: Transnational Publishers.

Ginsburg, F. (2003) 'Atanarjuat Off-Screen: From "Media Reservations" to the World Stage', *American Anthropologist* 105 (4): 827–831.

Ginsburg, F. (2008) 'Rethinking the Digital Age', in D. Hesmondhalgh and J. Toynbee (eds.), *The Media and Social Theory*. New York: Routledge.

Gleghorn, C. (2013) 'Revisioning the Colonial Record: *La relación de Michoacán* and Contemporary Mexican Indigenous Film', *Interventions: International Journal of Postcolonial Studies* 15 (2): 224–238.

Global Health Watch (2005) *Global Health Watch 2005–2006*. London: Zed Books.

Goddard, P. (1998) 'Converting the "Sauvage": Jesuit and Montagnais in Seventeenth-Century New France', *Catholic Historical Review* 84 (2): 219–239.

Goffman, E. (1959) *The Presentation of Self in Everyday Life*. Garden City, NY: Doubleday Anchor Books.

Goldenberg, S. M., Shoveller, J. A., Koehoorn, M. and Ostry, A. S. (2010) 'And They Call This Progress? Consequences for Young People of Living and Working in Resource-Extraction Communities', *Critical Public Health* 20 (2): 157–168.

González, G. and Fernandez, R. (2002), 'Empire and the Origins of Twentieth-Century Migration from Mexico to the United States', *Pacific Historical Review* 71 (1): 19–57.

González-Parra, C. and Simon, J. (2008) 'All That Glitters Is Not Gold: Resettlement, Vulnerability, and Social Exclusion in the Pehuenche Community Ayin Mapu, Chile', *American Behavioral Scientist* 51 (12): 1774–1789.

Good, K. (2008) *Diamonds, Dispossession and Democracy in Botswana*. Woodbridge: James Currey.

Gooda, M. (2011) 'One's Identity is for the Individual to Determine', *Sydney Morning Herald*, 24 November. Available at: http://www.smh.com.au/federal-politics/political-opinion/ones-identity-is-for-the-individual-to-determine-20111124-1nwew.html (Accessed 15 January 2015).

Gould, S. J. (1981) *The Mismeasure of Man*. New York: Norton.

Gordon, R. and Douglas, S. (2000) *The Bushman Myth: The Making of a Namibian Underclass*. Boulder, CO: Westview Press.

Graburn, N. (1969) *Eskimos without Igloos: Social and Economic Development in Sugluk*. Boston, MA: Little, Brown and Company.

Grant, R. (2003) *Ghost Riders: Travels with American Nomads*. London: Abacus.

Gray, A. (2009) 'Indigenous Peoples and their Territories', in A. de Oliveira (ed.), *Decolonising Indigenous Rights*. London: Routledge.

Griffin, C. (2012) 'Arctic Drilling Noise and Shipping Traffic May Cause Problems for Whales', Audubon Society, 9 July. Available at: http://www. audubon.org/news/arctic-drilling-noise-and-shipping-traffic-may-cause-problems-whales (Accessed 15 January 2015).

Grinde, D. and Johansen, B. E. (1995) *Ecocide of Native America: Environmental Destruction of Indian Lands and Peoples*. Santa Fe, NM: Clear Light Publishers.

Gupta, S. D. and Basu, R. S. (eds.) (2011) *Narratives from the Margins: Aspects of Adivasi History in India*. Delhi: Primus Books.

Haebich, A. (2000) *Broken Circles: Fragmenting Indigenous Families, 1800–2000*. Fremantle: Fremantle Arts Centre Press.

Hagan, W. T. (1988) 'How the West was Lost', in F. Hoxie (ed.), *Indians in American History*. Arlington Heights, IL: Harlan Davidson.

Hale, C. A. (1996) 'Political Ideas and Ideologies in Latin America, 1870––1930', in L. Bethell (ed.), *Ideas and Ideologies in Twentieth Century Latin America*. Cambridge: Cambridge University Press.

Hall, S. (1990) 'Cultural Identity and Diaspora', in J. Rutherford (ed.), *Identity: Community, Culture, Difference*. London: Lawrence & Wishart Ltd.

Hall, S. (1996) 'When Was the Post-Colonial? Thinking at the Limit', in I. Chambers and L. Curti (eds.), *The Post-Colonial Question: Common Skies, Divided Horizons*. London: Routledge.

Harada, M., Hanada, M., Miyakita, T., Fujino, T., Tsuruta, K., Fukuhara, A., Orui, T., Nakachi, S., Araki, C., Tajiri, M. and Nagano, I. (2005) 'Long-Term Study on the Effects of Mercury Contamination on Two Indigenous Communities in Canada (1975–2004)', trans. Tadashi Orui, *Research on Environmental Disruption* 34 (4). Available at: http://freegrassy. net/wp-content/uploads/2012/03/Harada_report_2004_FINAL.pdf (Accessed 15 January 2015).

Hardiman, D. (1987) *The Coming of the Devi: Adivasi Assertion in Western India*. Delhi: Oxford University Press.

Harper, K. (2001) *Give Me My Father's Body: The Life of Minik the New York Eskimo*. New York: Pocket Books.

Harvey, D. (2005) *A Brief History of Neoliberalism*. Oxford: Oxford University Press.

Hauanna Cassula, M. and Mendonça Bernardino, M. (2012) 'A importância da oralidade para a revitalização cultural dos guarani nhandewa'. Available at: http://www.portalanpedsul.com.br/admin/uploads/2012/Educacao_ Cultura_e_Relacoes_Etnico_Raciais/Trabalho/06_37_44_2764-6881-1-PB.pdf (Accessed 15 January 2015).

Hausbeck, K. (2008) 'Domestic Dependent Nation', in D. L. Fixico (ed.), *Treaties with American Indians: An Encyclopedia of Rights, Conflicts, and Sovereignty*. Santa Barbara, CA: ABC-CLIO.

Havemann, P. (2009) 'Ignoring the Mercury in the Climate Change Barometer: Denying Indigenous Peoples' Rights', *Australian Indigenous Law Review* 13 (2): 2–26.

Hayden, T. (ed.) (2002) *The Zapatista Reader*. New York: Thunder's Mouth Press/Nation Books.

HCA (High Court of Australia) (1992) *Mabo v. Queensland (No. 2)*. Available at: http://www.austlii.edu.au/au/cases/cth/HCA/1992/23.html (Accessed 15 January 2015).

Heggum, H. P. (2002) *The Batwa and the Hadzabe: An NCA Assessment*. Oslo: Norwegian Church Aid, Occasional Papers 4/02.

Heiss, A. and Minster, P. (2008) 'Aboriginal Literature', in A. Heiss and P. Minter (eds.), *Macquaire Pen Anthology of Aboriginal Literature*. Crows Nest, NSW: Allen & Unwin.

Heizer, R. and Almquist, A. (1971) *The Other Californians: Prejudice and Discrimination under Spain, Mexico, and the United States to 1920*. Berkeley, CA: University of California Press.

Hemming, J. (1987) 'Indian Frontier', in L. Bethell (ed.), *Colonial Brazil*. Cambridge: Cambridge University Press.

Hitchcock, R., Sapignoli, M. and Babchuk, W. (2011) 'What About Our rights? Settlements, Subsistence and Livelihood Security among Central Kalahari San and Bakgalagadi', *International Journal of Human Rights* 15 (1): 62–88.

Hobbes, T. (1958/1651) *The Leviathan Parts I and II*. Indianapolis: Bobbs-Merrill.

Hobsbawm, E. (1964) *The Age of Revolution: Europe 1789–1848*. London: Weidenfeld and Nicolson.

Hobson, J., Lowe, K., Poetsch, S. and Walsh, M. (eds.) (2010) *Re-Awakening Languages: Theory & Practice in the Revitalisation of Australia's Indigenous Languages*. Sydney: Sydney University Press.

Holden, W. and Ingelson, A. (2007) 'Disconnect between the Philippine Mining Investment Policy and Indigenous Peoples' Rights', *Journal of Energy & Natural Resources Law* 25 (4): 375–391.

Hooks, G. and Smith, C. (2004) 'The Treadmill of Destruction: National Sacrifice Areas and Native Americans', *American Sociological Review* 69 (4): 558–575.

House, D. (2005) *Language Shift Among the Navajos: Identity Politics and Cultural Continuity*. Tucson: University of Arizona Press.

Howell, D. (2005) *Geographies of Identity in Nineteenth Century Japan*. Berkeley: University of California Press.

Hoxie, F. (2008) 'Retrieving the Red Continent: Settler Colonialism and the History of American Indians in the US', *Racial and Ethnic Studies* 31 (6): 1153–1167.

HREOC (Human Rights and Equal Opportunity Commission Report) (1997) *Bringing Them Home: Report of the National Inquiry into the Separation of Aboriginal and Torres Strait Islander Children from Their*

Families. Available at: https://www.humanrights.gov.au/sites/default/files/content/pdf/social_justice/bringing_them_home_report.pdf (Accessed 15 January 2015).

HRW (Human Rights Watch) (2013a) *'They Say We Should Be Grateful': Mass Rehousing and Relocation Programs in Tibetan Areas of China.* Available at: https://www.hrw.org/report/2013/06/27/they-say-we-should-be-grateful/mass-rehousing-and-relocation-programs-tibetan (Accessed 15 January 2015).

HRW (Human Rights Watch) (2013b) *Those Who Take Us Away: Abusive Policing and Failures in Protection of Indigenous Women and Girls in Northern British Columbia, Canada.* Available at: http://www.hrw.org/reports/2013/02/13/those-who-take-us-away (Accessed 15 January 2015).

Hsieh, J. (2006) *Collective Rights of Indigenous Peoples: Identity-Based Movement of Plain Indigenous in Taiwan.* New York: Routledge.

Hubbard, T. (2014) 'Buffalo Genocide in Nineteenth Century North America: "Kill, Skin and Sell"', in A. Woolford, A. Hinton and J. Benvenuto (eds.), *Colonial Genocide in North America.* Durham, NC: Duke University Press.

Humphrey, C. and Sneath, D. (1999) *The End of Nomadism? Society, State and the Environment in Inner Asia.* Durham, NC: Duke University Press.

Hunt, S. (2013) 'Decolonizing Sex Work: Developing an Intersectional Indigenous Approach', in E. van der Meulen, E. Durisin and V. Love (eds.), *Selling Sex: Experience, Advocacy, and Research on Sex Work in Canada.* Vancouver: University of British Columbia Press.

Hunter, E., Milroy, H., Brown, N. and Calma, T. (2012) 'Human Rights, Health, and Indigenous Australians', in M. Dudley, D. Silove and F. Gale (eds.), *Mental Health and Human Rights: Vision, Praxis, and Courage.* Oxford: Oxford University Press.

Hurtado, A. (1988) *Indian Survival on the California Frontier.* New Haven, CT: Yale University Press.

Huseman, J. and Short, D. (2012) 'A Slow Industrial Genocide: Tar Sands and the Indigenous Peoples of Northern Alberta', *International Journal of Human Rights* 16 (1): 216–237.

IACHR (Inter-American Commission on Human Rights) (1985) *Resolution No 12/85. Case No 7615 Brazil,* 5 March. Available at: http://www.cidh.org/annualrep/84.85eng/Brazil7615.htm (Accessed 15 January 2015).

IACHR (Inter-American Commission on Human Rights) (2013) *Indigenous Peoples in Voluntary Isolation and Initial Contact in the Americas,* OEA/Ser.L/V/II. Doc. 47/13, 30 December. Available at: http://www.oas.org/en/iachr/indigenous/docs/pdf/Report-Indigenous-Peoples-Voluntary-Isolation.pdf (Accessed 15 January 2015).

IBGE (Instituto Brasileiro de Geografia e Estatística) (2010) *Censo 2010.* Available at: http://censo2010.ibge.gov.br (Accessed 15 January 2015).

Idle No More (2014) 'Turn the Tables: Reject the Interim Land Claims Policy', *IC Magazine,* 15 November. Available at: https://

intercontinentalcry.org/turn-the-tables-reject-the-interim-land-claims-policy/ (Accessed 15 January 2015).

ILO (International Labour Organization) (1957) *C107: Indigenous and Tribal Populations Convention*. Available at: http://www.ilo.org/dyn/normlex/en/f?p=NORMLEXPUB:55:0:::55:P55_TYPE,P55_LANG,P55_DOCUMENT,P55_NODE:REV,en,C107,/Document (Accessed 21 April 2016).

ILO (International Labour Organization) (1989) *C169: Indigenous and Tribal Peoples Convention*. Available at: http://www.ilo.org/dyn/normlex/en/f?p=NORMLEXPUB:12100:0::NO::P12100_ILO_CODE:C169 (Accessed 21 April 2016).

ILO/ACHPR (International Labour Organization/African Commission on Human and Peoples' Rights) (2009) *Country Report of the Research Project by the International Labour Organization and the African Commission on Human and Peoples' Rights on the Constitutional and Legislative Protection of the Rights of Indigenous Peoples: Botswana*. Available at: http://www1.chr.up.ac.za/chr_old/indigenous/country_reports/Country_reports_Botswana.pdf (Accessed 15 January 2015).

Imilán, W. A. (2010) *Warriache – Urban Indigenous: Mapuche Migration and Ethnicity in Santiago de Chile*. Berlin: Lit Verlag.

Indian Country Today (2011) 'Turtle Mountain Tribal Council Bans Fracking', 27 November. Available at: http://indiancountrytodaymedianetwork.com/2011/11/27/turtle-mountain-tribal-council-bans-fracking-64866 (Accessed 15 January 2015).

Indian Country Today (2014) 'Eastern Cherokee Band Forbids Fracking on Its Sovereign Lands', 20 October. Available at: http://indiancountrytodaymedianetwork.com/2014/10/20/eastern-cherokee-band-forbids-fracking-its-sovereign-lands-157437 (Accessed 15 January 2015).

Indian Law Resource Center (2010) *Safe Women, Strong Nations*. Available at: http://www.indianlaw.org/safewomen (Accessed 15 January 2015).

Ingold, T. (2000) *The Perception of the Environment: Essays on Livelihood, Dwelling and Skill*. London: Routledge.

Ingstad, B. and Fugelli, P. (2006) '"Our Health Was Better in the Time of Queen Elizabeth": The Importance of Land to the Health Perception of the Botswana San', in R. K. Hitchcock, K. Ikeya, M. Biesele and R. N. Lee (eds.), *Updating the San: Image and Reality of an African People in the 21st Century. Senri Ethnological Studies* 70. Osaka: National Museum of Ethnology.

Innu Nation and Mushuau Innu Band Council (1993) *Gathering Voices: Finding Strength to Help Our Children*. Sheshatshiu: Innu Nation.

IPACC (Indigenous Peoples of Africa Co-ordinating Committee) (2007) *Briefing Note on the Threat to the Hadzabe People of the Yaida Valley, Karatu District, United Republic of Tanzania*. Available at: http://www.ipacc.org.za/en/2007/6-briefing-note-on-the-threat-to-the-hadzabe-people-of-tanzania.html?path= (Accessed 21 April 2016).

Iriarte, J. A., and Jaksic, F. M. (1986) 'The Fur Trade in Chile: An Overview of Seventy-five Years of Export Data (1910–1984)', *Biological Conservation* 38: 243–253.

ISAWN/IWFNEI/AIPP (Inter State Adivasi Women's Network/Indigenous Women's Forum of North East India/Asia Indigenous Peoples Pact) (2014) *NGO CEDAW Shadow Report and Status of Adivasi/Tribal Women in India.* For the 58th Session of CEDAW (IV & V Periodic Report), June, Geneva. Available at: http://tbinternet.ohchr.org/Treaties/CEDAW/Shared%20Documents/Ind/INT_CEDAW_NGO_Ind_17414_E.pdf (Accessed 15 January 2015).

Ishii, L. (2011) 'Hopi Culture and a Matter of Representation', in S. Miller and J. Riding In (eds.), *Native Historians Write Back.* Lubbock: Texas Tech University Press.

Isuma TV (2009) *About Us.* Available at: https://www.isuma.tv/about-us (Accessed 15 January 2015).

IWGIA (International Work Group for Indigenous Affairs) (2015) *The Indigenous World 2015.* Available at: http://www.iwgia.org/iwgia_files_publications_files/0716_THE_INDIGENOUS_WORLD_2015_eb.pdf (Accessed 15 July 2015).

Jackson, H. H. (1965/1881) *A Century of Dishonor: The Early Crusade for Indian Reform.* New York: Harper and Row.

Jackson, R. H. (2015) *Demographic Change and Ethnic Survival among the Sedentary Populations on the Jesuit Mission Frontiers of Spanish South America, 1609–1803.* Boston, MA: Brill.

Jacob, M. M. (2013) *Yakama Rising: Indigenous Cultural Revitalization, Activism, and Healing.* Tucson: University of Arizona Press.

Jacobs, M. D. (2009) *White Mother to a Dark Race: Settler Colonialism and the Removal of Indigenous Children in the American West and Australia, 1880–1940.* Lincoln: University of Nebraska Press.

Jahoda, G. (1999) *Images of Savages: Ancient Roots of Modern Prejudice in Western Culture.* New York: Routledge.

Jaimes, M. A. (ed.) (1992) *The State of Native America: Genocide, Colonization, and Resistance.* Boston, MA: South End Press.

James, T. (2003) 'Indigenous Land Rights in Guyana: Past, Present and Future.' Presentation by the Amerindian Peoples Association, Indigenous Rights in the Commonwealth Conference, Georgetown, Guyana, 23–25 June.

Jefferson, T. (1975/1787) 'Notes on the State of Virginia', in M. Peterson (ed.), *The Portable Thomas Jefferson.* New York: Viking Penguin.

Jennings, F. (1975) *The Invasion of America: Indians, Colonialism and the Cant of Conquest.* New York: Norton.

Johannesen, M. (2014) 'The Discrimination of Women in Latin America', *Global Network for Rights and Development.* Available at: http://www.gnrd.net/seemore.php?id=1186 (Accessed 31 July 2015).

Johansen, B. E. (ed.) (1998) *The Encyclopedia of Native American Legal Tradition.* Westport, CT: Greenwood Press.

Johnson, H. B. (1987) 'Portuguese Settlement, 1500–1580', in L. Bethell (ed.), *Colonial Brazil*. Cambridge: Cambridge University Press.

Jung, C. G. (1916) *Psychology of the Unconscious: A Study of the Transformations and Symbolisms of the Libido: A Contribution to the History of the Evolution of Thought*. New York: Moffat, Yard and Co.

Karlsson, B. G. (2000) *Contested Belonging: An Indigenous People's Struggle for Forest and Identity in Sub-Himalayan Bengal*, 2nd ed. New York: Routledge.

Karlsson, B. G. (2003) 'Anthropology and the "Indigenous Slot": Claims to and Debates about Indigenous Peoples' Status in India', *Critique of Anthropology* 23 (4): 403–423.

Kaye, J. (2010) *Moving Millions: How Coyote Capitalism Fuels Global Immigration*. Hoboken, NJ: John Wiley and Sons.

Keal, P. (2003) *European Conquest and the Rights of Indigenous Peoples: The Moral Backwardness of International Society*. Cambridge: Cambridge University Press.

Kent, N. (2014) *The Sámi Peoples of the North*. London: Hurst.

Kessell, J. (1981) 'General Sherman and the Navajo Treaty of 1868: A Basic and Expedient Misunderstanding', *The Western Historical Quarterly* 12 (3): 251–272.

Kingsbury, B. (2008) '"Indigenous Peoples" in International Law: A Constructivist Approach to the Asian Controversy', in C. Erni (ed.), *The Concept of Indigenous Peoples in Asia*. Copenhagen/Chiang Mai: IWGIA/AIPP.

Kjosavik, D. J. (2011) 'Standpoints and Intersections: Towards an Indigenist Epistemology', in R. D. Rycroft and S. Dasgupta (eds.), *The Politics of Belonging in India*. London: Routledge.

Klare, M. (2012) *The Race for What's Left: The Global Scramble for the World's Last Resources*. New York: Macmillan.

Klein, H. (2015) *Compañeras: Zapatista Women's Stories*. New York: Seven Stories Press.

Kociumbas, J. (2004) 'Genocide and Modernity in Colonial Australia: 1788–1850', in D. Moses (ed.), *Genocide and Settler Society: Frontier Violence and Stolen Indigenous Children in Australian History*. New York: Berghahn Books.

Kolbert, E. (2006) *Field Notes from a Catastrophe*. London: Bloomsbury.

König, H.-J. (1998) '¿Bárbaro o símbolo de la libertad? ¿Menor de edad o ciudadano? Imagen del indio y política indigenista en Hispanoamérica', in H.-J. König (ed.), *El indio como sujeto y objeto de la historia latinoamericana: Pasado y Presente*. Madrid: Iberoamericana.

Kopenewa, D. and Aubert, B. (2013) *The Falling Sky: Words of a Yanomami Shaman*, trans. N. Elliot and A. Dundy. Cambridge, MA: Harvard University Press.

Korman, S. (2010) 'Protection of Indigenous Lands in Domestic Legal Regimes: The Importance of International Influences', *Northwestern Interdisciplinary Law Review* 3: 149–174.

Korsbaek, L. and Sámano Rentería, M. A. (2007) 'El Indigenismo en México: Antecedentes y Actualidad', *Ra Ximhai* 3 (1): 195–224.

Kurasawa, F. (2004) *The Ethnological Imagination: A Cross-Cultural Critique of Modernity*. Minneapolis: University of Minnesota Press.

Lacan, J. (2006) *Écrits: The First Complete Edition in English*, trans. B. Fink. New York: Norton.

Lacey, E. J. (2003) 'Manifest Destiny's New Face: Soft-Selling Tribal Heritage Lands for Toxic Waste', *Georgetown Law Journal* 92: 405–433.

LaForme, H. S. (2005) 'The Justice System in Canada: Does it Work for Aboriginal People?', *Indigenous Law Journal* 4: 1–17.

Lafitte, G. (2013) *Spoiling Tibet: China and Resource Nationalism on the Roof of the World*. London: Zed Books.

Lam, M. C. (1992) 'Making Room for Peoples at the United Nations: Thoughts Provoked by Indigenous Claims to Self-Determination', *Cornell International Law Journal* 25 (3): 603–622.

Lakhani, N. (2016) 'Berta Cáceres murder: four men arrested over Honduran activist's death. Honduras officials report arrests of two people linked to company building hydroelectric dam which Cáceres had fought', *Guardian*, 2 May. Available at: http://www.theguardian.com/world/2016/may/02/berta-caceres-murder-four-men-arrested-honduras (Accessed 4 May 2016).

Landman, T. (2006) *Studying Human Rights*. London: Routledge.

Langer, E. D. (2003) 'Introduction', in E. D. Langer and E. Muñoz (eds.), *Contemporary Indigenous Movements in Latin America*. Wilmington, DE: Scholarly Resources Inc.

LaRocque, E. (1997) 'Re-examining Culturally Appropriate Models in Criminal Justice Applications', in M. Asch (ed.), *Aboriginal and Treaty Rights in Canada: Essays on Law, Equity, and Respect for Difference*. Vancouver: University of British Columbia Press.

Las Casas, B. de (1992/1552) *A Short Account of the Destruction of the Indies*, trans. Nigel Griffin. London: Penguin.

Latta, A. (2007) 'Citizenship and the Politics of Nature: The Case of Chile's Alto Bío Bío', *Citizenship Studies* 11 (3): 229–246.

Law, B. (2008) 'Unease over Guatemalan Gold Rush', BBC Radio 4's *Crossing Continents*. Available at: http://news.bbc.co.uk/2/hi/programmes/crossing_continents/7569810.stm (Accessed 15 January 2015).

Lawrence, B. (2004) *'Real' Indians and Others: Mixed-blood Urban Native Peoples and Indigenous Nationhood*. Lincoln: University of Nebraska Press.

Lawrence, J. (2000) 'The Indian Health Service and the Sterilization of Native American Women', *The American Indian Quarterly* 24 (3): 400–419.

Lazreg, M. (1983) 'The Reproduction of Colonial Ideology: The Case of the Kabyle Berbers', *Arab Studies Quarterly* 5 (4): 380–395.

Leacock, E. B. (ed.) (1981) *Myths of Male Dominance: Collected Articles on Women Cross-Culturally*. New York: Monthly Review Press.

Lee, R. (1993) *The Dobe Ju/'Hoansi*, 2nd ed. Orlando, FL: Harcourt Brace College Publishers.

Legacy of Hope Foundation (n.d.) *Where Are the Children? Healing the Legacy of the Residential Schools*. Available at: http://wherearethechildren. ca/en (Accessed 15 January 2015).

Légaré, A. (2008) 'Canada's Experiment with Aboriginal Self-Determination in Nunavut: From Vision to Illusion', *International Journal on Minority & Group Rights* 15 (2): 335–368.

Lepore, J. (1998) *The Name of War: King Philip's War and the Origins of American Identity*. New York: Vintage.

Leslie, J. (2007) *Deep Water: The Epic Struggle over Dams, Displaced People, and the Environment*. London: Macmillan.

Leuthold, S. (1999) 'Native Media's Communities', in D. Champagne (ed.), *Contemporary Native American Cultural Issues*. Walnut Creek, CA: AltaMira Press.

Levene, M. (1999) 'The Chittagong Hill Tracts: A Case Study in the Political Economy of "Creeping" Genocide', *Third World Quarterly* 20 (2): 339–369.

Levin, M. (1999) 'Japan: *Kayano et al. v. Hokkaido Expropriation Committee*: The Nibutani Dam Decision', *International Legal Materials* 38 (2): 394–429.

Lewis, D. R. (2007) 'Skull Valley Goshutes and the Politics of Nuclear Waste', in M. Harkin and D. R. Lewis (eds.), *Native Americans and the Environment: Perspectives on the Ecological Indian*. Lincoln: University of Nebraska Press.

Lewis, J. (2000) *The Batwa Pygmies of the Great Lakes Region*. London: Minority Rights Group.

Li, T. M. (2010) 'Indigeneity, Capitalism and the Management of Dispossession', *Current Anthropology* 51 (3): 385–414.

Liberti, S. (2013) *Land Grabbing: Journeys in the New Colonialism*, trans. E. Flannelly. London: Verso.

Lindmark, D. (2006) 'Pietism and Colonialism. Swedish Schooling in Eighteenth-Century Sápmi', *Acta Borealia* 23 (2): 116–129.

Lindmark, D. (2013) 'Colonial Encounter in Early Modern Sápmi', in M. Naum and J. M. Nordin (eds.), *Scandinavian Colonialism and the Rise of Modernity: Small Time Agents in a Global Arena*. New York: Springer.

Lindqvist, S. (2007) *Terra Nullius: A Journey Through No One's Land*. London: Granta.

Lindsay, B. (2012) *Murder State: California's Native American Genocide, 1846–1873*. Lincoln: University of Nebraska Press.

Littlefield, A. (2001) 'Native American Labor and Public Policy in the United States', in S. Lobo and S. Talbot (eds.), *Native American Voices: A Reader*, 2nd ed. Upper Saddle River, NJ: Prentice-Hall.

Litvinoff, M. and Griffiths, T. (2014) *Securing Forests, Securing Rights: Report of the International Workshop on Deforestation and the Rights of Forest*

Peoples. Forest Peoples Programme, 5 December. Available at: http://www. forestpeoples.org/topics/rights-land-natural-resources/publication/2014/ securing-forests-securing-rights-report-intern (Accessed 15 January 2015).

Locke, J. (1965/1689) *Two Treatises of Government*, rev. ed. New York: New American Library.

Lonetree, A. (2012) *Decolonizing Museums: Representing Native America in National and Tribal Museums*. Chapel Hill: University of North Carolina Press.

López, A. (2005) *The Colonial History of Paraguay: The Revolt of the Comuneros, 1721–1735*. New Brunswick, NJ: Transaction Publishers.

Los Angeles Times (2008) 'Native Intelligence: Indigenous Peoples in South America are taking on Big Oil over Decades of Environmental Abuse', 29 March. Available at: http://articles.latimes.com/2008/mar/29/ opinion/ed-oil29 (Accessed 15 January 2015).

Luna, J. (1991) 'Allow Me to Introduce Myself: The Performance Art of James Luna', *Canadian Theatre Review* 68: 46–47.

Lund, R. (2000) 'Geographies of Eviction, Expulsion and Marginalization: Stories and Coping Capacities of the Veddhas, Sri Lanka', *Norsk Geografisk Tidsskrift* 54 (3): 102–109.

Lux, M. (2001) *Medicine that Walks: Disease Medicine and Canadian Plains Native People, 1880–1940*. Toronto: University of Toronto Press.

Macas, L. (2003) 'Luis Macas', in E. D. Langer and E. Muñoz (eds.), *Contemporary Indigenous Movements in Latin America*. Wilmington, DE: Scholarly Resources Inc.

MacDonald, R. (1995) *Between Two Worlds: The Commonwealth Government and the Removal of Aboriginal Children of Part Descent from the Northern Territory*. Alice Springs: IAD Press.

MacKenzie, J. M. (1988/1997) *The Empire of Nature: Hunting, Conservation and British Imperialism*. Manchester: Manchester University Press.

MacKinnon, A. (2015) 'Eyeing the Future on the Wind River', *Wyoming Law Review* 15: 517–548.

Maclellan, N. (2001) 'Indigenous Peoples in the Pacific and the World Conference Against Racism', in S. Chakma and M. Jensen (eds.), *Racism Against Indigenous Peoples*. Copenhagen: IWGIA.

Madani, B. (2003) 'Arabization of the Amazigh Lands', *International Journal of Francophone Studies* 6 (3): 211–213.

Madley, B. (2004) 'Patterns of Frontier Genocide 1803–1910: The Aboriginal Tasmanians, the Yuki of California, and the Herero of Namibia', *Journal of Genocide Research* 6 (2): 167–192.

Madley, B. (2012) 'California and Oregon's Modoc Indians: How Resistance Camouflages Genocide in Colonial Histories', in A. Woolford, J. Benvenuto and A. L. Hinton (eds.), *Colonial Genocide in Indigenous North America*. Durham, NC: Duke University Press.

Malinowski, B. (1945) *The Dynamics of Culture Change: An Inquiry into Race Relations in Africa*. New Haven, CT: Yale University Press.

Mamdani, M. (2012) *Define and Rule: The W. E. B. DuBois Lectures.* Cambridge, MA: Harvard University Press.

Mann, C. (2012) *1493: Uncovering the New World Columbus Created.* New York: Vintage.

Mantena, K. (2010) *Alibis of Empire: Henry Maine and the Ends of Imperial Liberalism.* Princeton, NJ: Princeton University Press.

Marcus, A. R. (1995) *Relocating Eden: The Image and Politics of Inuit Exile in the Canadian Arctic.* Hanover: University Press of New England.

Marlowe, F. (2002) 'Why the Hadza are Still Hunter Gatherers', in S. Kent (ed.), *Ethnicity, Hunter-Gatherers, and the 'Other': Association or Assimilation in Africa.* Washington DC: Smithsonian Institution Press.

Martinez, D. (2011) *The American Indian Intellectual Tradition: An Anthology of Writings, 1772–1992.* Ithaca, NY: Cornell University Press.

Marzal, M. (2000) 'Las Misiones Jesuitas, una Utopía Posible?', in S. Negro and M. Marzal (eds.), *Un Reino en la Frontera: Las Misiones Jesuitas en la América Colonial.* Quito: Ediciones ABYA-YALA.

Masefield, J. (ed.) (1910) *Chronicles of the Pilgrim Fathers.* No. 480. London: Dent & Sons.

Mathur, H. M. (2003) *Displacement and Resettlement in India: The Human Cost of Development.* Abingdon: Routledge.

Maylam, P. (2001) *South Africa's Racial Past: The History and Historiography of Racism, Segregation, and Apartheid.* Aldershot: Ashgate.

Mayorga, F. and Córdoba, E. (2009) *El Movimiento Antiglobalización en Bolivia: Procesos globales e iniciativas locales en tiempo de crisis y cambio.* La Paz: Plural Editores.

McCarthy, T. (2009) *Race, Empire and the Idea of Human Development.* Cambridge: Cambridge University Press.

McCarty, T. L. (2002) *A Place to be Navajo: Rough Rock and the Struggle for Self-Determination in Indigenous Schooling.* London: Routledge.

McCarty, T. L., Watahomigie, L. J., Yamamoto, A. Y. and Zepeda, O. (1997) *School–Community–University Collaborations: The American Indian Language Development Institute.* ERIC Clearinghouse. Available at: http://aildi.arizona.edu/sites/default/files/aildi-30-year-book-01-school-community-university-collaborations.pdf (Accessed 21 April 2016).

McGhee, R. (2004) *The Last Imaginary Place: A Human History of the Arctic World.* Toronto: Key Porter Books and the Canadian Museum of Civilization.

McGoey, L. (2015) *No Such Thing as a Free Gift: The Gates Foundation and the Price of Philanthropy.* London: Verso.

McGrane, B. (1989) *Beyond Anthropology: Society and the Other.* New York: Columbia University Press.

McGrath, M. (2006) *The Long Exile: A True Story of Deception and Survival in the Canadian Arctic.* London: Harper Perennial.

McGregor, R. (1993) *Imagined Destinies: Aboriginal Australians and the Doomed Race Theory, 1880–1939.* Melbourne: Melbourne University Press.

McIvor, S. D. (2004) 'Aboriginal Women Unmasked: Using Equality Litigation to Advance Women's Rights', *Canadian Journal of Women & the Law* 16 (1): 106–136.

McMichael, P. (2009) 'The Agrofuels Project at Large', *Critical Sociology* 35 (6): 825–839.

McNiven, L. (2015) *A Short History of Indigenous Filmmaking*. Australia's Audiovisual Heritage Online. Available at: http://aso.gov.au/titles/collections/indigenous-filmmaking/ (Accessed 15 January 2015).

Mead, G. H. (1934) *Mind, Self, and Society*. Chicago, IL: University of Chicago Press.

Medak-Saltzman, D. (2010) 'Transnational Indigenous Exchange: Rethinking Global Interactions of Indigenous Peoples at the 1904 St. Louis Exposition', *American Quarterly* 62 (3): 591–615.

Medak-Saltzman, D. (2015) 'Empire's Haunted Logics: Comparative Colonialisms and the Challenges of Incorporating Indigeneity', *Critical Ethnic Studies* 1 (2): 11–32.

Mercer, D. (2003) '"Citizen Minus"?: Indigenous Australians and the Citizenship Question', *Citizenship Studies* 7 (4): 421–445.

Mey, W. (ed.) (1984) *They are Now Burning Village After Village. Genocide in the Chittagong Hill Tracts, Bangladesh*. Copenhagen: IWGIA.

Mignolo, W. (ed.) (2011) *The Darker Side of Western Modernity: Global Futures, Decolonial Options*. Durham, NC: Duke University Press.

Milan, S. (2013) *Social Movements and their Technologies*. Basingstoke: Palgrave Macmillan.

Miller, B. (2003) *Invisible Indigenes: The Politics of Nonrecognition*. Lincoln: University of Nebraska Press.

Miller, R., Ruru, J., Behrendt, L. and Lindberg, T. (2010) *Discovering Indigenous Lands: The Doctrine of Discovery in the English Colonies*. Oxford: Oxford University Press.

Miller, S. (1998) 'Licensed Trafficking and Ethnogenetic Engineering', in D. Mihesuah (ed.), *Natives and Academics: Researching and Writing about American Indians*. Lincoln: University of Nebraska Press.

Miller, S. (2011) 'Native Historians Write Back: The Indigenous Paradigm in American Indian Historiography', in S. Miller and J. Riding In (eds.), *Native Historians Write Back*. Lubbock: Texas Tech University Press.

Mills, A. (1994) 'Reincarnation Belief among Indians and Inuit', in A. Mills and R. Slobodin (eds.), *Amerindian Rebirth: Reincarnation Belief among North American Indians and Inuit*. Toronto: University of Toronto Press.

Minde, H. (2003) 'Assimilation of the Sami: Implementation and Consequences', *Acto Borealia* 20 (2): 121–146.

Molintas, J. M. (2004) 'The Philippine Indigenous Peoples' Struggle for Land and Life: Challenging Legal Texts', *Arizona Journal of International & Comparative Law* 21 (1): 269–306.

Molyneaux, S. and Imai, S. (2014) 'Speaker's Corner: Mining Company Lawsuit Shows Need for International Law Reform', *Law Times*, 20

October. Available at: http://www.lawtimesnews.com/201410204263/commentary/speaker-s-corner-mining-company-lawsuit-shows-need-for-international-law-reform (Accessed 15 January 2015).

Momaday, N. S. (1964) 'The Morality of Indian Hating', *Ramparts* 3 (1): 29–40.

Momaday, N. S. (1997) *The Man Made of Words: Essays, Stories, Passages*. New York: St. Martin's Press.

Monroy, D. (1993) *Thrown Among Strangers: The Making of Mexican Culture in Frontier California*. Berkeley: University of California Press.

Montaigne, M. (1993/1580) 'On the Cannibals', in M. A. Screech (ed.), *Michel de Montaigne: The Complete Essays*. London: Penguin.

Montreal Gazette. (2016) 'Quebec Coroner to Probe Five Innu Suicides', 3 February. Available at: http://montrealgazette.com/news/quebec-coroner-to-probe-five-innu-suicides (Accessed 14 February 2016).

Mooney, J. (1965/1896) *The Ghost Dance Religion and the Sioux Outbreak of 1890*. Chicago, IL: University of Chicago Press.

Moorhouse, B. (1996) *A Place Called Grand Canyon: Contested Geographies*. Tucson: University of Arizona Press.

Moreno Yañez, S. and Figueroa, J. (1990) *El Levantamiento Indígena del Inti Raymi de 1990*. Quito: ABYA-YALA.

Moreton-Robinson, A. (ed.) (2004) *Whitening Race: Essays in Social and Cultural Criticism*. Canberra: Aboriginal Studies Press.

Morgan, L. H. (1962/1851) *League of the Iroquois*. New York: Corinth Books.

Morgan, R. (2009) 'Forging Indigenous Rights at the United Nations: A Social Constructionist Account', in R. Morgan and B. S. Turner (eds.), *Interpreting Human Rights: Social Sciences Perspectives*. Abingdon: Routledge.

Morgan, R. (2011) *Transforming Law and Institution: Indigenous Peoples, the United Nations and Human Rights*. Farnham: Ashgate.

Morris, G. (1992) 'International Law and Politics: Toward a Right to Self-Determination for Indigenous Peoples', in M. A. Jaimes (ed.), *The State of Native America: Genocide, Colonization, and Resistance*. Boston, MA: South End Press.

Morris, L. (ed.) (2006) *Rights: Sociological Perspectives*. Abingdon: Routledge.

Moseley, C. W. R. D. (1983) *The Travels of Sir John Mandeville*. London: Penguin.

Muggah, R. (2003) 'A Tale of Two Solitudes: Comparing Conflict and Development-induced Internal Displacement and Involuntary Resettlement', *International Migration* 41 (5): 5–31.

Murray, K. (1959) *The Modocs and Their War*. Norman: University of Oklahoma Press.

Nabhan, G. and Antoine, S. St. (1993) 'The Loss of Floral and Faunal Story: The Extinction of Experience', in S. Kellert and E. O. Wilson (eds.), *The Biophilia Hypothesis*. Covelo, CA: Island Press.

Nagel, J. (1994) *American Indian Ethnic Renewal: Red Power and the Resurgence of Identity and Culture*. New York: Oxford University Press.

Nakamura, N. (2007) 'The Representation of Ainu Culture in the Japanese Museum System', *Canadian Journal of Native Studies* 27 (2): 331–365.

Nash, S. and Colwell-Chanthaphonh, C. (2010) 'NAGPRA after Two Decades', *Museum Anthropology* 33 (2): 99–104.

Ndagala, D. K. (1985) 'Attempts to Develop the Hadzabe of Tanzania', *Nomadic Peoples* 18: 17–26. Available at: http://cnp.nonuniv.ox.ac.uk/pdf/NP_journal_back_issues/Attempts_to_Develop_Hadzabe_of_Tanzania_DK_Ndagala.pdf (Accessed 15 January 2015).

Nettle, D. (1999) *Linguistic Diversity*. Oxford: Oxford University Press.

Nettle, D. and Romaine, S. (2000) *Vanishing Voices: The Extinction of the World's Languages*. Oxford: Oxford University Press.

Nettleton, C., Napolitano, D. and Stephens, C. (2007) 'An Overview of Current Knowledge of the Social Determinants of Indigenous Health.' Working Paper. London School of Hygiene and Tropical Medicine.

Newman, D. G. (2010) 'Africa and the United Nations Declaration on the Rights of Indigenous Peoples', in S. Dersso (ed.), *Perspectives on the Rights of Minorities and Indigenous Peoples in Africa*. Pretoria: Pretoria University Law Press.

Nicholas, C. (2000) *The Orang Asli and the Contest for Resources: Indigenous Politics, Development and Identity in Peninsular Malaysia*. Copenhagen: IWGIA.

Nicholas, C. (2002) 'Organizing Orang Asli Identity', in G. Benjamin and C. Chou (eds.), *Tribal Communities in the Malay World: Historical, Cultural, and Social Perspectives*. Singapore: Institute of Southeast Asian Studies.

Nielsen, M. O. (2009) 'Introduction to the Context of Native American Criminal Justice System Involvement', in M. O. Nielsen and R. Silverman (eds.), *Criminal Justice in Native America*. Tucson: University of Arizona Press.

Niezen, R. (ed.) (2000) *Spirit Wars: Native North American Religions in the Age of Nation Building*. Berkeley: University of California Press.

Niezen, R. (2003) *The Origins of Indigenism: Human Rights and the Politics of Identity*. Berkeley: University of California Press.

Niezen, R. (2005) *A World Beyond Difference: Cultural Identity in the Age of Globalization*. Oxford: Blackwell.

Nomura, G. (1992) Inauguration Speech, UN General Assembly, 10 December, Ainu Association of Hokkaido (Japan). Available at: https://www.ainu-assn.or.jp/english/inaugu.html (Accessed 5 May 2016).

Norget, K. (2015) '"Knowing Where We Enter": Indigenous Theology and the Popular Church in Oaxaca, Mexico', in E. L. Cleary and T. J. Steigenca (eds.), *Resurgent Voices in Latin America: Indigenous Peoples, Political Mobilization and Religious Change*. New Brunswick, NJ: Rutgers University Press.

Noriega, J. (1992) 'American Indian Education in the United States: Indoctrination for Subordination to Colonialism', in A. Jaimes (ed.), *The State of Native America: Genocide, Colonization, and Resistance*. Boston, MA: South End Press.

Norman, D. W. (2014) 'Control Mapping: Peter Pitseolak and Zacharias Kunuk on Reclaiming Inuit Photographic Images and Imaging', *Decolonization: Indigeneity, Education & Society* 3 (1): 48–72.

Nugent, M. (2015) 'Encounters in Country', in G. Sculthorpe et al. (eds.), *Indigenous Australia: Enduring Civilisation*. London: British Museum.

NWAC (Native Women's Association of Canada) (n.d.) *Fact Sheet: Missing and Murdered Aboriginal Women and Girls*. Available at: http://www.nwac. ca/wp-content/uploads/2015/05/Fact_Sheet_Missing_and_Murdered_ Aboriginal_Women_and_Girls.pdf (Accessed 22 January 2016).

Okada, M. V. (2012) 'The Plight of Ainu, Indigenous People of Japan', *Journal of Indigenous Social Development* 1 (1): 1–14.

Oliveira, A. de (ed.) (2009) *Decolonising Indigenous Rights*. London: Routledge.

Oliver-Smith, A. (1996) 'Anthropological Research on Hazards and Disasters', *Annual Review of Anthropology* 25: 303–328.

Olmsted, N. (2004) 'Indigenous Rights in Botswana: Development, Democracy and Dispossession', *Washington University Global Studies Law Review* 3: 799–866.

Olusoga, D. and Erichsen, C. (2010) *The Kaiser's Holocaust: Germany's Forgotten Genocide and the Colonial Roots of Nazism*. London: Faber and Faber.

Ong, A. (2006) *Neoliberalism as Exception: Mutations in Citizenship and Sovereignty*. Durham, NC: Duke University Press.

Ontebetse, K. (2014) 'Hunting Ban Aimed at Starving Basarwa out of CKGR', *Sunday Standard*. Available at: http://www.sundaystandard. info/'hunting-ban-aimed-starving-basarwa-out-ckgr'-sesana (Accessed 15 January 2015).

Opie, J. (1998) *Nature's Nation: An Environmental History of the US*. Fort Worth, TX: Harcourt Brace College Publishers.

Ornelas, R. (2014) 'Implementing the Policy of the UN Declaration on the Rights of Indigenous Peoples', *The International Indigenous Policy Journal* 5 (1). Available at: http://ir.lib.uwo.ca/iipj/vol5/iss1/4 (Accessed 15 January 2015).

Owens, L. (2001) 'As If an Indian Were Really an Indian', in G. Bataille (ed.), *Native American Representations: First Encounters, Distorted Images, and Literary Appropriations*. Lincoln: University of Nebraska Press.

Pagden, A. (1995) *Lords of All the World: Ideologies of Empire in Spain, Britain and France c.1500–1800*. New Haven, CT: Yale University Press.

Pairican, F. (2014) *Malon: La Rebelión del Movimiento Mapuche 1990–2013*. Santiago: Pehuén Editores.

Panday, P. K. and Jamil, I. (2009) 'Conflict in the Chittagong Hill Tracts of Bangladesh: An Unimplemented Accord and Continued Violence', *Asian Survey* 49 (6): 1052–1070.

Parker, L. (1996) *Native American Estate: The Struggle over Indian and Hawaiian Lands*. Honolulu: University of Hawaii Press.

Pasqualucci, J. (2006) 'The Evolution of International Indigenous Rights in the Inter-American Human Rights System', *Human Rights Law Review*, 6 (2): 281–322.

Pasqualucci, J. (2009) 'International Indigenous Land Rights: A Critique of the Jurisprudence of the Inter-American Court of Human Rights in Light of The United Nations Declaration on the Rights of Indigenous Peoples', *Wisconsin International Law Journal* 27: 51–98.

Pauketat, T. R. and Emerson, T. E. (eds.) (1997) *Cahokia: Domination and Ideology in the Mississippian World*. Lincoln: University of Nebraska Press.

Pearce, R. H. (1988/1953) *Savagism and Civilization: A Study of the Indian and the American Mind*. Berkeley: University of California Press.

Pearson, W. G. and Knabe, S. (eds.) (2015) *Reverse Shots: Indigenous Film and Media in an International Context*. Waterloo: Wilfrid Laurier University Press.

Pedlowski, M. A. (2013) 'When the State Becomes the Land Grabber: Violence and Dispossession in the Name of "Development" in Brazil', *Journal of Latin American Geography* 12 (3): 91–111.

Peloso, V. C. (2014) *Race and Ethnicity in Latin American History*. New York: Routledge.

Penn, N. (2005) *The Forgotten Frontier: Colonist and Khoisan on the Cape's Northern Frontier in the 18th Century*. Athens: Ohio University Press.

Perry, R. (1996) *From Time Immemorial: Indigenous Peoples and State Systems*. Austin: University of Texas Press.

Peters, E. and Andersen, C. (eds.) (2013) *Indigenous in the City: Contemporary Identities and Cultural Innovation*. Vancouver: University of British Columbia Press.

Philpott, D., Nesbit, W., Cahill, M. and Jeffery, G. (2004) *An Educational Profile of the Learning Needs of Innu Youth*. St. Johns: Memorial University of Newfoundland.

PIB (Povos Indigenas no Brasil) (2015) *Localização e extensão das Tis*. Available at: http://pib.socioambiental.org/pt/c/terras-indigenas/demarcacoes/localizacao-e-extensao-das-tis (Accessed 15 January 2015).

Poirier, C. (2013) *Indigenous Rights under Assault in Brazil*. Available at: http://amazonwatch.org/news/2013/0808-indigenous-rights-under-assault-in-brazil (Accessed 15 January 2015).

Poirier, R. and Ostergren, D. (2002) 'Evicting People from Nature: Indigenous Land Rights and National Parks in Australia, Russia and the United States', *Natural Resources Journal* 42: 331–351.

Poitras, G. (2009) 'Canada's Bloody Oil', *Guardian*, 24 August. Available at: http://www.theguardian.com/commentisfree/2009/aug/24/climate-camp-canada-oil-tar-sands (Accessed 15 January 2015).

Polanyi, K. (1944) *The Great Transformation: The Political and Economic Origins of Our Time*. Boston, MA: Beacon Books.

Porteous, J. and Smith, S. E. (2001) *Domicide: The Global Destruction of Home*. Montreal: McGill-Queens University Press.

Porter, J. (2014) 'Ontario Gives Green Light to Clearcutting at Grassy Narrows', CBC News, 30 December. Available at: http://www.cbc.ca/news/canada/thunder-bay/ontario-gives-green-light-to-clearcutting-at-grassy-narrows-1.2885801 (Accessed 15 January 2015).

Porter, J. (2015) 'Grassy Narrows First Nation Declares Emergency over Bad Water', CBC News, 28 August. Available at: http://www.cbc.ca/news/canada/thunder-bay/grassy-narrows-first-nation-declares-emergency-over-bad-water-1.3204974 (Accessed 4 October 2015).

Pretty, J. (2013) 'The Consumption of a Finite Planet: Well-Being, Convergence, Divergence and the Nascent Green Economy', *Environmental and Resource Economics* 55 (4): 475–499.

Quane, H. (1998) 'The United Nations and the Evolving Right to Self-Determination', *International and Comparative Law Quarterly* 47 (3): 537–572.

Quinn, W. (1992) 'Federal Acknowledgment of American Indian Tribes: Authority, Judicial Interposition, and 25 CFR §83', *American Indian Law Review* 17 (1): 37–69.

Ramnarine, T. K. (2013) 'Sonic Images of the Sacred in Sámi Cinema', *Interventions: International Journal of Postcolonial Studies* 15 (2): 239–254.

Ramos, A. R. (1998) *Indigenism: Ethnic Politics in Brazil*. Madison: University of Wisconsin Press.

Ramos, A. R. (2003) 'The Special (or Specious?) Status of Brazilian Indians', *Citizenship Studies* 7 (4): 401–420.

Rata, E. (2003) 'Late Capitalism and Ethnic Revivalism: A New Middle Age?', *Anthropological Theory* 3 (1): 43–63.

RCAP (Royal Commission on Aboriginal Peoples) (1996) *Looking Forward, Looking Backward*, vol. 1. Ottawa: Minister of Supply and Services Canada.

Republic of Bolivia (2009) *Constitución Política del Estado Plurinacional de Bolivia*. Available at: http://www.harmonywithnatureun.org/content/documents/159Bolivia%20Constitucion.pdf (Accessed 21 April 2016).

Republic of the Congo (2011) *Act No. 5: On the Promotion and Protection of Indigenous Populations*. Parliament of Congo. Available at: http://www.iwgia.org/iwgia_files_news_files/0368_Congolese_Legislation_on_Indigenous_Peoples.pdf (Accessed 21 April 2016).

Republic of Ecuador (2008) *Constitución de la República del Ecuador*. Available at: http://www.asambleanacional.gov.ec/documentos/constitucion_de_bolsillo.pdf (Accessed 15 January 2015).

Republic of the Philippines (1997) *The Indigenous Peoples' Rights Act (IPRA) No. 8371*. Available at: http://www.gov.ph/1997/10/29/republic-act-no-8371/ (Accessed 15 January 2015).

República Federativa do Brasil (1988) *Constituição da República Federativa do Brasil*. Available at: http://www.planalto.gov.br/ccivil_03/Constituicao/Constituicao.htm (Accessed 15 January 2015).

Reynolds, H. (2005) *Nowhere People*. New York: Penguin.

Riesman, D. (1961) *The Lonely Crowd: A Study of the Changing American Character*. New Haven, CT: Yale University Press.

Rist, G. (1997) *The History of Development: From Western Origins to Global Faith*, trans. P. Camiller. London: Zed Books.

Robbins, R. (2006) 'The Guaraní: The Economics of Ethnocide', in R. Maaka and C. Andersen (eds.), *The Indigenous Experience: Global Perspectives*. Toronto: Canadian Scholars' Press.

Robertson, L. (2005) *Conquest by Law: How the Discovery of America Dispossessed Indigenous Peoples of their Lands*. New York: Oxford University Press.

Rodríguez, A. and Vergara, P. (2015) *La Frontera. Crónica de la Araucanía rebelde*. Santiago: Catalonia y Ediciones UDP.

Roque de Pinho (2013) 'Shooting Climate Change in the Maasai Mara: Aesthetics and Expectations in Participatory Filmmaking with Kenyan Pastoralists', *Anthropology Now* 5 (2): 74–86.

Rostow, W. W. (1990/1960) *The Stages of Economic Growth: A Non-Communist Manifesto*. Cambridge: Cambridge University Press.

Roy, R. C. (2000) *Land Rights of the Indigenous Peoples of the Chittagong Hill Tracts Bangladesh*. Copenhagen: IWGIA.

Roy, R. D. (2009) 'The ILO Convention on Indigenous and Tribal Populations, 1957, and the Laws of Bangladesh: A Comparative Review', *Project to Promote ILO Policy on Indigenous and Tribal Peoples and ILO Office*. Dhaka, Bangladesh.

Russett, C. E. (1976) *Darwin in America: The Intellectual Response 1865–1912*. San Francisco: W. H. Freeman.

Sale, R. and Potapov, E. (2010) *The Scramble for the Arctic: Ownership, Exploitation and Conflict in the Far North*. London: Frances Lincoln.

Sale, K. (1991) *The Conquest of Paradise: Christopher Columbus and the Columbian Legacy*. New York: Plume.

Salidjanova, N. (2011) *Going Out: An Overview of China's Outward Foreign Direct Investment*. US–China Economic & Security Review Commission. Available at: http://www.bioin.or.kr/InnoDS/data/upload/policy/13140 79084656.pdf (Accessed 15 January 2015).

Salisbury, N. (1974) 'Red Puritans: The "Praying Indians" of Massachusetts Bay and John Eliot', *The William and Mary Quarterly* 31 (1): 27–54.

Salisbury, N. (2003) 'Embracing Ambiguity: Native Peoples and Christianity in Seventeenth-Century North America', *Ethnohistory* 50 (2): 247–259.

Samson, C. (2003) *A Way of Life That Does Not Exist: Canada and the Extinguishment of the Innu*. London: Verso Press.

Samson, C. (2008) 'The Rule of *Terra Nullius* and the Impotence of International Human Rights for Indigenous Peoples', *Essex Human Rights Review* 5 (1): 69–82.

Samson, C. (2013) *A World You Do Not Know: Settler Societies, Indigenous Peoples and the Attack on Cultural Diversity*. London: School of Advanced Studies Press.

Samson, C. (2016) 'Canada's Strategy of Dispossession: Aboriginal Land and Rights Cessions in Comprehensive Land Claims', *Canadian Journal of Law and Society / Revue Canadienne Droit et Société*: 1–24

Samson, C. and Cassell, E. (2013) 'The Long Reach of Frontier Justice: Canadian Land Claims "Negotiation" Strategies as Human Rights Violations', *International Journal of Human Rights* 17 (1): 35–55.

Samson, C. and Short, D. (2006) 'Sociology and the Human Rights of Indigenous Peoples', in L. Morris (ed.), *Rights: Sociological Perspectives.* Abingdon: Routledge.

Sand, H. P. (2014) 'Norwegian Sociology and the Recognition of the Saami Minority', *Advances in Applied Sociology* 4 (5): 135–140. Available at: http://dx.doi.org/10.4236/aasoci.2014.45017 (Accessed 15 January 2015).

Sanders, E. (2015) 'Canadian Industry Lags Behind in Human Rights', *Cultural Survival Quarterly*, 14 January. Available at: http://www.culturalsurvival.org/news/canadian-industry-lags-behind-human-rights (Accessed 15 January 2015).

Sando, J. (1976) *The Pueblo Indians.* San Francisco, CA: Indian Historical Society Press.

Sarkin, J. (2011) *Germany's Genocide of the Herero: Kaiser Wilhelm II, His General, His Settlers, His Soldiers.* Woodbridge: James Currey.

Saugestad, S. (2001) *The Inconvenient Indigenous: Remote Area Development in Botswana, Donor Assistance and the First People of the Kalahari.* Oslo: The Nordic Africa Institute.

Saugestad, S. (2008) 'Beyond the "Columbus Context": New Challenges as the Indigenous Discourse is Applied to Africa', in H. Minde (ed.), *Indigenous Peoples: Self-Determination, Knowledge, Indigeneity.* Delft: Eburon.

Schedneck, B. (2015) *Thailand's International Meditation Centers: Tourism and the Global Commodification of Religious Practices.* Abingdon: Routledge.

Schendel, W. (2011) 'The Dangers of Belonging: Tribes, Indigenous Peoples and Homelands in South Asia', in R. D. Rycroft and S. Dasgupta (eds.), *The Politics of Belonging in India.* London: Routledge.

Scheper-Hughes, N. (2002) 'Coming to Our Senses: Anthropology and Genocide', in A. L. Hinton (ed.), *Annihilating Difference: The Anthropology of Genocide.* Berkeley: University of California Press.

Schneider, R. R., Hauer, G., Adamowicz, W. L. and Boutin, S. (2010) 'Triage for Conserving Populations of Threatened Species: The Case of Woodland Caribou in Alberta', *Biological Conservation* 143: 1603–1611.

Schwartz, S. B. (1987) 'Plantations and Peripheries, c.1580–c.1750', in L. Bethell (ed.), *Colonial Brazil.* Cambridge: Cambridge University Press.

Seed, P. (2001) *American Pentimento: The Invention of Indians and the Pursuit of Riches.* Minneapolis: University of Minnesota Press.

Sejersen, F. (2015) *Rethinking Greenland and the Arctic in the Era of Climate Change.* London: Routledge.

Shelton, A. A. (2000) 'Museum Ethnography An Imperial Science', in
E. Hallam and B. Street (eds.), *Cultural Encounters: Representing Otherness*.
London: Routledge.

Short, D. (2003) 'Reconciliation, Assimilation and the Indigenous Peoples
of Australia', *International Political Science Review* 24 (4): 491–513.

Short, D. (2008) *Reconciliation and Colonial Power: Indigenous Rights in
Australia*. Aldershot: Ashgate.

Shulman, D. (2014) 'Gaza: The Murderous Melodrama', *New York Review
of Books*, 20 November: 32–34.

Siddle, R. (1996) *Race, Resistance and the Ainu of Japan*. London: Routledge.

Silva, E. (2009) *Challenging Neoliberalism in Latin America*. New York:
Cambridge University Press.

Silverberg, R. (1970) *The Pueblo Revolt*. Lincoln: University of Nebraska
Press.

Simmons, L. (1942) *Sun Chief: The Autobiography of a Hopi Indian*. New
Haven, CT: Yale University Press.

Simon, J. (1998) 'Anthropology, "Native Schooling" and Maori: The
Politics of Cultural Adaptation Policies', *Oceania* 69 (1): 61–78.

Simon, S. (2007) 'Paths to Autonomy: Aboriginality and the Nation in
Taiwan', in C. Storm and M. Harrison (eds.), *The Margins of Becoming.
Identity and Culture in Taiwan*, vol. 5. Weisbaden: Harrassowitz Verlag.

Simon, S. (2011) 'Multiculturalism and Indigenism: Contrasting the
Experiences of Canada and Taiwan', in T.-W. Ngo and W. Hong-Zen
(eds.), *Politics of Difference in Taiwan*. London: Routledge.

Simpson, A. (2011) 'On Ethnographic Refusal: Indigeneity, "Voice" and
Colonial Citizenship', *Junctures: The Journal for Thematic Dialogue* 9:
67–80.

Siver Times (2016) 'Kuujjuaq Shaken by a Series of Suicides', 17 February.
Available   at: http://sivertimes.com/kuujjuaq-shaken-by-a-series-of-
suicides/9786 (Accessed 18 February 2016).

Slattery, B. (2005) 'Aboriginal Rights and the Honour of the Crown',
Supreme Court Law Review 20: 433–445.

Slezkine, Y. (1994) *Arctic Mirrors: Russia and the Small Peoples of the North*.
Ithaca, NY: Cornell University Press.

Slowey, G. (2008) *Navigating Neoliberalism: Self-Determination and the Mikisew
Cree First Nation*. Vancouver: University of British Columbia Press.

Smith, A. (2005) *Conquest: Sexual Violence and American Indian Genocide*.
Durham, NC: Duke University Press.

Smith, A. (2009) 'Indigenous Peoples and Boarding Schools: A Comparative
Study.' Paper for the Secretariat of the UN Permanent Forum on
Indigenous Issues. New York: United Nations.

Smith, L. T. (2012) *Decolonizing Methodologies: Research and Indigenous
Peoples*. London: Zed Books.

Smith, P. C. and Warrior, R. A. (1997) *Like a Hurricane: The Indian
Movement from Alcatraz to Wounded Knee*. New York: New Press.

Smith-Oka, V. (2009) 'Unintended Consequences: Exploring the Tensions Between Development Programs and Indigenous Women in Mexico in the Context of Reproductive Health', *Social Science & Medicine* 68 (11): 2069–2077.

SNZ (Statistics New Zealand) (2013) *Census QuickStats about Māori*. Available at: http://www.stats.govt.nz/Census/2013-census/profile-and-summary-reports/quickstats-about-maori-english/population.aspx (Accessed 15 January 2015).

Sontag, D. and MacDonald, B. (2014) 'In North Dakota, a Tale of Oil, Corruption and Death', *New York Times*, 28 December. Available at: http://www.nytimes.com/2014/12/29/us/in-north-dakota-where-oil-corruption-and-bodies-surface.html?_r=0 (Accessed 15 January 2015).

Soruco Sologuren, X., Franco Pinto, D. and Durán, M. (2014) *Composición Social del Estado Plurinacional: Hacia la Descolonización de la Burocracia*. La Paz: Fondo Editorial de la Vicepresidencia.

Soto, S. (2015) '"A World Where Many Worlds Fit": Zapatismo and the Reconstruction of a Post 1994 Mayan World in Chiapas.' Latina/o Studies Speaker Series Program. University of Wyoming, 20 October.

SSB (Statistics Norway) (2014) *Sami, 2011–2013*. Available at: https://www.ssb.no/en/befolkning/statistikker/samisk/hvert-2-aar/2014-02-06#content (Accessed 15 January 2015).

Stahler-Sholk, R. (2007) 'Resisting Neoliberal Homogenization: The Zapatista Autonomy Movement', *Latin American Perspectives* 34 (2): 48–63.

Stavenhagen, R. (2007) *Adoption of Declaration on Rights of Indigenous Peoples a Historic Moment for Human Rights, UN Expert says*. Available at: http://www.ohchr.org/EN/NewsEvents/Pages/DisplayNews.aspx?NewsID=1721&LangID=E (Accessed 15 January 2015).

Stavenhagen, R. (2008) 'Los Derechos de los Pueblos Indígenas: Desafíos y Problemas', *Revista IIDH* 48: 257–268.

Stavenhagen, R. (2010) *Los Pueblos Originarios: El Debate Necesario*. Buenos Aires: CLACSO.

Stegeborn, W. (2004) 'The Disappearing Wanniyala-Aetto ('Veddahs') of Sri Lanka: A Case Study', *Nomadic Peoples Journal* 8(1): 43–63.

Steinmetz, G. (ed.) (2013) *Sociology and Empire: The Imperial Entanglements of a Discipline*. Durham, NC: Duke University Press.

Stocks, A. (2005) 'Too Much For Too Few: Problems of Indigenous Land Rights in Latin America', *Annual Review of Anthropology* 34: 85–104.

Stone, J. (1988) 'Imperialism, Colonialism and Cartography', *Transactions of the Institute of British Geographers* 13: 57–64.

Stout, M. (2012) *Native American Boarding Schools*. Santa Barbara, CA: ABC-CLIO, LLC.

Strohmeyer, J. (1993) *Extreme Conditions: Big Oil and the Transformation of Alaska*. New York: Simon and Schuster.

Strong, P. T. (2004) 'Representational Practices', in T. Biolsi (ed.), *A Companion to the Anthropology of American Indians*. Oxford: Blackwell.

Supreme Court of Belize (2007) *Aurelio Cal et al v. Attorney General of Belize.* Available at: http://www.tjsl.edu/slomansonb/10.3_Indigenous_Case.pdf (Accessed 15 January 2015).

Survival International (n.d.) *Wanniyala-Aetto.* Available at: http://www.survivalinternational.org//tribes/wanniyala (Accessed 21 June 2016).

Survival International (1990) *Yanomami: Survival Campaign.* London: Survival International.

Tauli-Corpuz, V. (2007) *Message by Victoria Tauli-Copuz.* Available at: http://undesadspd.org/indigenouspeoples/declarationontherightsofindigenouspeoples.aspx (Accessed 15 January 2015).

Tauli-Corpuz, V. (2014) *Interview with Victoria Tauli-Corpuz, Recently Appointed Special Rapporteur on the Rights of Indigenous Peoples.* UN-NGLS, Available at: http://www.un-ngls.org/spip.php?article4446 (Accessed 15 January 2015).

Taussig, M. (1987) *Shamanism, Colonialism and the Wild Man: A Study in Terror and Healing.* Chicago: University of Chicago Press.

Tenenbaum, D. (2009) 'Oil Sands Development: A Health Risk Worth Taking?', *Environmental Health Perspectives* 117 (4): A150–A156.

Tester, F. and Kulchyski, P. (1994) *Tammarniit (Mistakes): Inuit Relocation in the Eastern Arctic, 1939–63.* Vancouver: University of British Columbia Press.

The Magazine (2008) *Universe of Marcus Amerman.* Available at: http://www.santafe.com/article/universe-of-marcus-amerman (Accessed 15 January 2015).

Thompson, P. (2000) *The Voice of the Past,* 3rd ed. Oxford: Oxford University Press.

Thuen, T. (1995) *Quest for Equity: Norway and the Saami Challenge.* St. John's, Newfoundland: Institute of Social and Economic Research.

Thwaites, R. G. (1896–1901) *The Jesuit Relations and Allied Documents,* 73 vols. Cleveland: Burrows Brothers.

Tierraviva (2015) *Corte Suprema de Justicia viola garantías judiciales admitiendo doble juzgamiento en caso Sawhoyamaxa.* Available at: http://www.tierraviva.org.py/?p=4731 (Accessed 15 January 2015).

Tischler, J. (2013) *Light And Power for a Multiracial Nation: The Kariba Dam Scheme and the Central African Federation.* Basingstoke: Palgrave Macmillan.

Tobin, B. (2014) *Indigenous Peoples, Customary Law and Human Rights – Why Living Law Matters.* Abingdon: Routledge.

Tocqueville, A. de. (1945) *Democracy in America,* vol. 1, trans. P. Bradley. New York: Vintage Books.

Todorov, T. (1984) *The Conquest of America: The Question of the Other.* New York: Harper and Row.

Tonge, J. (2006) 'Don't Romanticise the Kalahari Bushmen. They're Part of the Modern World, Too', letter to *The Guardian,* 24 March.

Trafzner, C. and Hyer, J. (1999) *Exterminate Them! Written Accounts of the Murder, Rape, and Enslavement of Native Americans During the California Gold Rush.* East Lansing: Michigan State University Press.

Treaty 7 Elders and Tribal Council, Hildebrand, W., First Rider, D. and Carter, S. (1996) *The True Spirit and Original Intent of Treaty 7*. Montreal: McGill-Queen's University Press.

Trejos Romero, L. F. (2013) 'Ejes Articuladores del Discurso Internacional del Presidente del Estado Plurinacional de Bolivia, Evo Morales Ayma', *Revista Encrucijada Americana* (5) 2: 43–53.

Trudel, M. (1973) *The Beginnings of New France 1524–1663*, trans. P. Claxton. Toronto: McClelland and Stewart.

Truman, H. S. (1949) Inaugural Address before Congress, 20 January.' Available at: https://www.trumanlibrary.org/whistlestop/50yr_archive/inagural20jan1949.htm (Accessed 21 April 2016).

Truth and Reconciliation Commission of Canada. (2015) *Honouring the Truth, Reconciling for the Future*. Available at: http://www.trc.ca/websites/trcinstitution/File/2015/Findings/Exec_Summary_2015_05_31_web_o.pdf (Accessed 27 July 2015).

Tuisku, T. (2001) 'The Displacement of Nenets Women from Reindeer Herding and the Tundra in the Nenets Autonomous Okrug, Northwestern Russia', *Acta Borealia* 18 (2): 41–60.

Tum, R. M. (1992) 'The Nobel Peace Prize Acceptance Speech', 10 December. Available at: http://www.nobelprize.org/nobel_prizes/peace/laureates/1992/tum-lecture.html (Accessed 15 January 2015).

Tupper, J. (2014) 'Social Media and the Idle No More Movement: Citizenship, Activism and Dissent in Canada', *Journal of Social Science Education*. 13 (4): 87–94.

Turner, D. (2006) *This Is Not a Peace Pipe: Towards a Critical Indigenous Philosophy*. Toronto: University of Toronto Press.

Tylor, E. B. (1964/1878) *Early History of Mankind: and the Development of Civilization*. Chicago, IL: University of Chicago Press.

UN DESA (United Nations, Department of Economic and Social Affairs) (2009) *State of the World's Indigenous Peoples*. New York: United Nations.

UNDP (United Nations Development Programme) (2012) *Media and Technology Help Boost Indigenous Peoples' Political Participation*. Available at: http://www.undp.org/content/undp/en/home/presscenter/articles/2012/08/09/media-and-technology-help-boost-indigenous-peoples-political-participation/ (Accessed 15 January 2015).

UNDRIP (2007) *Declaration of the Rights of Indigenous Peoples*, Available at: http://www.un.org/esa/socdev/unpfii/documents/DRIPS_en.pdf (Accessed 4 May 2016).

UNESCO (United Nations Educational, Scientific and Cultural Organization) (2003) *Convention for the Safeguarding of the Intangible Cultural Heritage*. Available at: http://www.unesco.org/culture/ich/index.php?lg=en&pg=00006 (Accessed 15 January 2015).

UNESCO (United Nations Educational, Scientific and Cultural Organization) (2011) *ICTs and Indigenous People*. Available at: http://iite.

unesco.org/files/policy_briefs/pdf/en/indigenous_people.pdf (Accessed 15 January 2015).

UN General Assembly (1948) *Universal Declaration of Human Rights* (UDHR). Available at: http://www.un.org/en/universal-declaration-human-rights/index.html (Accessed 15 January 2015).

UN General Assembly (2007) *United Nations Declaration on the Rights of Indigenous Peoples*, 13 September. A/RES/61/295. Available at: http://www.un.org/esa/socdev/unpfii/documents/DRIPS_en.pdf (Accessed 21 April 2016).

UNHRC (United Nations Human Rights Council) (2008) *Report of the Special Rapporteur on the Situation of Human Rights and Fundamental Freedoms of Indigenous People*. James Anaya, 11 August. A/HRC/9/9. Available at: http://www.ohchr.org/EN/Issues/IPeoples/SRIndigenousPeoples/Pages/SRIPeoplesIndex.aspx (Accessed 21 April 2016).

UNHRC (United Nations Human Rights Council) (2009) *Report on the Situation of Human Rights of Indigenous Peoples in Brazil*. James Anaya, 26 August. A/HRC/12/34/Add.2. Available at: http://unsr.jamesanaya.org/country-reports/report-on-the-situation-of-human-rights-of-indigenous-peoples-in-brazil-2009 (Accessed 21 April 2016).

UNHRC (United Nations Human Rights Council) (2012) *Report of the Special Rapporteur on the Rights of Indigenous Peoples*. James Anaya, 30 August. A/HRC/21/47/Add.1.

UNICEF (United Nations Children's Fund), UN Women (United Nations Entity for Gender Equality and the Empowerment of Women), UNFPA (United Nations Population Fund), ILO (International Labour Organisation), OSRSG/VAC (Office of the Special Representative of the Secretary-General on Violence against Children) (2013) *Breaking the Silence on Violence against Indigenous Girls, Adolescents and Young Women*. Available at: http://www.unwomen.org/en/digital-library/publications/2013/5/breaking-the-silence-on-violence-against-indigenous-girls#sthash.VcGVf4mO.dpuf (Accessed 15 January 2015).

UNPFII (United Nations Permanent Forum on Indigenous Issues) (2014) *Report of the International Expert Group Meeting on the Theme 'Sexual Health and Reproductive Rights: Articles 21, 22(1), 23 and 24 of the United Nations Declaration on the Rights of Indigenous Peoples': note/by the Secretariat*, 3 March. E/C.19/2014/8. Available at: http://www.refworld.org/docid/534bd3284.html (Accessed 21 April 2016).

USCB (United States Census Bureau) (2010) Available at: http://www.census.gov/2010census/ (Accessed 15 January 2015).

Vanderklippe, N. (2013) 'Toxic Waste Spill in Northern Alberta Biggest of Recent Disasters in North America', *Toronto Globe and Mail*, 12 June. Available at: http://www.theglobeandmail.com/report-on-business/industry-news/energy-and-resources/apache-pipeline-leaks-60000-barrels-of-salty-water-in-northwest-alberta/article12494371/ (Accessed 15 January 2015).

Veltmeyer, H. and Petras, J. (2014) *The New Extractivism: A Post-Neoliberal Development Model or Imperialism of the Twenty-first Century?* London: Zed Books.

Vidal, J. (2009) 'We Are Fighting for Our Lives and Our Dignity', *Guardian*, 12 June. Available at: http://www.theguardian.com/environment/2009/jun/13/forests-environment-oil-companies (Accessed 21 April 2016).

Vidal, J. (2014) 'Mining Threatens to Eat Up Europe's Last Wilderness', *Guardian*, 3 September. Available at: http://www.theguardian.com/environment/2014/sep/03/mining-threat-northern-europe-wilderness-finland-sweden-norway (Accessed 15 January 2015).

Viljoen, F. (2010) 'Reflections on the Legal Protection of Indigenous Peoples' Rights in Africa', in S. Dersso (ed.), *Perspectives on the Rights of Minorities and Indigenous Peoples in Africa*. Pretoria: Pretoria University Law Press.

Villa, W. and Houghton, J. (2005) *Violencia Política contra los Indígenas en Colombia 1974-2004*. Bogotá: CECOIN–OIA–IWGIA.

Vinding, D. (2003) *The Indigenous World, 2002–03*. Vancouver: University of British Columbia Press.

Vitebsky, P. (2005) *Reindeer People: Living with Animals and Spirits in Siberia*. London: Harper Collins.

Vitoria, F. de. (1991) *Political Writings*. Cambridge: Cambridge University Press.

Vizenor, G. (1984) *The People Named the Chippewa: Narrative Histories*. Minneapolis: University of Minnesota Press.

Vizenor, G. (1994) *Manifest Manners: Postindian Warriors of Survivance*. Hanover, NH: Wesleyan University Press.

Vizenor, G. and Lee, A. R. (1999) *Postindian Conversations*. Lincoln: University of Nebraska Press.

Vrdoljak, A. F. (2008) 'Reparations for Cultural Loss', in F. Lenzerini (ed.), *Reparations for Indigenous Peoples: International & Comparative Perspectives*. Oxford: Oxford University Press.

Wachira, G. M. and Karjala, T. (2014) 'Advocacy for Indigenous Peoples' Rights in Africa: Dynamics, Methods and Mechanisms', in R. Laher and K. Sing'Oei (eds.), *Indigenous People in Africa: Contestations, Empowerment and Group Rights*. Pretoria: Africa Institute of South Africa.

Wade, P. (1997) *Race and Ethnicity in Latin America*. London: Pluto Press.

Wadi, R. (2011) '"A Poetic Concept of Identity": An Interview with Mapuche Poet David Aniñir Guilitraro', *Upside Down World*. Available at: http://upsidedownworld.org/main/chile-archives-34/3260-a-poetic-concept-of-identity-an-interview-with-mapuche-poet-david-aninir-guilitraro- (Accessed 15 January 2015).

Waldram, J. (1993) *As Long as the Rivers Run with Hydroelectric Development and Native Communities in Western Canada*. Winnipeg: University of Manitoba Press.

Walker, B. (2001) *The Conquest of Ainu Lands: Ecology and Culture in Japanese Expansion, 1590–1800*. Berkeley: University of California Press.

Walker, S., Spohn, C. and DeLone, M. (2011) *The Color of Justice: Race, Ethnicity, and Crime in America*. Belmont, CA: Cengage Learning.

Watson, B. (2011) 'The Doctrine of Discovery and the Elusive Definition of Indian Title', *Lewis & Clark Law Review* 15 (4): 995–1024.

Watson, F. (2013) 'Brazil's Treatment of its Indigenous People Violates Their Rights', *Guardian*, 29 May. Available at: http://www.theguardian.com/commentisfree/2013/may/29/brazil-indigenous-people-violates-rights (Accessed 15 January 2015).

Watson, M. K. (2014) *Japan's Ainu Minority in Tokyo: Diasporic Indigeneity and Urban Politics*. Abingdon: Routledge.

Weaver, J. C. (2003) *The Great Land Rush and the Making of the Modern World, 1650–1900*. Montreal: McGill-Queen's University Press.

Weinberg, A. (1935) *Manifest Destiny: A Study of Nationalist Expansionism in American History*. Chicago, IL: Quadrangle Books.

Weir, J. K. (2008) 'Connectivity', *Australian Humanities Review* 45. Available at: http://www.australianhumanitiesreview.org/archive/Issue-November-2008/weir.html (Accessed 15 January 2015).

Weist, K. (1995) 'Development Refugees: Africans, Indians and the Big Dams', *Journal of Refugee Studies* 8 (2): 163–184.

West, P., Igoe, J. and Brockington, D. (2006) 'Parks and People: The Social Impact of Protected Areas', *Annual Review of Anthropology* 35: 251–277.

Wheeler, S. (2010) *The Magnetic North: Travels in the Arctic*. London: Vintage.

Whitmore, A. (ed.) (2012) *Pitfalls and Pipelines: Indigenous Peoples and Extractive Industries*. Baguio City: Tebtebba Foundation and IWGIA.

Wiessner, S. (2011) 'The Cultural Rights of Indigenous Peoples: Achievements and Continuing Challenges', *The European Journal of International Law* (22) 1: 121–140.

Wilkins, D. E. and Lomawaima, K. T. (2001) *Uneven Ground: American Indian Sovereignty and Federal Law*. Norman: University of Oklahoma Press.

Williams, H. and Hoffmann, H. (2015) 'Fracking Near Indian Country: The Federal Trust Relationship, Tribal Sovereignty, and the Beneficial Use of Produced Water', *Yale Journal on Regulation* 32: 453–494.

Wilson, J. (1998) *The Earth Shall Weep: A History of Native America*. New York: Grove Press.

Witz, L., Rassool, C. and Minkley, G. (2001) 'Repackaging the Past for South African Tourism', *Daedalus* 130 (1): 277–296.

Wolf, E. R. (1982) *Europe and the People Without History*. Berkeley: University of California Press.

Woodward, G. S. (1982) *The Cherokees*. Norman: University of Oklahoma Press.

Woollacott, A. (2015) *Settler Society in the Australian Colonies: Self-Government and Imperial Culture*. Oxford: Oxford University Press.

World Commission on Dams (2000) *Dams and Development: A New Framework for Decision-Making*. London: Earthscan.

World Conference on Indigenous Women (2013) *Lima Declaration*. Available at: http://www.forestpeoples.org/sites/fpp/files/news/2013/11/182171104-Lima-Declaration_web_0.pdf (Accessed 15 January 2015).

Wright, S. (2014) *Our Ice Is Vanishing/Sikuvut Nunguliqtuq: A History of Inuit, Newcomers, and Climate Change*. Montreal: McGill-Queen's University Press.

Xanthaki, A. (2010) *Indigenous Rights and United Nations Standards: Self-Determination, Culture and Land*. Cambridge: Cambridge University Press.

Yamada, T. (2001) 'Gender and Cultural Revitalization Movements among the Ainu', in I. Keen and T. Yamada (eds.), *Identity and Gender in Hunting and Gathering Societies*. Osaka: National Museum of Ethnology.

Yazzie, R. (2000) 'Postcolonial Colonialism', in M. Battiste (ed.), *Reclaiming Indigenous Voice and Vision*. Vancouver: University of British Columbia Press.

Yellow Bird, M. (1999) 'What We Want to Be Called: Indigenous Peoples' Perspectives on Racial and Ethnic Identity Labels', *American Indian Quarterly* 23 (2): 1–21.

Zusman, P. (2007) 'Paisajes de Civilización y Progreso: El Viaje de Sarmiento a los Estados Unidos', in P. Zusman, C. Lois and H. Castro (eds.), *Viajes y Geografía*. Buenos Aires: Prometeo Libros.

Index